Transformed
by Love

Transformed *by* Love

THE VERNON GROUNDS STORY

BRUCE L. SHELLEY

Discovery House Publishers

Books, music, and videos that feed the soul with the Word of God

Box 3566 Grand Rapids, MI 49501

Transformed by Love: The Vernon Grounds Story
© 2002 by Bruce L. Shelley

Discovery House Publishers is affiliated with RBC Ministries,
Grand Rapids, Michigan, 49512.

Discovery House books are distributed to the trade exclusively by
Barbour Publishing, Inc., Uhrichsville, Ohio, 44683.

Library of Congress Cataloging-in-Publication Data
Shelley, Bruce L. (Bruce Leon), 1927–
    Transformed by love : the Vernon Grounds story / Bruce L.
    Shelley.
              p. cm.
Inlcudes bibliographical references.
    ISBN: 1-57293-065-9
1. Grounds, Vernon C. 2. Evangelists—Biography.   I. Title.
    BV3785.G75 S54 2002
    269'.2'092—dc21
                                                    2002014005

Printed in the United States of America

02 03 04 05 06 07 08 09 / CHG/ 10 9 8 7 6 5 4 3 2 1

Contents

Preface

The strength of a man's virtue must not be measured
by his efforts, but by his ordinary life.

— BLAISE PASCAL

In many ways the long life of Vernon Grounds has been an ordinary life. He has held no position of power in Washington, has won no great medals of honor, has had no national platform from which to speak to the masses, no TV program, no radio talk show. Yet there is nothing ordinary about this multifaceted man. He is a scholar, a speaker, a counselor, a pastor, a poet, a singer, a weight lifter, and a hiker. Above all, he is a man who has a deep understanding of the love of God.

For most of his life, Vernon has been an itinerant speaker, a man with a message and always on his way somewhere to deliver it. And that message is: "How faith activates love." In a multitude of ways he has lived out the answer to that question every day of his life. But the love that Vernon Grounds exhibits and so often speaks of is not a self-generated, manufactured love. No, the love he speaks of and lives out is from God.

Vernon knows and speaks the language of the heart; and with the gesture, the touch, the smile, the pause, the silence of understanding, he uses it to communicate with others like few men I have ever known. Good counselors—and Vernon is a good counselor—can, and must, learn to listen, but Vernon does more. He responds. Time after time, grieving or anxious or troubled souls have sensed his love and his eagerness to do anything he can to help those who are hurting and in pain.

But what made this man the person he is? That's the question the biographer must always ask, and answer. The Bible says, "Man looks at the outward appearance, but the Lord looks at the heart." So when I was encouraged to write this book, I started to search for the real heart story of Vernon Grounds. Why did he rise early, morning after morning, year after year, to meet some student or sufferer for breakfast? What was it that made him grab his huge book bag and head to the airport weekend after weekend, leaving his home and family, to minister across the country? What made him keep a fresh supply of coffee and a variety of mugs in his office, always ready for the next person who came through the door? Why did he instinctively refrain from the slightest criticism of others? What I discovered was a story worth telling.

Vernon's eighty-eight years have spanned the beginning and maturing of the evangelical movement in the United States, and through the years he has been an influential presence in the development of the movement. Vernon is by nature a gentle man, but even he has had his adversaries, men who objected to his teaching or viewed him as a rival for power with "the people." Most of these individuals were themselves persons in positions of power, and they sometimes resented the growing influence of this gentle man who speaks of love and lives it. This, too, is part of his story.

The most extraordinary thing about this ordinary man, however, is the way he has lived his personal life. Unlike the vast majority of Americans, he has refused to pursue his own happiness. In a thousand ways his life says, "I am no consumer, no pursuer of happiness; I am a debtor to grace."

When he retired from the presidency of Denver Seminary in 1979, Vernon looked back across the years and said, "I stand here and I gladly confess my gratitude. And I am thinking of the unpayable debt of love I owe to God for His goodness and mercy, for His unchanging faithfulness, for the wonder of His redemptive grace, and for the privilege of His fellowship. Robert McCheyne, that great Scottish preacher who shook his country, wrote:

'Chosen not for good in me,
Wakened up from wrath to flee,
Hidden in the Saviour's side,
By the Spirit sanctified.
Teach me, Lord, on earth to show
By my love how much I owe.'"[1]

In the course of writing this biography, Vernon himself gave freely of his time for interviews, as did several of his colleagues who have known him at various points along his journey. Douglas Birk and James Beck were especially helpful.

The written sources I have quoted were just being assembled and organized in the Carey S. Thomas Library archives at Denver Seminary by my friend Sarah Miller, who had served as the school's librarian for over three decades. Sarah was extremely helpful to me, as was Jeanette France, who was her assistant for many years. It was Jeanette, another friend, who provided the original bibliography with which I began my work.

In using these sources I had to decide at every point what to use from the institutional files of Denver Seminary, which Vernon Grounds led for so many years, and what to use from the personal correspondence he kept. I also relied heavily on Vernon's letters, especially his wonderful annual Christmas letters.

Finally, at the risk of sounding like the sixteenth chapter of Romans, I must acknowledge a few friends and helpers:

Carol Holquist and her able staff at Discovery House have been a constant source of encouragement. My special thanks to Judith Markham for her skillful touch and helpful suggestions. She made this a much better book.

Many of the stories in the book came from interviews with or letters from Dr. Grounds's many friends. They have now become my friends too.

Carol Rebell, who served for a time as Dr. Grounds's assistant, secured a number of sources for me, and I am grateful.

My colleague Gordon Lewis provided some details and pictures for chapter 3.

Barbara Owen, Vernon's daughter and the family's historian, generously shared the family history she has compiled about her parents and grandparents and supplied most of the pictures included in the book. She also took time to review the chapters related to the Grounds family.

And, finally, I thank my journalist friend Krista Nash, who, while carrying her second baby, read ten chapters of the manuscript and offered many valuable suggestions about the development of the material.

Deeply grateful, I thank them all, even little Caroline, who was born before the book itself saw the light of day.

CHAPTER 1

Finding the Way

No one writes hymns praising the hangman's noose, wears a replica of the guillotine, or decorates a church with an electric chair. Why, then, do Christians glory in the cross—that ghastly symbol of cruelty, shame, and death? We do so for one overwhelming reason. The cross of Calvary is the time-abiding, heart-assuring, all-sufficient revelation of God's love. Apart from Calvary, there is no convincing evidence to support the New Testament claim, "God is love."

— VERNON GROUNDS, *The Splendor of Easter*

Almost everyone calls him "Dr. Grounds." It seems the only appropriate name for this dignified white-haired gentleman. He is not a large or imposing figure of a man, standing now about five feet, seven, but he has strong arms from lifting weights, and his gentle, understanding face is compelling. As soon as he gets a stranger's name, a subtle smile curls across his face. Warmth and strength with dignity! Yes, "Dr. Grounds" sounds just right.

Usually these impressions of dignity, strength, and gentleness come after Dr. Grounds has spoken for about forty-five minutes, in his rich, mellifluous voice, on some contemporary issue of importance, sprinkling the truth with a dozen or so multisyllabic words, but always with a delicate touch of humor. Bookish but stimulating, that is "Dr. Grounds," and always something of a mystery, both to his audience and to himself. When someone dares to ask him, "Why do you do this or that?" he often pleads ignorance and almost never tries to explain himself.

"I have taught a whole range of courses," Dr. Grounds confesses. "And I have read quite incessantly. And yet I am aware of how little I know. I am relatively ignorant of history; I'm almost totally ignorant of science; I'm a moron in mathematics; and even in theology I realize how little I know. By God's grace I have been able to put some things together, but my mood as I muse on the mystery of life, despite the light shed by biblical revelation, is frequently one of bemusement. There are certainties—absolute certainties—but there is this awareness of ignorance. I have to repeat often:

'My knowledge of that life is small;
The eye of faith is dim.
But 'tis enough that Christ knows all
And I shall be with Him.'"[1]

Where did Vernon Grounds find such faith and humility?

The Mysteries of Life

Vernon Grounds was born into a working-class, nominally Lutheran household on Liberty Avenue in Jersey City, New Jersey, July 19, 1914. Both of Vernon's maternal grandparents, Richard Heimburge and Elizabeth Lentz, were born in Germany but did not meet until after each had immigrated to America and settled near Albany, New York. His paternal grandparents, John Thomas Grounds and Lena Felts, who was also a German immigrant, were from the same area.

Richard Heimburge was a man of strong beliefs who worked hard to gain a foothold in the rich earth of America. He was also a lay preacher. "In my birth-family, because of its German roots, we celebrated the Savior's advent on Christmas Eve rather than Christmas morning," recalls Vernon. "I recall walking home after one candlelight service holding my grandfather's hand as snow was falling."

Vernon also has a few distinct memories of his Grandmother Lena, his father's mother. He remembers a time when she took him to her Pentecostal church. When the two returned home after the service, Vernon was asked what he learned at church. "All the people crazy," he replied. When his concerned parents threw questioning glances at his grandmother, she explained. One of the hymns that morning encouraged the worshipers to raise their hands and dance happily in the aisles. Witnessing this behavior, which was quite unlike any Lutheran service he'd attended, Vernon misunderstood the words the Pentecostals were singing. To him, "All the people praise Thee" sounded like "all the people crazy."

Both of Vernon's parents came from strong religious backgrounds. Unfortunately, these backgrounds did not result in much spiritual training in the home they established, and they did not attend church regularly. "Though my parents came out of rather staunch religious backgrounds, we had no Bible reading in our home, no hymn singing, no family prayers. There was that Sunday evening at the Calvary Baptist Church in Clifton, New Jersey, that my father raised his hand for prayer and rededicated himself to Christ. But as far as I can remember, that made no difference in the family lifestyle."

Like many of his generation, John Charles Grounds, Vernon's father, knew the meaning of hard work and the trials of raising a family. He was only a boy when his own father, John Thomas, died. To put food on the table, his widowed mother, Lena, turned to the only skill she knew. She began baking bread and sent her boys, John Charles and Harry, throughout the neighborhood, door-to-door, selling those very edible loaves.[2]

The death of his father meant that John Charles, though only thirteen, became the man of the house. He quit school and found work at the nearby rail yards of the New York Central. He worked first as a wiper boy, where his job was to climb up into the big cabs of the steam engines and wipe the excess grease from everything in sight. John Charles would stay with the railroad for the rest of his life, working his way up through the tough and grimy jobs to the position of engineer, all to make a living and provide for his family.

After their marriage, John Charles and Bertha left the Albany area and moved to Jersey City, New Jersey, where all four of their children were born: Mildred (1909), John (1913), Vernon (1914), and Raymond (1916). Their neighborhood in Jersey City was a friendly place where children could safely wander about.

"Our home in Jersey City was within a neighborhood where everyone took a kind and active interest in everyone else. My neighbors, however, must have taken an especially enthusiastic interest in me, because I still have a faint remembrance of my own little self toddling from one home to another munching thick slices of bread weighed down with raspberry jam or marmalade. What an amicable little pest I must have been! I strayed through neighbors' domiciles with cheerful disregard, big inquiring eyes, prying little fingers, and an eager tongue."

Early on, Vernon developed a spirit of independence, and one of his earliest memories is his discovery of the public library on a cool winter's day. "I wandered in," he recalls, "awed and rather bashful, and strayed with amazed eyes through the rows and rows and rows of books, until the kind old librarian put a slender volume in my hands and placed me at a little table. I read page after page completely entranced. The story told of a great big grizzly bear and a hunter of a boy. But I never finished the story. My sister, coming in search of me, literally tore me away from my treasure while I whimpered in protest."

In 1922 the family moved about thirty miles north to a two-story house in Clifton, New Jersey. Vernon, of course, had no say in the matter and "suffered the first great tragedy" of his life. "I was wrenched away from everything I knew and loved and found myself transplanted to some wilderness of hostile things." It was during that first winter in his new home that Vernon wrote his first poem. "It was really a silly little thing (at least I think so now), but at that time my parents seized it with wonder and joy, and for a little while I was regarded as little lower than the angels!"

The following year brought the first great sadness and loss into Vernon's life when his younger brother, Raymond, died of throat cancer on August 17, 1924. After trying everything they knew to relieve the pain, the doctors had sent the eight-year-old boy home to die. Vernon's parents put Raymond in a bedroom near them upstairs and sent for Grandma Heimburge, Bertha's mother, to come to help with the other children.

For weeks Vernon tried to sleep downstairs with his brother John, but night after night Raymond's painful cries pierced the darkness and haunted Vernon's dreams. After weeks of tears and pain, the end came. Grandma Heimburge, who did her best to console the other children, had taken Mildred, John, and Vernon for a walk in the neighborhood. As they returned and were approaching the front door, they were suddenly struck by the silence. No more crying! "We knew at once that Raymond was gone!"

Ten-year-old Vernon was left with two things: vivid memories of those agonizing cries in the darkness, and a tender heart for suffering people.

***

John Grounds had not had much of a home life as a boy, so he loved his wife and children and wanted to create a warm and happy home life for them. He worked hard to provide for his family and saw home as a place of relaxation and enjoyment. A rather large, jovial man, John loved to cook. Vernon often said, "In our home, food was king."

Shortly after Raymond's death, Vernon's father was promoted to locomotive engineer for the Erie Railroad. Through a correspondence school, John had studied for the test he needed to pass to qualify as an engineer.

Hoping to share his working world with his sons, he took Vernon and John to the rail yards where they were given a short ride around the yard in the huge engine he drove. Vernon was fascinated watching the firemen tossing their shovelfuls of coal into the roaring furnace that supplied the steam, but he found the steam and soot almost unbearable. John, however, enjoyed the whole experience immensely.

At home it was the same story. When John Charles led his sons to his workbench in the basement to teach them how to use his tools, he found young John was a natural, handling tools with ease, but Vernon was all thumbs. One day, after his father's saw cut into one of Vernon's bent nails, making the horrible screeching noise of metal on metal, his father said, "Vernon! Why don't you go upstairs?" And up he went, leaving his brother and his father to finish the job without him.

As a teenager, Vernon continued to gain a reputation for mechanical incompetence. His sister, Mildred, often spoke of the time her kid brother was learning to drive, and the day he could not get the car started. Vernon had to call for his brother to get the car started; and when John rushed to the rescue, he found the car was simply out of gas!

But there was one place Vernon had no problem excelling, and that was in Scout Troop #3 at the Clifton Reformed Church. At the weekly Boy Scout meetings he learned camping skills, from pitching tents to tying knots. More importantly he learned the Scout Oath:

> On my honor, I will do my best:
> To do my duty to God and my country
> and to obey the Scout Law.
> To help other people at all times
> To keep myself physically strong
> mentally awake
> and morally straight.

He also memorized the Scout Law: "A Scout is . . . helpful . . . friendly . . . courteous . . . and kind," and practiced it faithfully enough to gain the rank of Eagle Scout, the highest rank in Scouting.

In their early teens Vernon and John delivered newspapers together in Clifton, seven days a week, but they seemed to have little else in common. John loved cars and machines. He seemed to be able to do almost anything physically, and he was prepared to fight anyone who challenged him. Vernon, who always had his nose in a book, was calm, even-tempered, optimistic, and—to borrow the King James English—"not easily provoked."

Years later, after he had read stacks of books about human psychology, Vernon described his own temperament as "sanguine, phlegmatic," and "hopefully empathic." His friends often described him as "tender-hearted" and "kind." He shunned competitive sports, except tennis, because he knew someone always had to lose, and that seemed unfair, even cruel. The loser or the little guy always had Vernon's sympathy.

During his years at Clifton High, "Vern" Grounds became a campus leader, not by excelling in sports, but by expressing his thoughts. He joined the Debating Club, the Footlights Club (the dramatic society), and was chosen editor-in-chief of *The Reflector*, the school's yearbook, when he was a junior. Traditionally a senior held the post. His picture with *The Reflector* staff shows Vern—in his white shirt, tie, vested suit, and serious expression—looking every bit the all-business editor-in-chief.

From the time he encountered the written word in his discovery of the public library excursion and his first venture into poetry, Vernon knew that words were his world. Words read, words spoken, and words written. In high school he wrote,

> Dust that was rose,
> Dust that was jade—
> Poets may die,
> But words never fade.

During his years in the Debating Club and on *The Reflector* staff, he began to express his deepest feelings in both the spoken and the written word, in his debates and in his poetry. In his debating he soon became known for his smooth delivery. In his poetry he revealed some of his deepest thoughts, as when he expressed his humanistic philosophy in "The Wizard of Menlow."

> And there in the dark—in the gloom of night—
> He raised his hand—and his hand held LIGHT.
> And old men saw through the haze of years,
> And children laughed and forgot their fears.
> And knowledge gleamed where voids had been,
> And Wisdom banished the curse of sin.
> And peace came where his feet had trod—
> For GOD is LIGHT—and LIGHT is GOD.
>
> (February 1932)

But in a matter of months this humanism would combine with a growing cynicism bordering on an arrogant atheism. Even though he continued to attend church and to participate in the church's Christian Endeavor meetings, he now considered himself nothing less than an enlightened atheist!

Pagan Philosophy

> God does not want us to be gay
> If we don't feel at all that way,
> For any heathen can rejoice
> If all his pots of flesh are choice.
> God does not want us to attend
> His holy teachings without end,
> If we know fields and little streams
> Can better help us live our dreams.
> God does not want us all to roam

Within His walls when we leave home,
So when angelic trumpets blow
A horde of us will squat below.

(written during his last year of high school)

What had happened? "We had at one time the largest [Christian Endeavor] society in all of New Jersey, and we would take the prize for attendance at annual conventions. I was the fair-haired boy in our church, sometimes sharing in a worship service, offering prayer or leading a hymn. But all during those early adolescent years I began to suspect that Christianity was mythological."

———

Approaching graduation from high school in the winter of 1932, Vernon Grounds had more than one reason to be cynical and discouraged. His father had always neglected his health. He smoked and was overweight. Then, in the winter of 1931, after suffering from chest pains, he finally saw the doctor, who told him that he had contracted acute lobar pneumonia and needed to have complete bed rest. But John Charles Grounds would not stay in the hospital bed as the doctors ordered, and in only a matter of days he was dead, at the age of forty-eight.

Along with the shock and sorrow of losing his father came the realization that the family's primary means of support was gone. On top of that, it was 1932, only three years since Wall Street had collapsed, plunging the entire country into the Great Depression. Vernon's brother, John, was now out of school but had no work. His sister, Mildred, daily rode the train into Manhattan where she worked for the Metropolitan Life Insurance Company. Her meager salary helped to put food on the table but it was far from enough. In the depths of their grief at the loss of husband and father, the Grounds family now faced the daunting struggle just to survive. For a time, Vernon's mother tried to operate a little millinery shop, but this quickly proved a total fiasco. No one was buying hats! Long unemployment lines were everywhere.

Vern had no hope of going to college as he had always dreamed. As soon as he graduated, he tried everywhere to find work, including Metropolitan Life where Mildred worked, but he found nothing to help relieve his family's financial burden, absolutely nothing.

Out of school, with no work in sight, Vernon turned to books more than ever. He spent his days reading and began to question both the American myth and the Christian faith. *Is making it to the top what life is all about? Do I really want to spend my life climbing over other people just to make more money and gain the world's applause?* he wondered. He also began to think about the little guy, the poor, and the oppressed.

When he learned that the high school had a program for advanced study after graduation, he took several English classes and found the library a treasure trove of books—at no cost. He read, and read, and read, keeping a notebook of unfamiliar words, laboring to make every one his own. He thought about words, played with words, and created words . . . long lines of words, especially verse. He sent several poems to the *Passaic Herald,* and was pleased to see them published. But he received nothing more than the satisfaction of seeing his name in print.

While Vernon had no heart for true faith, he had been drawn to the Clifton Reformed Church by the Scouting program and even found himself, as a teenager, teaching Sunday school—with no knowledge of the Bible whatsoever. During the week he helped with the Scouting program and on Sundays he led the large Christian Endeavor group, numbering two hundred young people, perhaps the largest in the state. His leadership, speaking ability, and mannerly behavior soon caught the pastor's eye.

"Vernon," he said one day, "may I see you for a few minutes?"

They found a quiet place to talk, and the pastor told Vernon about a scholarship for ministerial candidates that was available from the Reformed Church of America. This offered him an opportunity to attend Rutgers University at New Brunswick. All he had to do was apply and meet with a group of pastors to answer a few questions.

Vernon could scarcely believe his ears. But he was pleased—and eager—to jump at the chance of going to college. The only problem was the interview! How could he satisfactorily answer the pastors' questions at the interview? He no longer firmly believed that God even existed. Still, he had been to church and he knew what the selection committee wanted to hear. Believing this would be his only chance at a college education and that "the ministry was a genteel profession affording abundant opportunity for social uplift and humanitarian service," he met with the pastors. By telling them what they wanted to hear, he gained their approval and left for Rutgers University in the fall of 1933.

The Rutgers Years

Once on the university campus, Vern's great opportunity for learning also became his great test of faith as he faced squarely the case for unbelief. Slightly bewitched by the academic environment, he plunged into new experiences and new ideas with a passion. He eagerly joined the Men's Glee Club and sat in awe of his professors. After completing a course in Contemporary Civilization taught by Professor Mark Heald, an historian who reflected the "enlightened" view of modern times, Vernon wrote a letter thanking Heald for "delivering me from the chains of Christian superstition."

He read scores of books he had only heard about: Nietzsche, Hume, Freud, and Russell. And he wrote for the college publications, defiantly expressing his unbelief. "I found my studies so confirmatory of my latent skepticism that by the end of my freshman year I made up my mind to leave the church and join the American Humanist Society."

The young anti-militant was becoming increasingly militant in his attitude. He decided that he not only wanted nothing to do with the ROTC program, but he eagerly joined in the student-led, anti-war effort and went public with his pacifism because he was convinced that Europe was once again heading for a bloodbath. His roommate that year was C. Kilmer Myers, who would years later become the Episcopal bishop of Northern California, succeeding Bishop James Pike. The two Rutgers freshmen, both conscientious objectors and campus liberals, along with a few other quasi-radicals, helped to organize a "Strike Against War and Fascism." Vernon rode around the campus in a sound truck announcing the rally, urging students to cut classes and join the strike. A few hundred students showed up for the open-air rally to protest passionately, and Vernon Grounds, now the young radical, considered the strike a great success. Only much later did he come to see that the big anti-war effort was also a student front for communism![3]

After a year of classes at Rutgers, with whatever minimal faith he'd had in tatters, Vernon faced a tough question: How could he continue to train for the ministry if there was nothing to believe in? The summer of 1933 would answer that question and prove a major turning point in his life.

In May, when Vernon returned home to Clifton for the summer break, he heard that a number of his high school friends and acquaintances would be attending the Clifton Reformed Church one Sunday evening. While church no longer had any place in his life, he wanted to investigate the reports that had reached him at Rutgers of a revival in his hometown. Some of his former friends and acquaintances were being saved and holding meetings in various churches. *Saved,* he thought cynically. *Saved from what?* He went to that Sunday evening service and was reunited with an enthusiastic group of young people. He noticed that they seemed different somehow, and none more than Mike Birkner. Vernon and Mike lived near each other, and he knew Mike as a Catholic kid who hung around poolrooms, drank some, and used foul language. But here was Mike at church on a Sunday night carrying a large Thompson Chain Reference Bible under his arm.

Following the service, Vernon was standing around talking with several friends, when someone mentioned that they were "going over to Francis Ternigan's house for fellowship." That was when Vernon learned that during the year he had been away at college, a number of his high school friends had been active in a loosely organized prayer fellowship. Now about fifty of them gathered in different homes after Sunday evening services to sing, give their testimonies, and pray together.

"Why don't you come along, Vern?" they said. His friends Bill Orange and Johnny Van Houten, who were now members of a Gospel quartet, were going. And so was Mike Birkner.

Why not? Vern thought. *This might be an interesting psychological study.* But once the group had settled into the Ternigans' second-floor apartment on Ward Street in the heart of Clifton, Vern, listening to the singing and testifying, began to sense a strange reality that was unlike anything he had ever experienced in a church meeting. The Ternigan apartment had two bedrooms, and the girls went into one to pray together and the boys went into the other. During this time of prayer, Vernon, kneeling beside the bed, felt within his heart an urge to pray out loud, as he had done in the past while leading worship. Half-sincerely, half insincerely, he asked God, if God was real, to help him believe in Jesus Christ, if Jesus was actually alive and able to save.

As soon as one of the boys prayed the last prayer of the meeting, two of Vernon's friends led him aside and explained to him what it meant to accept Jesus as Savior and what he must do as a new believer. "You have to pray every day," they said. "And read your Bible. And you'll have to find Christian fellowship every chance you get. You won't make it in the Christian life alone."

When Vernon left the Ternigans' apartment, he turned around, lifted his hand toward the house, and said, "I'll never forget this place."

That summer was, in Vernon's words, "the great continental divide in my life." Although "God took me at my word, revealed Jesus Christ to me, and saved my soul," scores of questions continued to swirl through the canyons of his mind. He was puzzled by Christian friends who rejected the scientific theory of evolution and other secular ideas. And many times he found himself thinking, *There is nothing to this! My prayer was only emotionally motivated.*

In the weeks that followed, Vernon served as director of the Scout camp at Camp Kaheka on Kanawakee Lake, about sixty miles from Clifton in New York State. Every afternoon, while the young scouts were in their tents supposedly taking a siesta, he climbed the mountain overlooking the lake, found a boulder to sit on, read his Bible, and prayed. At first the Bible didn't seem especially meaningful, and prayer was a strange monologue. Gradually, though, the Bible became intelligible, and prayer started to feel like a conversation with an invisible but real Person. When Thursdays rolled around, his day off each week, Vern got into his car and drove back to Clifton for one, single purpose: to have fellowship with his friends. He found that being with other Christians was a uniquely uplifting experience. The young people in the prayer fellowship had joined with a dedicated layman, Martin Kuiper, to erect a tent seating hundreds of people, and every night during the summer an evangelistic service was held. Vern, now definitely headed for the ministry, was occasionally asked to preach.

On July 23, after one of these services, he wrote in his journal:

"Last night I made a hurried visit home to attend Christian Endeavor and the Tent Meeting afterward. Again my presence seemed to be doubly blessed: Mother in tears confessed at a prayer meeting . . . that she had slid in grace and desired in penitence to return to the security of the Fold; and Walter and Louise [two young people from the neighborhood] acknowledged publicly their belief in the saving power of Christ Jesus . . . I may write that their doing so filled me with an unreasoning ecstasy. I was more joyous than I had ever been, over what I know not. Examined in the cold light of reason, their emotional reactions and my own excess of sentiment were psychologically explicable, though practically unsound. When I am in the midst of the Saved an elation takes possession of me. I throw discretion and sense to the winds, indulging in an orgy of rankest emotionalism. Nor will I permit myself to reason, for commonsense saps such experiences of their meanings.

"This leaves me with a profound paradox still unsolved. How can joy come from what one does not truly believe? Philosophically Christianity to me is still untenable. Whenever I think of its dogmas of Hell, Eternal Damnation, Divine Wrath, Washing in the Blood, Crucifixion, Self Abnegation, a shudder of repulsion runs through my intellectual being. Yet to convert others to this thralldom of mind brings me peculiar happiness, such as I have not tasted of formerly. Is there something in this mystery of existence which logic cannot explain?"[4]

Obviously, for Vernon Grounds, the journey of faith was no easy road. He was tempted many times to give up, but he didn't. Through Bible reading, prayer, and Christian fellowship, God became more and more real to him. And when he returned to

Rutgers in the fall, he was a different person. Rooming in Herzog Hall on the campus of New Brunswick Theological Seminary and now convinced that Christian faith required separation from worldliness, he wrote:

"Having returned to school and announced that my ideas have altered considerably during the summer, I find myself living as an alien among the men in the Hall. I am regarded as an object of curiosity. I am no more to be considered as entirely sane; part of my reason has left me, apparently. . . . I find myself regarded as a curio chiefly because I have changed so decidedly. I object to off-color stories. I refuse to attend the theater, and I object to dancing, not for the group as a whole, but for myself as an individual. A genuine Christian, satisfied with Christ, is a rare thing in this age of unbelief.

"Very seriously I wonder whether I can remain here with my convictions intact, or if I retain them, without coming into desperate conflict with the entire community. There is smut, unbelief, mockery of things sacred, actual agnosticism and borderline atheism in this training school for the Christian ministry. There is no faith in the Atonement of Christ; that is an antiquity which must be discarded promptly. There is no acceptance of Calvary save as a mystical symbol of man's love for his fellows. . . . When belief is professed, an effort is made at once to destroy it. With God's help, though, I am confident that I shall conquer, and moreover be the means of preaching a Crucified Saviour to the future ministers of Protestantism."

Years later, looking back on his experience, Vernon Grounds called his childhood faith "a pre-critical stage." In those early years, he simply accepted what he was taught, and not much of that. But through his reading, and then through his educational experiences at Rutgers, he passed into "a critical stage." This period of questioning and doubt culminated with his decision to join the Humanist Society on campus. Then, after his experience of grace during the summer at the end of his freshman year, he entered "a post-critical stage," moving to a much deeper level of faith and commitment. He called this "living, hopefully, in that post-critical stage aware of what can be said against the faith, sensitive to the difficulties people have with the Gospel, and yet myself passionately persuaded that this is the Truth."

Books and More Books

During his last three years at Rutgers, Vernon, as a Language and Literature major, continued his reading and writing with a passion, but now he tended to view life from the widest possible perspective. Two books proved especially helpful in strengthening his faith and in deepening his understanding of Christian truth. Thomas Mann's novel *The Magic Mountain* raised the issues that seemed to persist and confront people. Mann offered him no solutions to the problems but "starkly revealed that without the gospel all culture and philosophy and experience reach a self-destructive impasse." In sharp contrast, James Orr's *The Christian View of God and the World* proved a great help in Vernon's inward struggle to reconcile the Christian faith and human reason.

As he later wrote in an article about "Books That Helped Shape My Life," the Orr book freed him "from the haunting suspicion that belief in the gospel must be maintained by faith alone in defiance of learning and logic. It made me realize that the Christian has no rival when it comes to seeing life steadily and seeing it whole.

"I confess to you that the resurrection is the anchor of my hope, because as I reflect on it and reflect on life I come to perceive that by means of man's worst—the crucifixion of Jesus—God achieves His best. And out of injustice and hatred and falsehood and cruelty and death, God brings glorious fulfillment. And a hope grounded in Jesus Christ, His cross, and His empty tomb . . . that beyond all our human failure and frustration God will bring glorious fulfillment."5

In 1937, Vernon Carl Grounds received his Bachelor of Arts degree, and Rutgers recognized his academic excellence by awarding him the Greek Prize and Phi Beta Kappa honors.

At this juncture in his life journey he was already intensely interested in people, in human nature, and had devoured hundreds of books and pages of poetry. But he was now also captivated by the apostle Paul's two affirmations in his letter to the Romans: First, "God commendeth his love toward us, in that, while we were yet sinners, Christ died for us." And second: "the love of God is shed abroad in our hearts by the Holy Spirit given unto us."

Vernon knew that he had been profoundly changed by Calvary love. Now he wanted to know the personal and ethical implications of that in his own life and in the lives of others.

CHAPTER 2

The Reason for Our Hope

Since Jesus Christ cannot be pushed aside as a liar or waved away as a lunatic, what conclusion must we draw? Jesus Christ is what He claimed to be! He is the Lord of glory, Deity incarnate, God humbling Himself to become man in order to redeem his lost creation. And since that is so, it is blasphemy for us to talk patronizingly about Him as a teacher or a martyr or a religious genius. Instead, we must bow down at his nail-pierced feet in adoration and faith exclaiming, "My Lord and my God!"

— VERNON GROUNDS, *Reason for Our Hope*

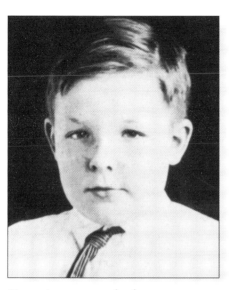

Vernon in grammar school,
Jersey City, NJ

Vernon at Rutgers University

Vernon, about 1938

Vernon, director at Scout Camp
Kaheka

Vernon and the Harmony Gospel Quartet, 1936

Vernon at Faith Seminary, 1935-1936

Studying at Faith Seminary

First Baptist Church, Johnson City, NY, home of Baptist Bible Seminary, 1945

Dean Grounds, Baptist Bible Seminary, 1950

Addressing students at Baptist Bible Seminary, 1948

Preaching the Word, 1943

Vernon and Ann with Barbara Ann, 1943

Vernon and Ann with Barbara Ann

Vernon with Barbara Ann

The Bonfils mansion, home of "the new Baptist seminary in the West"

The lobby, with its rich mahogany and white marble staircase

"The French Room"

VCG, about 1958

VCG in the early 1960s

Denver Seminary faculty 1964-65
Top, left to right: Edward Hayes, Bruce Shelley,
Raymond Baker
Bottom, left to right: Joseph Edwards,
Raymond McLaughlin, Douglas Birk, VCG,
Earl Kalland, Gordon Lewis, Donald Burdick

Dean Grounds with one of the
first seminary students

Vernon and Ann celebrate their 25th wedding anniversary on a trip to Hawaii, June 1964

VCG and his collection of walking canes

"The troika" in 1970: Earl Kalland, Vernon, Douglas Birk

Dean Edward Hayes, Vernon, Douglas Birk, 1975

Speaking at a Jews for Jesus meeting, 1977

President Grounds at Denver Seminary commencement, wearing the presidential medallion

Dedication of Vernon and Ann's great-grandson, Noah. *On the left:* their granddaughter, Emily, her husband Mike Gagnebin, and Noah; *on the right,* their daughter Barbara and her husband Robert Owen

Presentation of Vernon's portrait for the halls of Denver Seminary

The Denver Seminary campus, 1982

50th reunion of Faith Seminary graduates; Vernon is at bottom right

Vernon and Ann's 50th wedding
anniversary celebration, 1989

Vernon and Ann Grounds, 1996

To understand certain fish, we must plunge into water; to understand Vernon Grounds, we must consider his times. The leader he became and the positions he held become much more understandable when viewed in the light of the events of his day—events in Christian churches and events in American society.

It was the great American pamphleteer, Thomas Paine, who wrote in a desperate hour of the American Revolution, "These are the times that try men's souls." Truly, during the first twenty years of Vernon's life, the souls of many Americans were being tried by the flames of great events.

In the year of his birth, 1914, war erupted in Europe. While the United States was not immediately drawn into the conflict, the mood in the country was, as one historian describes it, "about as unwarlike as the sun ever shone upon." President Woodrow Wilson was a student and teacher of history, a "scholar in politics," and many believed that he was a pacifist. His secretary of state, William Jennings Bryan, was a foe of imperialism and a crusader for world peace. According to one student of the times, America's initial reaction to the European tragedy was one of "sheer humanitarian horror."

Then, on May 7, 1915, German ships torpedoed the British steamship *Lusitania* off the southern coast of Ireland. The ship sank in less than twenty minutes, taking 1,198 lives—including 128 Americans—to a watery grave. The resulting shock wave changed the mood throughout the United States and led to a declaration of war. America sent thousands of doughboys off to Flanders fields.

In later years Vernon would have only one vivid memory relating to those war years. He recalls "standing at the age of four in the midst of a very noisy crowd on the boulevard in Jersey City gazing at an effigy of Kaiser Wilhelm dangling high above the street. That was at the end of World War I in 1918." He could not recall his feelings at that moment "other than bewilderment that everybody seemed to hate the man whose image was hanging in midair."

Still, growing up within the shadows of New York City's towering skyline, young Vern Grounds could not escape for long the impact of "the times that try men's souls." Like millions of other American schoolboys, he devoured the tales of Horatio Alger, the nineteenth-century best-selling author whose *Bound to Rise, Rags to Riches, Struggling Upward*, and scores of other stories told of underprivileged youth from the streets of New York who made it big in America by the virtues of honesty, perseverance, and hard work.

For a time in the 1920s life matched the myth. After the boys came marching home from Europe, America experienced a period of great prosperity. The "Roaring Twenties" brought dramatic changes: new buildings, new fashions, new music, and new ideas. With this desire for the new, even the inherited faith of the nation seemed dated and out of style. The nation was turning more and more from its roots in the Judeo-Christian tradition to a religious humanism inspired by advances in science and technology.

The Bible on Trial

The greatest demonstration of this cultural shift came in the summer of 1925 when Vern Grounds was an eleven-year-old schoolboy reading his Horatio Alger stories. In a hot courtroom in tiny Dayton, Tennessee, nestled in the Cumberland Mountains, traditional Christianity was put on trial before the nation.

The state of Tennessee had brought charges against a young schoolteacher named John Scopes, who, in defiance of a state law prohibiting the teaching of doctrines contrary to the Bible, was teaching the theory of evolution to his Tennessee pupils. The trial, held in Dayton's red brick courthouse, attracted as an associate prosecutor a highly popular political figure from American's traditional heartland, William Jennings Bryan. The defense, thanks to the American Civil Liberties Union, was led by Clarence Darrow, an outspoken agnostic, widely known for his defense of radicals.

Many people considered Bryan the heroic figure in the courtroom. Raised in southern Illinois on pork, potatoes, and the *McGuffey Reader,* he had risen to the heights of power as a three-time presidential candidate and secretary of state under Woodrow Wilson. Even after resigning from his post as head of the State Department during the war in Europe, Bryan remained an eminent national figure by standing on moral principle. He stumped for a woman's right to vote and played a significant role in gaining the passage of the Eighteenth Amendment outlawing alcoholic beverages across the country.

In the spring of 1921, the "Great Commoner," as they called Bryan, had issued a series of attacks on evolution that instantly placed him in the forefront of fundamentalist forces, most importantly his lecture "The Menace of Darwinism." Bryan argued that morality is dependent upon religion and a belief in God, and anything that weakens this faith in God weakens man and makes him unable to do good. The evolutionary theory, he said, does this. It robs man of his major incentive for moral living.

William Jennings Bryan was the traditional "common man" from a small town who lived for faith, family, and the common good. He was the obvious choice to lead the charge against evolution.

Since both Darrow and Bryan were well-known public figures, more than one hundred journalists descended on Dayton to report on the "monkey trial," which would become the most publicized trial of the decade. Both prosecuting and defense attorneys knew that the nation would be listening to this first made-for-radio trial, and both tried to appeal to the larger audience.

On the fifth day of the trial in the stifling courthouse, Bryan, in his shirtsleeves, rose to speak for the first time. "The principal attorney [Darrow] has suggested that I am the arch conspirator and that I am responsible for the presence of this case, and I have almost been credited with leadership of the ignorance and bigotry which he thinks could alone inspire a case like this."

Not so, Bryan said, and went on to mock evolution by citing Darwin and thundering, "Never have they traced one single species to any other."

But Clarence Darrow presented what proved to be the most effective strategy of the trial when he called Bryan himself to the stand. Over the objections of his colleagues, Bryan agreed to testify.

Darrow's clear purpose was to weaken the prosecution's case by making the star attorney look foolish. The testimony had little bearing on the case itself, but in the heated two-hour exchange between Darrow and Bryan, the greatly admired Bryan was made to look like a closed-minded fundamentalist.

Darrow kept pressing Bryan for the age of the earth and the age of man on the earth. At one point he pushed him for the date of the Flood and asked, "What do you think that the Bible itself says?"

"I never made a calculation," Bryan responded.

"What do you think?" Darrow pressed.

"I do not think about things I do not think about," quipped Bryan.

"Do you think about things you do think about?" Darrow snapped.

"Well, sometimes."

The court rippled with laughter.

When one of Bryan's colleagues at the prosecution desk finally complained, "What is the purpose of this examination?" Bryan interrupted with his own answer, "The purpose is to cast ridicule on everybody who believes in the Bible. . . . I am simply trying to protect the Word of God against the greatest atheist or agnostic in the United States."

The crowd applauded, and in the end Bryan won the case. Scopes was found guilty and fined $100. But Darrow's humiliating cross-examination of Bryan painted this once immensely popular man as a bigoted, Bible-Belt fundamentalist. And that was the image most Americans remembered, not only of Bryan but of all fundamentalists.

The Scopes trial raised a hornet's nest of questions. Is the Bible true? What is man? Does science have the final answer? What about the soul? Is it a special creation by God—as Western civilization had taught for centuries—endowed with the power of moral choice with eternal consequences, or is it merely a development of natural existence, some strange by-product of age-after-age of natural selection?

The Scopes trial also made a profound impact upon American life and the popular faith of the people. The traditional vision of a Christian America suddenly appeared to be nothing more than an outdated fantasy of the past. Naturalistic evolution spread throughout the public schools, making traditional faith in the Bible an antiquated belief and portraying Bible-believing Christians as bigoted, uneducated, and unthinking.[1]

The new religion in America was now "modernism," and "fundamentalism" was its ardent foe. Modernism drew life from the universities and cities; fundamentalism from revivals and radio.

From Sawdust to Radio

The story of Christian evangelism in America is filled with colorful men and women who were eager to go anywhere and do almost anything to catch a complacent public's attention: George

Whitefield in Puritan Massachusetts, James McGready in the Kentucky wilderness, Aimee Semple McPherson in Hollywood, and the list goes on and on.

In the summer of 1933, when Vernon Grounds began to read his Bible in search of God, the most popular evangelist in America was a converted baseball player named Billy Sunday. In 1917, during Sunday's New York campaign for souls, the *Times* reported, "He poses on one foot like a fast ball pitcher winding up. He jumps upon a chair. In the stress of his routine he may stand with one foot in the chair and another on the lectern. All the while he is flaying the 'whiskey kings,' the German war lords, slackers, suffragettes or the local ministry."[2]

Few evangelists did more to create the public image of the Sawdust Trail, with its revival tents, its sawdust aisle leading to a crude altar or "mourner's bench" at the front of the tent, than Billy Sunday. Along with this went the assortment of means that fundamentalists used to preach the gospel to the lost, such as summer Bible conferences, radio broadcasts, camp meetings, and "Gospel Tabernacles."

But the trail of sawdust wasn't the only prevailing image of fundamentalism. Even as fundamentalists were engaged in a campaign to overthrow modernism in America's schools (for example, the Scopes trial), they were also militantly opposed to modernism in the churches. On the one hand, they treasured a deep conviction, inherited from their Puritan forefathers, that America was indeed "one nation under God," with a holy calling and a manifest destiny. On the other hand, many fundamentalists also had come to believe that the Bible taught that in the last days Christian churches, including America's, would fall from God's favor into unbelief. In the last days there would be a great apostasy, and fundamentalists were convinced that modernism in the nation's churches was a sure sign of that end-of-the-age apostasy. God had used revivals in the past to bring America back to God and He had promised to do it again.

Vernon Grounds grew up in the New York City area, a world away from the Bible Belt. New York was the home of the Yankees, the *New York Times*, and Harry Emerson Fosdick, the nation's best-known religious liberal. But Clifton, New Jersey, Vernon's hometown, was also near Princeton, where J. Gresham Machen, professor of New Testament since 1915, had challenged liberalism and gained national attention with his thoughtful defense of orthodoxy in his writings in the *New York Times*.

Then, in the late 1930s, the area experienced a strange new event: a *youth* revival. In New Jersey, where the colonial Great Awakening once flourished, young people rallied to sing and preach the old-fashioned gospel. One of the pioneers in this movement was Lloyd Brandt, who had grown up in a tough neighborhood in Boston and, as a teenager, was converted to faith in Christ. After a stint in business, Brandt enrolled in the National Bible Institute and caught the eye of Will Houghton, the pastor of New York City's Calvary Baptist Church. In 1932 Houghton hired Brandt to revive the youth ministry in his Manhattan church, and during the next eight years Brandt conducted more than five hundred rallies at the old Alliance Tabernacle in the heart of Manhattan.

At about the same time in Philadelphia, Pennsylvania, Percy Crawford, a hard-driving, Canadian-born preacher, and his talented wife, Ruth, began holding youth rallies along the Atlantic seaboard and broadcasting their popular program, *Young People's Church of the Air.*

The young friends Vern Grounds joined in the summer of 1933 were actively fanning the flames of this teenage revival, giving their personal testimonies of faith and fervently preaching the good news to their high school friends. Like them, once Vernon experienced his own personal faith in Christ, he discovered that the love of Christ has a strange power that compels a believer to pass on the gospel story. He soon joined his friends in the Harmony Gospel Quartet, traveling throughout the area evangelizing—a youth rally here, a church service there. John Van Houten, Martin Brown, Frank Boyko, and Bill Orange sang and Vernon preached! And Vern loved it. The high school debater had become the youth evangelist.

The New York area was a long way from Tennessee's Cumberland Mountains, but this too was fundamentalism. After the Harmony Gospel Quartet sang about "Calvary covering it all," the young debater-turned-evangelist preached the glories of the cross from his Scofield Reference Bible. During the service the quartet members shared their testimonies and reminded the listeners that "we are saved to carry the Good News to others." As part of their evangelizing effort, the group and their friends would "go out early in the morning, placing tracts under milk bottles and newspapers."[3]

In the 1920s fundamentalism had been all about the war within the traditional denominations and the struggle against evolution in the public schools. In the public press, fundamentalism lost both wars. But once fundamentalists withdrew from the denominations, they were forced to create new, independent agencies for ministry: schools, missions, publication houses, youth ministries, radio broadcasts, and a host of other independent organizations to "get the message out." Thus, the 1930s marked a significant shift in American Christianity. The tide of evangelistic and missionary fervor was ebbing from the mainstream denominations and rising in interdenominational channels.

The 1930s also saw the advent of "Christian radio." With stations popping up all over the country on coast-to-coast networks, fundamentalist preachers seized this opportunity for preaching the gospel to larger audiences. All America could tune in for President Roosevelt's "Fireside Chats" from Washington or Charles E. Fuller's "Old-Fashioned Revival Hour" from Los Angeles. For years to come, Christian radio would be the movement's primary means of communicating to millions of people.

Buoyed along by this swift current of change and controversy, young Vernon Grounds was also making life-changing encounters.

Ann

When Vernon had returned to Rutgers in September 1934 for the beginning of his sophomore year and discovered what a misfit he now was on campus, he decided to stay home in Clifton and commute to school. So each morning during the week he caught the train and rode the sixty miles to New Brunswick; then after his classes he caught the train again for the ride back home. This way he could pray with his friends any evening of the week and travel with the quartet on weekends, and this became his lifestyle for the next three years: classes during the week; ministry on the weekend. He was also establishing a pattern that he would follow for the rest of his life.

After a year traveling with the Harmony Gospel Quartet, Vernon heard about a ministry in Paterson, New Jersey, a larger, industrial town, where a group of about thirty Christians had resuscitated a comatose, independent Baptist church on the corner of North Ninth and Jefferson streets and were looking for a pastor. Vernon, though young, was already an able communicator, so the two—small church and eager young preacher—found each other, and Vernon began to preach regularly at the Gospel Tabernacle in Paterson. At a mere twenty-one years of age, he found himself pastor of a congregation and a traveling evangelist, making friends wherever he went. Among the friends Vernon met in this itinerary ministry was Ann Barton.

Sarah Ann Isabelle Barton was the daughter of Sarah (Woods) and Oliver Barton, both immigrants from Northern Ireland. Oliver had followed Sarah to America, and they had been married on April 16, 1912, the day the *Titanic* sank.

Both Sarah and Oliver were devout believers, Sarah from a strong Protestant background, and Oliver after a conversion to Christ as an adult. Their lives centered around the church, attending Christian conferences, and ministry together. They enjoyed short trips by car, and often drove to Ocean Grove, New Jersey, to hear Christian speakers. In this way Ann spent her youth in the company of a number of popular Christian leaders. She met Billy Sunday, heard Gypsy Smith at Ocean Grove, and met William Newell, who wrote the popular gospel hymn "At Calvary."

During these years, Ann accepted her parents' beliefs as her own, and on her tenth birthday accepted Christ as her personal Savior. A few years later she dedicated her life to Christ and began accompanying her father when he preached on street corners, and in prisons and homes for the aged. Her father's devotion impressed Ann with the importance of faithful Christian service. Nothing, she came to believe, should keep a committed Christian from attending church or from Christian ministry. Quitting was never an option.

Ann's parents came from music-loving families, and Ann inherited both the love and the talent. When her mother inherited a small family legacy, she decided to buy a piano for Ann, and at twelve years of age Ann began lessons. Through her lessons and practice, she became an accomplished and popular pianist.

During the first year of the Harmony Quartet ministry, Ann joined the group and spent many happy weeks in ministry. She later said that these were some of the happiest times of her young life, despite the brutal schedule. Usually Ann had to be ready to go by 6:00 A.M. on Saturday and did not return home until late Sunday evening. Many times after a fatiguing schedule of weekend services the young men would stop at the Barton home, where Ann's mother served them hot tea and thick slices of her Irish soda bread. Ann's parents basked in the glow of these young folks who were serving the Lord so diligently.

During these weekends traveling together, Vernon and Ann began to enjoy each other's company. Their first formal date was to a football game between Rutgers and Yale, but most of their "dates" were the weekends they spent traveling with the quartet. Still, when Vernon finally asked Ann to marry him, she happily said yes.

August 24 proved to be a significant date in Ann Barton's life. In 1914 she had come into the world on that date at her parents' small apartment at E. 87th Street in New York City. Ten years later she experienced her spiritual birth on that date when she accepted Christ as her Savior. And on her twenty-third birthday, she and Vernon announced their engagement.

Too excited to sleep that night after the party their friends had given to celebrate, Ann sat in her tiny bedroom and watched the diamond on her finger sparkle in the lamplight. She was going to be a pastor's wife. Was that possible? Her parents were wonderful Christians, but she knew they had little education and less money. Vernon was a graduate of Rutgers University and was at the time attending Faith Theological Seminary. Ann now recalls how nervous she was the first time he met her parents. She had told Vernon they lived in a humble little home and warned him that her father was not highly educated. He studied his Bible and preached whenever and wherever he could, often at the Littleton Chapel, but he'd had to work hard all his life to support his family and had had no opportunities for formal education.

After the meal, Ann helped her mother in the kitchen while Vernon visited with her father in the living room. What would a bright young seminary student think of her father, she wondered.

When Vernon was ready to leave, he and Ann spent a few minutes together at the door saying goodnight. "You know, Ann," he said, "when your father and I began talking I thought I was so superior in my knowledge of theology and God. But as I listened to your dear father talk about the Bible, I realized that compared to him I am spiritually just in kindergarten."

Has God been preparing me all my life to be a pastor's wife, Ann thought. After her high school graduation, she had attended Drake

Business School in East Orange, New Jersey, and later she took a job at the Morrison Mission. Then, about a year later, a Christian friend hired her to work at the Morristown branch office of the Metropolitan Insurance Company, where she learned the ins and outs of the business world. She knew Vernon had no interest in money, so perhaps these years, she thought, were preparing her to handle the family's finances—which proved to be true.

That night at the Barton home God spoke to Ann's heart, telling her not to worry. She would be equal to her calling. She had no way of knowing at that point that one day she would be the wife of a seminary president, would travel extensively, and would entertain leaders in the evangelical Christian world. That night it was enough for her to be assured that she could handle the task of pastor's wife and "helpmeet to my dear Vernon."

In response, Vernon shared his own feelings for Ann in a poem he wrote just before their marriage.

> I needed someone, dearest,
>   To take this heart of mine
> And fill it with an ardour
>   Akin to that divine.
>
> I needed someone, dearest,
>   To love me as I am,
> In spite of shameful failure,
>   In spite of petty sham.
>
> I needed someone, dearest,
>   To soothe my childlike grief,
> To ease the trying burden
>   And give me kissed relief.
>
> I needed someone, dearest,
>   To share my fairest dreams,

And yet to point out firmly
　　The folly of some schemes.

I needed someone, dearest,
　　To labour at my side,
To smile with eyes ashining
　　At every shift of tide.

I needed someone, dearest,
　　To keep me staunchly true,
To urge me ever on for Christ—
　　And so God gave me you.

(April 26, 1939)

The Seminary Years

In 1937, Vernon graduated Phi Beta Kappa in Language and Literature from Rutgers University. His original plan, after graduation, was to attend Westminster Seminary in Philadelphia. Flames of controversy had smoldered for years regarding liberal professors on the faculty of Princeton Seminary. The controversy had erupted openly in 1929 when the well-known J. Gresham Machen and his colleagues Robert Dick Wilson, Cornelius Van Til, and others withdrew from Princeton and, under the leadership of Machen, formed the staunchly conservative Westminster Seminary in Philadelphia.

But in the spring of 1937 another option appeared on the horizon when Faith Theological Seminary was organized as an alternative to Westminster because, according to its founder Carl McIntire, Westminster did not adhere to "the separated life or premillennialism." Many of Vernon's friends counted both points of vital importance, and one evening some of these friends invited Vernon and Ann to dinner so they could meet Dr. James Graham, who was home from his missionary ministry and had joined forces with McIntire in starting the new seminary.

Driving to dinner Vernon vowed to Ann, "I am determined! I will not budge from my decision to go to Westminster." But in his conversation with Dr. Graham, as he later explained, "the immovable object met the irresistible force," and that evening Vernon decided it was God's will for him to attend the new Faith Seminary in Wilmington, Delaware.

In the late summer of that year when he arrived in Wilmington, he found that there was no campus. Classes were to be held in the First Independent Presbyterian Church, and students would room in some apartments a short walk from the church. Vernon and a few other students spent the first few days of their first term painting walls and helping to prepare the quarters for the other men who would be joining them.[4]

The excitement of a new school, new classmates, and new professors carried Vernon along in those early days. He found one professor, Dr. Griffith, a particularly colorful character. Griffith would occasionally place a chair on top of his desk and lecture from that elevated position. And it was from Griffith that Vernon first heard the little jibe, "Fundamentalism is too much fun, too much damn, and too little mental."

The central figure in the infant seminary, however, was Carl McIntire, the militant young pastor from Collingswood, New Jersey, who not only formed his own seminary but also his own denomination in the new Bible Presbyterian movement. McIntire spoke weekly in chapel to update the faculty and student body on the latest developments in apostasy and to inspire new crusaders for his "Twentieth-Century Reformation." Still, in most classes Vernon received a classical seminary education in the Reformed tradition, reading the Bible in the original languages and learning systematic theology from Charles Hodge's three-volume classic, *Systematic Theology*.

In this school, soon to be the center of much controversy, Vernon also met at least a dozen men who would become well-known names in evangelical Christian circles. Among them were Francis Schaeffer, who became internationally known as the founder of L'Abri Fellowship in Switzerland and author of books focused on the cultural crisis in the West; Kenneth Kantzer, who became the dean of Trinity Evangelical Divinity School and editor of *Christianity Today;* Arthur Glasser, who, after serving as a missionary to China and fleeing when the Communist regime assumed power, became head of Fuller Seminary's School of World Missions; Joseph Bayly, who would become the editor of InterVarsity's *His* magazine, vice-president of David C. Cook Publishing, and a widely read author; and Douglas Young, the Old Testament scholar who founded the Institute for Holy Land Studies in Israel. All these, and more, became Vernon's lifelong friends and evangelical colleagues.

Vernon continued to pastor the church in Paterson, New Jersey, while he attended seminary. His church ministry extended from Friday evening to Monday morning. On Monday afternoon he caught the train for Wilmington, Delaware, where his classes at Faith ran from Tuesday morning through Friday noon. Then it was back to Paterson, and so the cycle continued.

After two years of this schedule, Vernon and Ann were married on June 17, 1939, at Gospel Tabernacle. Ann had played the piano at the Rescue Mission in Morristown, and the superintendent, L. B. Haynes, and his wife, Kitty, were good friends of the Barton family, so Ann asked him to perform the marriage ceremony. Jacob Stam was Vernon's best man. Stam was an attorney who also served for a time as chairman of the board for the Latin American Mission and as a dynamic member of many other Christian agencies. Though thirteen years older than Vernon, Jacob attended Vernon's church and often served as a spiritual guide for the young pastor. Through the years the Stams and the Groundses became close friends.

Three hundred family members and friends filled the church for the wedding on that hot, sultry June day. After the service, the twenty members of the wedding party drove to Morristown for a lawn reception at the Bartons' modest home. They celebrated and enjoyed Mrs. Barton's delicious home-cooked food.

Vernon and Ann moved into a small apartment on Ninth Street in Paterson. United now in marriage, they were united as well in ministry. Vernon was often away preaching, and Ann nearly always traveled with him. She continued to play the piano for the quartet and for Bible conferences. On Sunday mornings at the Gospel Tabernacle, when Vernon was preaching, Ann played for the congregational singing, the offertory, and the radio broadcasts.

For a time, in their early days together, Vernon and the Harmony Gospel Quartet had beamed a radio broadcast from Brooklyn. This brief experience was enough to encourage Vernon to try a radio broadcast once he began to preach at the church in Paterson. He started broadcasting over WPAT in Paterson and later moved to WAAT to broadcast "The Lighthouse Hour" after the Sunday evening service.

At home and in ministry, Vernon and Ann were a team in the truest sense.

In the spring of 1940, as he approached his graduation from Faith, Vernon received a call to lead the Bible Presbyterian Church in St. Louis, which some called "one of the largest independent Presbyterian churches in the county." He accepted the invitation to candidate, caught the train for St. Louis, and was genuinely impressed by the possibilities. Bible Presbyterian was not only a large church but also had many professional people in its congregation. Vernon knew that he would find a challenge in preaching thoughtfully to such a congregation.

After the Sunday morning service some of the leaders took him to the country club for lunch and urged him to become their pastor. Vernon felt drawn to the church, and during the return train trip to Paterson he decided to accept the invitation. Upon arriving home he called the leaders in St. Louis and told them he accepted the call. They were delighted. But then came the hard part. He had to stand before his friends at the Tabernacle and announce his resignation, which he did on the following Sunday, and then came the tears.

The next day, with a heavy heart, he caught the train for Wilmington and his final exams at Faith. But he was smitten with conviction as a voice within said, "You don't really believe it!"

He had read Calvin, Hodge, Warfield, and many other greats of the Reformed tradition and knew their case for infant baptism, which he had decided he could accept. But as he continued to ponder the issue, he felt increasing doubt. So even in the midst of final exams and events surrounding his graduation from seminary, he was trapped in a strange emotional crisis. He didn't like the thought of leaving his friends in Paterson; he became more and more certain that he could not agree with the Presbyterian position on baptism; and he realized he would be a deceitful man if in such a state of mind he accepted the attractive post in St. Louis.

For the next three days he read and read. He read the Scriptures again, and he read books presenting the Baptist case for faith-baptism. After three days, he said to himself, *I can't accept the Presbyterian position, and I can't serve a Presbyterian church.*

On Thursday morning Vernon felt driven to call Clarence Hellar, head deacon at the Tabernacle, just to tell the church leaders what a terrible mistake he had made in resigning. After listening to his pastor's story, Hellar said, "Vernon, you wait right there. I'm coming down to Wilmington."

Within a few hours, he arrived. Then, as they drove back to Paterson, Mr Hellar listened sympathetically as Vernon described his confusion and mental struggle. Just as Vernon entered the apartment where Ann awaited him, the telephone rang and the leaders of the church in St. Louis told him excitedly, "We have found a home for you!"

Vernon thanked them graciously but then confessed, painfully, that he had had second thoughts and that he could not, in good conscience, accept the call to the St. Louis church. Emotionally exhausted, he took Ann to visit friends in New York State, and there he spent the weekend relaxing and walking through the countryside. When they returned to the Tabernacle the following Sunday, Vernon simply told his congregation the whole story, including his now firm convictions about faith baptism. The people gladly welcomed him back, and within a few weeks Vernon himself was baptized by immersion and proceeded to baptize thirty others from the congregation.

In mid-May, 1940, Vernon graduated from seminary, and that fall, with Ann's strong encouragement, he enrolled in a Ph.D. program at Drew University, which was only twenty-six miles away in Madison, New Jersey. Sensing the need of struggling Christians for pastoral care, Vernon chose to concentrate his studies in the area of psychology, and focused especially on the importance of love.

At Drew he was introduced not only to the Wesleyan tradition in theology but also to Blaise Pascal, Søren Kierkegaard, Walter Rauschenbusch, Emil Brunner, Reinhold Niebuhr, and, in his own words, "many other seminal thinkers whom previously I had known only nominally and, as a rule, negatively. It was an exciting, consciousness-raising exposure and experience."[5] His problem was how to integrate any valid insights from such sources with biblical truths. That problem was to be his ongoing concern.

The War Years

A year later the United States was plunged into war when the Japanese attacked Pearl Harbor. For Vernon and Ann and the members of the Gospel Tabernacle, like the rest of the country, the war years (1941–1945) meant sacrifice, hard work, and devastating loss. The war demanded that the country live with little and appreciate everything as people throughout the nation threw themselves sacrificially into the conflict. New Jersey shipyards turned out aircraft carriers, battleships, heavy cruisers, and destroyers for the U.S. Navy. The Curtiss-Wright Company in Paterson built thousands upon thousands of aircraft engines. But the war also brought ration cards, nightly blackouts, and the sight of the gold and silver stars in house windows announcing the loss of a son.

Though by nature a gentle man, Vernon began to acquire a special touch in rescuing the perishing and healing the emotionally wounded. He genuinely loved people and made friends everywhere. It was love, more than any other single factor, that made the Tabernacle a family. Vernon once described it as "a thriving testimony."

The Tabernacle did not, however, claim all of Vernon's time. With the quartet he had gotten a taste of itineration and found he liked it. He loved to travel, to meet people and to befriend them in Jesus' name. While serving the church and pursuing his education, he also managed to teach at two small Bible schools in the area: the Hawthorne Evening Bible School and the American Seminary of the Bible. He also taught one day a week at King's College, which Percy Crawford, a well-known youth evangelist, had established in New Castle, Delaware.

In the middle of the war, life suddenly brought great joy and delight to Vernon and Ann when, on June 16, 1943, their daughter Barbara Ann was born. With a new baby in the home, Vernon's extensive travel became more of a problem, but Ann learned to adjust, not only to having him gone but to staying home herself. Her favorite verses had long been Isaiah 12:2–3, and these sustained her more than ever now. "Behold, God is my salvation; I will trust, and not be afraid; for the LORD Jehovah is my strength and my song; he also is become my salvation. Therefore, with joy shall ye draw water out of the wells of salvation" (KJV).

But the war years also brought great sadness to the Grounds family. In late October of 1944, Ann's father died suddenly. Bypass surgery did not exist in those days, and so, at age fifty-nine, Oliver Barton died of "an enlarged heart." After his death, Ann's mother, Sarah Barton, came to live with the Groundses, sharing a bedroom with two-year-old Barbara.

Then, on July 12, 1945, Vernon's brother John died of cancer, leaving behind his wife, Rita, and their two daughters, Carol and Janet. Vernon stood at the bedside of his brother, holding his hand as he slipped into eternity.

About the time Oliver Barton died, Vernon gave a series of radio messages in which he made the case for Christianity and appealed to listeners to turn to Christ in personal faith. In one talk he referred to "the colossal disaster of the present war," decrying the mangled bodies of little children, the carnage of the bombings, and the misery of the masses. The scenes raised within his own soul that irrepressible question, "Oh, God, why?"

"Let us frankly recognize the limits of our minds," he appealed. Many times in some misery we must wait and trust. But we can know that "judgment is falling." The Scriptures speak of "calamity as a divine visitation." The "long-restrained judgment of outraged Deity is now being unleashed upon a Bible-hating, Christ-rejecting civilization. . . . Judgment is falling."

Current events, however, played only a tiny part in the series. Beyond the war in Europe, beyond the bombings and bloodshed in the Pacific, Vernon saw a larger warfare: the ageless conflict between faith and unbelief—the struggle for the truth. Like Augustine centuries before, he saw historical events against the backdrop of divine events, the saga of human redemption.

The dozen or so talks were later published in his first book, *The Reason for Our Hope*. So on radio and then on the printed page he made his case for faith in God, in Jesus, and in the Bible. Influenced by J. Gresham Machen's well-reasoned books, Vernon engaged in the cultural conflict between faith and unbelief with the determination and passion of a Marine hitting the beach at Normandy.

Dr. Allan MacRae, president of Faith Seminary, wrote the introduction to *The Reason for Our Hope* and noted that "the Church no longer has the place of influence in American society that it once had." But, as Dr. MacRae indicated, Vernon Grounds made his case for faith drawing from "a wide section of contemporary opinion." Books and more books! Already, at thirty years of age, Vernon was developing into a scholar, with books the mark of the man.[6]

In *The Reason for Our Hope,* Vernon argued for faith in a living Creator, faith in a supernatural Christ, and faith in the credibility of the Bible. He challenged and sought to refute the case for unbelief. He never suggested that anyone could reason his way to God, but he did speak of "the godly faculty of reason."

Calling the case for unbelief "incredible" and "illogical," he wanted every listener and every reader to know that the Bible-believing Christian was not some brainless scarecrow from the cornfields of Kansas. According to naturalism, he said, "everything in the world, including the human mind, can be explained quite easily in terms of evolving mud. Just give mud enough time and it will produce all by itself the dramas of Shakespeare, the music of Handel, the paintings of Michaelangelo and the teachings of Jesus Christ!" Mud and time the explanation for man and the world? "Now why such nonsense is unquestionably accepted as the essence of truth is to me a dark enigma."

Grounds had found such arguments in James Orr, G. K. Chesterton, and other Christian apologists, but he made *his* case for Christianity by mustering the testimonies of an impressively wide range of witnesses on both sides of each question. He knew the arguments, and he always concluded his talk with a clear appeal to "come to God in the name of Jesus, confessing that you are a blinded, bewildered sinner."

When the book appeared in 1945, as the war in Europe and the Pacific was moving at last to its long-awaited conclusion, the author dedicated it to his church family at the Gospel Tabernacle in Paterson. After more than ten years of ministry there, it also served as a fond farewell, for Vernon was leaving. Through the decade of his leadership, the congregation had grown from about thirty people to more than three hundred. But Vernon was now ready to move into a teaching post and had accepted an invitation to become Professor of Theology and Apologetics at the Baptist Bible Seminary, in Johnson City, New York. There he would meet his next test of faith and work of love.

CHAPTER 3

A Fork in the Road

Because of God's forgiving love, we can press upon Christian hearts and minds *the ethic of forgiving love*. We can remind pardoned transgressors of Paul's entreaty in Ephesians 4:32: "And be ye kind one to another, tenderhearted, forgiving one another, even as God for Christ's sake hath forgiven you."

– VERNON GROUNDS,
The Love That Keeps on Forgiving

In the late summer of 1945, Vernon and Ann Grounds, their daughter, Barbara, and Ann's mother, Sarah Barton, rode the Lackawanna Railroad from Paterson, New Jersey, to Binghamton, New York, for their move to Baptist Bible Seminary in nearby Johnson City. Vernon was eager to join the faculty of the young school that was meeting in the educational wing of the imposing First Baptist Church in Johnson City, at the corner of Main and Baldwin Streets.

The "seminary" label was somewhat misleading, however; "Bible school" would have been more accurate. But the name represented a dream as much as a fact, and the school did offer courses in theology. Still, Vernon, now thirty years old, with his Phi Beta Kappa key from Rutgers, eagerly anticipated his ministry in Christian education.

Vernon and Ann found an attractive, three-bedroom house on Grand Avenue in Johnson City. The place also had a detached garage, but they had no immediate need for the garage since they had sold their car in Paterson to be able to afford a house. Soon they had little Barbara and Mrs. Barton settled in one bedroom and had rented the third bedroom to two young women students from the school. "Mr. Grounds," now sporting a dapper bow tie, made an immediate impact upon the school. In his first year he taught a string of courses, stretching from English Composition to Christian Apologetics. In the second year he became "Dean Grounds" when he also assumed that role, working hard to strengthen the academic program. When Vernon arrived, the three-year program of study at Baptist Bible Seminary earned a student no degree of any kind. Four years after he became dean, the school had state certification, having added two years of liberal arts.

Vernon, with his own liberal arts background, also changed the atmosphere in the classroom. One student described his teaching as turning on "the lights everywhere." As he taught philosophy, theology, and Christian apologetics (or, as it was often called at the time, "evidences"), his vocabulary was free of the sometimes deadening clichés and trite formalities of traditional fundamentalism, and the students found his insights offered a refreshingly new perspective on their study of Scripture. Perhaps most importantly, he took a pastoral, personal interest in every student.[1]

It was this concern for students that soon led him to spend hour after hour in counseling the young people around him. He took time to sit down with discouraged freshmen and bewildered upperclassmen, have coffee with them at Nick's Sandwich Shop or Larry's Diner down on Main Street, and share what one student called "little pieces of advice and love for the Word." When he traveled to speak in the area, Vernon often took students with him— sometimes to drive, sometimes to sing. Whatever he did, he made friends of the students, many of them for life. Years afterward, many still had stories to tell.

One midwinter day Dean Grounds was scheduled to conduct a wedding rehearsal in Ithaca, New York, about fifty miles north of Johnson City, so he asked two students, Hank Beukema and his girl friend, Peggie, to drive him. When the three left Johnson City, they headed into a horrible snowstorm, with Hank behind the wheel of a borrowed car without snow tires. The further they drove, the worse the storm became. Arriving in Ithaca, a city surrounded by steep hills, Hank headed down one of the steepest. Midway down, the car began to skid, then turned completely around and gently slid down the hill backward.

Peggie was praying, Hank was valiantly trying to steer the car, and Dean Grounds was trying to get the door open. As Vernon said later, "I never thought to pray, only to get out!" When the car came to rest against a curb at the bottom of the hill, Dean Grounds finally managed to open the door. "Mr. Beukema," he said, "if you don't mind, I will walk the rest of the way." And that is just what he did.

Not long after their "wild" Ithaca experience, Vernon sang at Hank and Peggie's wedding, and in 1950 he preached the message at Hank's ordination service. Hank and Peggie Beukema agree that Vernon Grounds was a great professor and a trustworthy friend.[2]

Travel and Talk

Along with his responsibilities as professor and dean, Vernon continued to travel whenever and wherever he was invited, speaking at university centers, churches, and student conferences. One of his favorite trips was the drive up the old two-lane highway from Johnson City to Ithaca, where he went to speak to the InterVarsity Christian Fellowship meetings at Cornell University. The meetings drew about a hundred collegians, and more than half of the young men who attended were veterans just back from the war.

Before long, the Cornell students knew that when Dean Grounds spoke, they could expect something intellectually challenging from a Christian perspective. There and elsewhere, Vernon was gaining a reputation for his wide reading and scholarship. In fact, some of the students, knowing that Dean Grounds would answer their questions reasonably and without apology, brought, as they called them, their "hard nut philosophy major" non-Christian friends.

Vernon had now built his own rational case for Christianity, based on Christ's redeeming and revealing acts. These "evidences," as he presented them, gave his listeners "a reason" to hope for God's

mercy even beyond the grave. Vernon's demeanor also invited questions from the groups he spoke to, and he was always available to
talk after the meetings.

Following one InterVarsity meeting in the fall of 1948, a freshman from Cornell drove to Johnson City with his own troubling
questions about Christianity. John Warwick Montgomery spent
an hour with Vernon and found his responses to the questions so
convincing that by the Christmas holiday, as he later reported, "I
had passed into the Kingdom. For that one hour alone, I am forever in your debt." Montgomery went on to gain his own Ph.D.
and to write extensively in defense of the Christian faith.[3]

Earlier that same year, after professor Edward John Carnell's *An
Introduction to Christian Apologetics* appeared, Vernon wrote to
"Brother Carnell" at Fuller Seminary in Pasadena, California. "I am
anxious to make whatever contacts I can with brothers like yourself," his letter began. "Intellectual comradeship is a real and most
precious thing. . . . You are spearheading a kind of intellectual renaissance among American evangelicals."

Making it clear that he wanted to be a part of this "intellectual
renaissance," Vernon continued, "I am anxious to help in any way
I possibly can to bring about a stirring of the mind as a prelude to
reaching of souls."

For his part, Carnell was especially interested in the fact that
Vernon Grounds was working on his doctorate under Edwin Lewis
at Drew Seminary, and he urged Vernon to "garner any rumblings
from Lewis about my book." But, more significantly, he was
impressed with Vernon's passionate zeal for an evangelical "intellectual renaissance."

"I am glad," Carnell wrote in response to Vernon's letter, "that
you feel like we do that it is high time that the evangelicals gird
themselves about and revive learning. I feel that we are on the verge
of great things. The Fuller faculty . . . is tingling with long range

plans for the attack." Then he asked Vernon what he thought about the organization of an evangelical scholars' fellowship.[4]

In just this sort of exchange, the "new evangelical" movement within traditional fundamentalism was slowly forming.

―――

By now, Vernon was deep into his doctoral program at Drew. On certain days of the week he would catch the train in Binghamton and ride the rails to Madison, New Jersey, to complete his class work and begin research for his dissertation. For the latter, he had settled on a study of the concept of love, and he began to read widely in psychology, Scripture, theology, and studies on human nature.

In the course of his reading and research, he came upon an old brown book written by Ernest Sartorius, a leader in the evangelical church in Germany in the late nineteenth century. Vernon read every word of *The Doctrine of Divine Love* and in his copy marked significant passages with two or three red lines in the margins. It was Sartorius, far beyond all others, who convinced Vernon Grounds that God's love is indeed the dominant theme of the whole Bible.[5]

"The love of God, our Creator and Redeemer," wrote Sartorius, "begets in us the love to love Him and keep His commandments. This is a basic principle of evangelical morality." Love is "the supreme virtue and the sum-total of all virtues. Love is the fulfilling of the law (1 Corinthians 13; Romans 13:10). Love is the sacrifice of the heart, the perfect self-denial, the resignation of all self-love and self-pleasing, and the humble readiness to serve our brethren." Love, Sartorius said, casts out every fear (1 John 4:18).

Once Vernon discovered this unbreakable bond between Christian faith and Christian love, the conviction grew and grew within him until it took hold of his life. Distinctive Christian love, he came to believe, is Calvary love, and only a Christian faith that is growing and active in the expression of Calvary love is worthy of the name of Christ. It is also this bond between faith and love that makes sense out of life's joys and sorrows.

At about the same time, a course with Professor Stanley Hopper at Drew introduced Vernon to Søren Kierkegaard's *Works of Love,* and Vernon soon made a habit of reading a few of the Dane's thought-provoking passages before heading off to his classes. As he delved deeper into the book, Vernon marveled at Kierkegaard's treatment of the major New Testament passages speaking of God's love.

In one of his meditations upon the Lord's Supper, Kierkegaard ponders the words, "Love covers a multitude of sins." What a wonder that man endeavors to be loving, he writes, "seeing that he himself is in need of love, and to that extent is really looking after his own interest by being loving. . . . Luther says that every man has a preacher with him, a preacher called flesh and blood, lusts and passions . . . yet it also is certain that every man has a confidant who is privy to his inmost thoughts, namely conscience." A man, says Kierkegaard, cannot hide his sins from himself. "This privy confidant which follows man everywhere is in league with God. . . . The true preacher is the confidant of thine inmost thoughts." As a consequence, we all feel a need to hide ourselves. "Oh that there were a place of refuge, a pardon to take away my sin from me!"

Well, there is! The love of Christ hides the sins. At the Lord's Table the Savior stretches out His arms for the fugitive who would flee from the consciousness of his sin. "'Come to me' He invites us. 'Love hides the multitude of sins.'"

"Oh, believe Him!" writes Kierkegaard. "He hides them quite literally. . . . Oh, blessed hiding place! It is not a doctrine He communicates to thee; no, He gives thee Himself."[6]

When Vernon read these words, he saw his ambivalent prayer that night in the Ternigan home in an entirely new light. Now, he knew he had found his central purpose in life: to love God in every possible way . . . in thought, deed, and motive. True faith energizes love; it empowers love to live, and die, for others.

A Sense of Restlessness

In his soul, however, Vernon was beginning to sense a strange discomfort and at times felt out of place at the Johnson City school. For one thing, he could not dismiss the memory of his early days there when the president of the school had been accused of "inappropriate" conduct toward a female graduate and the board of trustees had launched an inquiry. Three women teachers at the school reported that the investigating board members had treated them "roughly" in the course of the investigation. One of the faculty members who spoke up in their defense was Professor Frank Neuberg, a Jewish believer with a Johns Hopkins doctorate who taught the Old Testament courses at the seminary. He had commented to Vernon, "Gangsters in Chicago have higher ethical standards than these men!"

In the midst of this controversy at the school Vernon was walking down Main Street one day, engaged in subvocal prayer, when he recalled Peter's encounter with Jesus on the shore of the Sea of Galilee. Suddenly, Jesus' words to His questioning disciple reached out and grabbed him: "What is that to thee? Follow thou me." That was enough reassurance at the time of crisis, and Vernon determined to focus on being a steadfast follower of Christ.

Two years later, in 1947, with the school under the leadership of a new president, Dr. Paul R. Jackson, the Baptist Bible *Seminarian*, the school's yearbook, featured both the new president and the dean in a two-page spread. Each wrote about the need of the hour.

Baptist Bible Seminary of Johnson City was approved by the General Association of Regular Baptist churches and was publicly promoted as militantly fundamentalist. Not surprisingly, then, Dr.

Jackson spoke of apostasy and doctrinal purity. "Fifteen years ago Baptist Bible Seminary was but a dream child, forming in the hearts of faithful men of God. . . . Apostasy was attacking Christendom insidiously. The call to separation was heeded by only a few. It was during those days that Baptist Bible Seminary was established. Now Christendom is torn by the apostasy which has grown into a Goliath. Churches by the hundreds are obeying the clarion call to separation. And our Seminary stands ready to train, for these churches, leaders."

On the opposite page, Dean Vernon Grounds, smiling through his rimless glasses above a bright tartan tie, wrote, "In this challenging hour the Church of Jesus Christ needs many things, but it needs nothing more desperately than men and women who know God not as a datum of theology but as a Person and a Friend. It is dismayingly possible for one to be, technically, a servant of God, occupying a sacred office, and in spite of that know Him not."

He recalled that Phineas and Hophni, the two sons of Eli the priest, could, no doubt, have creditably passed an examination in doctrine. "They may even have been rigid fundamentalists who cried out against any deviation from orthodoxy. *But they knew not the Lord.* And their ignorance was mirrored in the shameless sin which proved a stumbling-block to Israel. . . . Zeal for the faith once delivered is contemptible when united with a profound ignorance of God in personal experience."

The contrast in these two pieces clearly reveals the fresh perspective that Vernon was bringing to the school. But it also reveals why, as time passed, he felt more and more like a misfit in the militantly fundamentalist school. The administrators of the school were kind and generous to Vernon and his family, and he was extremely happy in the classroom where he was having an impact on students. He also enjoyed his informal contacts with younger believers over coffee, and he enjoyed the opportunities he had to speak every Sunday in some church in the area. But Vernon knew something simply wasn't right!

His feelings and concerns began to crystallize when school leaders subtly criticized his philosophical background. The General Association of Regular Baptists (GARB) and the Johnson City school were now allied with Carl McIntire's American Council of Christian Churches (ACCC), and the chairman of the school's board of trustees would occasionally, from his pulpit at the First Baptist Church in Johnson City, ridicule philosophy as "the wisdom of the world." Students in the audience were naturally inclined to think of the one man in the school who had a Phi Beta Kappa key on his key chain and taught philosophy.

By 1950, Vernon had decided that he could not continue on the faculty of the school with a clear conscience because he could not accept the doctrine of "separation" espoused by the American Council of Christian Churches. He did not believe in "separating" from Christian believers who happened to be in a church or ministry that the ACCC called "questionable" or tainted with what they termed outright "apostasy."

It had been fourteen years since Vernon had graduated from Rutgers—fourteen years spent in the heart of fundamentalism, where he had discovered firsthand its highs and lows, its evangelistic passion and its separatist zeal. Now, after five years in Johnson City, Vernon and Ann decided that he should resign and move on. But where?

⸻

By the spring of 1951, Vernon had received several invitations from other institutions. Kenneth Kantzer, his friend from their days at Faith Seminary who was teaching at Wheaton College's Graduate School, wrote at the dean's request to ask Vernon to consider joining Wheaton's graduate faculty. Los Angeles Baptist

Seminary was urging him to consider the presidency of their school, and a third overture had come from Denver, Colorado, where some of his friends in ministry were supporting the creation of a new Baptist seminary.

This third possibility intrigued Vernon most. Drawn to the prospect of helping to shape a graduate school of theology, he checked specifically on the Denver school's spirit of cooperation with other evangelical believers. What he learned assured him that this position offered him a greater opportunity to minister in wider Christian circles.

Still, a decision of this magnitude was not easy, especially since Vernon was unusually sensitive to the consequences his decision would have on his relationships with people he had come to respect. He shared these concerns in a letter—which was, in effect, his resignation—to seminary president Dr. Paul Jackson.

"I am desperately anxious to do nothing which will in the least hurt the rest of the faculty or injure the Seminary as a whole. But you are before anything else a man of principle, and the school exists because it is committed to the defense and propagation of certain great convictions. And, as God knows my heart, I desire to be free from hypocrisy in any aspect of my life. Christian ethics, therefore, to say nothing of common decency, demand that I make a few matters crystal-clear."

He went on to explain that he had not abandoned any of his basic beliefs. "But to put it bluntly," he said, "I have reached the place where I am not in agreement with the American Council." Indeed, he said, he was in "rather serious disagreement" with its major premise—"a refusal to cooperate with evangelicals who maintain certain ecclesiastical connections."

When Vernon met with President Jackson face to face to tender his resignation, Jackson asked, "Won't you change your mind and stay?"

At this point Vernon told him that he was seriously considering a position with a new Baptist seminary in Denver. "The Conservative Baptist school?" the president asked. "Look, Vernon, I know that you are no enemy of the gospel. But I fear that you will be endorsing those who are enemies. You will be giving aid and comfort to the enemies because the Denver school is not fully separated from unbelief."[7]

That was the final confirmation for Vernon that he was taking the right step, and in June he traveled to Buffalo, New York, to meet with the board and several faculty members of the seminary in Denver. Shortly after the meeting he received a phone call, from the dean and the acting president, offering him the position. Vernon, with Ann's full approval, accepted the position, and the Grounds family prepared to cut their eastern roots and begin a new life in the West.

CHAPTER 4

In Search of Camelot

I Corinthians, chapter 13 . . . is a piece of poetry, though we know now, that love is far more than poetry: it is a measureless force. As a matter of fact, this passage is a hymn in which Paul sings the praises of love—not ordinary love, of course, but the supernatural love which the Holy Spirit creates within us when we accept Jesus Christ as our Savior. And this hymn voices one major idea: love, God's redemptive love in Jesus Christ working out in our own lives by faith, is the greatest thing in all the world.

– VERNON GROUNDS,
Love: Poetry or Power

When Vernon and Ann Grounds, with Ann's mother and eight-year-old Barbara in the back seat, drove their Chevrolet up Denver's Eighth Avenue and turned right on Humbolt in late July of 1951, they gazed wide-eyed at the stately old homes in the area old timers called "Capital Hill." At the corner of Tenth and Humbolt, they got their first view of the impressive mansion on the edge of Cheesman Park that was the home of the new Baptist seminary.

The mansion had been the home of Frederick G. Bonfils, multimillionaire owner of the *Denver Post*. When the mansion was built early in the twentieth century, the Rocky Mountain region was a young empire. Capitalists exploited the area's countless resources, but the empire had no czar. As Gene Fowler puts it in his biography, *Timberline*, Bonfils had "the Napoleonic awareness of the hour." He, above all others, carried his dark head high and kept his eye on the horizon. For forty years Bonfils and his roly-poly, blond partner, Harry Tammen, ruled the Rocky Mountain empire from their offices at the *Denver Post* and shaped history when they uncovered the Teapot Dome Scandal.

By the time Bonfils was sixty-three, he was working and scheming as hard as ever, and telling friends that he was worth $60 million. Still, he was a lonely man, stern and unyielding. He had won notoriety and fortune but didn't know what to do with either. Now, in his declining years, his gods of money and power were of little solace.

As Fowler tells it, when the *Post's* managing editor put his head through the doorway and said, "Coolidge is dead," Bonfils stared incredulously. He had always admired the silent New Englander who had become president of the United States. Had he now lost his last friend on earth?

When two of his intimates visited Bonfils a bit later, he emerged from his office in a mood to talk of life and death. "Coolidge has gone," he said, "And one wonders why we keep up the struggle, and what it all means."

He waved toward a door leading to the reception room. "By stepping through the doorway called death, we could find peace and enter upon the larger experience. It all seems so simple. Why should a man depend solely on material things, on wealth?"

One of the listeners, a longtime associate, asked, "Don't you think you might concentrate on religion?" Bonfils's eyes flashed. "No!" he said.

The woman who raised the question persisted. "Many persons find something in religion to buoy them in troublesome time. Many have found peace in the Catholic faith. Why don't you seek admission to the Catholic Church?"

Bonfils drew a deep breath and roared, "Never! Never!"

The next day he became ill with influenza, with a threat of pneumonia. A few days later he grew worse, suffering from toxic encephalitis. His family gathered beside his bed.

Now, with his eyes fixed on something other than life, Bonfils spoke weakly, "Send for a priest."

On the morning of February 2, 1933, the Reverend Father Hugh L. McMenamin, rector of the Cathedral of the Immaculate Conception, arrived at the mansion and baptized Bonfils in the Catholic faith. Bonfils looked at the crucifix and then lapsed into a long sleep—his last sleep.[1]

Bonfils had wanted nothing to do with religion, until faced with eternity. Now, just seventeen years after his death, the former residence of the czar of the Rocky Mountain empire was home to a seminary.

Could This Be Camelot?

Just over a year before Vernon and his family first climbed the front steps of the mansion at Tenth and Humboldt, in May 1950, several conservative Baptist pastors in Colorado had agreed that their fledgling but growing association of churches needed a new seminary to train men and women to serve in their churches and as missionaries on foreign fields. The pastors moved quickly on the idea, and within just four months had formed a committee, located a building to house the new school, turned to a banker in the Beth Eden Church in Denver to arrange the loan, formed the board of trustees, and invited four graduates and faculty members from Northern Baptist Seminary in Chicago to teach the first year of classes. They hired William Kerr for theology, Donald Burdick for New Testament, Raymond McLaughlin for homiletics, and Douglas Birk for Christian education. Two students who were enrolling at the seminary to finish their degrees, Joseph Edwards and Jack Fall, were prepared to serve as instructors in Old Testament and Church History. And by September, thirty-one students had enrolled as the entering class.

Helen Bonfils, one of Frederick's two daughters, had agreed to sell the old mansion for $55,000, so the school moved in with a huge debt, a glorious view, and some prominent neighbors. The Humphreys mansion, with its thirty rooms of classic Denver grandeur, was across the street. (Ira B. Humphreys had made his millions from mining and oil in the region.) Two blocks away lived Mamie Eisenhower's mother, Mrs. Dowd. After "Ike" became president in 1952, professors and seminarians could occasionally catch a glimpse of the presidential motorcade and the war-hero president in the neighborhood.

The Bonfils mansion itself was something to behold: three stories of classical grandeur surrounded by gardens, lawn, and wrought-iron fencing. Four huge Ionic columns framed the north entrance, where two beveled-glass doors led into a lobby whose walls were covered with tapestry and rich mahogany. To the left was an exquisitely formal parlor, which could be divided in half by cut-glass sliding doors. From day one the seminary family called the north half "The French Room" because it was a copy of a room in the Versailles Palace: silver-leaf ceiling, bright tapestry walls, mirrors all around, and floors with an inlaid hardwood pattern. What elegance for seminary receptions! But faculty meetings were also held around the imposing table under the sparkling, crystal chandelier.

Seminary chapel services were conducted in the more spacious south half of the parlor, where the windows looked out onto the terraced gardens. Here the tapestry walls were darker, with wildlife scenes from the French countryside; the ceiling was gold leaf and reflected the light of another huge chandelier. The sliding glass doors between the two large rooms were covered on the chapel side by maroon ceiling-to-floor draperies, which soon served as backdrop for nationally known speakers such as Lorne Sanny of the Navigators; Bill Bright, founder of Campus Crusade for Christ; Francis Schaeffer of L'Abri, Switzerland; and Dr. Carl Henry of Fuller Seminary.

Ascending from the first-floor foyer to the second-floor bedrooms was the most impressive feature of the mansion: a beautiful, spiral stairway of radiant white Italian marble.

The word that comes to mind in describing this setting is *Camelot*. Within a decade the music of Lerner and Loewe's Broadway musical *Camelot* would sweep across the country, and writers would borrow the image of the classic legend of noble King Arthur and his magnificent court for President John Kennedy's administration in Washington. But something of the same idealism—an evangelical Camelot, if you will—marked the dreams of pastors, professors, and students during the early years of the seminary in Denver. Most students who stepped through the doors of the school in the early years did so with a sense of awe—if not of the professors, then of the beautiful building and its picturesque location on the edge of wooded Cheesman Park. But Camelot is a mythic place, and this was the real world.

Vernon and Ann Grounds were in their late thirties by now—old enough to have had their share of shattered dreams yet young enough to still be surprised by life. And some surprises awaited them. They encountered the first surprise on their very first day in the city.

That evening, they were invited to meet the faculty and their wives for a welcoming picnic supper at the home of Joseph Edwards, but they soon discovered that no one had brought the hot dogs and chips for the picnic because no one had enough money to buy them. Once the guests of honor sensed the situation, and as soon as it was graciously possible, they slipped away to the nearest grocery store and bought the food for their own welcome to the seminary family.

During the evening the conversation turned, quite naturally, to the problems facing the faculty. Surprisingly, considering the picnic food situation, financial concerns were among the least of the problems. As the heat of the day faded into cool evening breezes, Vernon and Ann listened to the story of the school's first year of survival—its dreams, conflicts, intrigues, and suspense.

The Struggle

Conservative Baptists were, at the time, a youthful missionary movement supported by Baptist churches stretching from Maine to California. The movement's overseas agency was the Conservative Baptist Foreign Mission Society (CBFMS), founded in 1941. Its roots were deep in the history of fundamentalism within the Northern Baptist Convention, but it was more moderate and cooperative than the General Baptists the Groundses had known in Johnson

City. Vernon had checked on this before he ever agreed to accept the position in Denver. But he had no idea how passionate and unreasonable a small minority of critics could be.[2]

On that first Friday night in the Edwardses' backyard Vernon and Ann learned that two groups of Baptist churches in Colorado, with about thirty on each side, were in sharp disagreement over what it meant to be a "Conservative Baptist." One group was "the militants," the other "the moderates." Both sides in the conflict supported the idea of a new Baptist seminary in Denver, but they had no essential unity on the question, "What is our purpose?" The constitution of the new school stated, "The Seminary is in fellowship with all who share the basic principles of the Conservative Baptist movement, and stands to serve the worldwide Baptist cause." But, in practical terms, who decided the identity of the genuinely Conservative Baptists?

Controversy had erupted in Colorado among a few influential pastors in the Baptist churches, namely, Sam Bradford of the Beth Eden Church on Denver's near north side; William Spratt of the Judson Baptist Church on the west side of Denver; and William Whittemore of the First Baptist Church in Fort Collins. Pastor Bradford had been around for a long time and through the years had rallied a loyal following in many of the churches. He had recommended a number of young pastors to the smaller churches scattered around the state and had gained a reputation for his courage in challenging theological modernism by leading his Beth Eden congregation to sever ties with the Northern Baptist Convention. Some called him "a prophet of God."

Whittemore and Spratt were colleagues in Conservative Baptist churches, but both were more moderate than Bradford and were not militant separatists. They had fought their own battles with the Northern Baptist Convention but were eager to put controversy behind them and move on in their ministries.

The proposal to start the new seminary in Denver had probably originated with Pastor Bradford. In May 1950, while he was serving as president of the new state association, the Baptist fellowship had endorsed the creation of a committee to consider establishing a seminary. And there were a number of signs during that summer that Sam Bradford had hopes of controlling the new school's future.

Bradford's dreams were frustrated, however, at the first meeting of the board of trustees on August 31–September 1. Since the school was intended to serve a national constituency, thirty-nine board members were selected from three geographical regions to represent the fledgling Conservative Baptist movement throughout the country. Naturally the Colorado pastors had in mind their own candidates to serve as chairman of the board and president of the school, but after two days of meetings the board rather surprisingly announced that the chairman would be I. Cedric Peterson, a moderate pastor from Chicago. And within weeks the board had selected Pastor William Whittemore as acting president for the first year. These announcements were difficult for Bradford and his followers to accept, since they indicated that they were not yet in a position to determine the direction of the new school.

Then another wrinkle appeared in this web of design and from unexpected quarters. The dean of the school, Dr. William Kerr, and the first-year faculty were all hired from Northern Baptist Seminary in Chicago. Those three faculty members had all been students of Dr. Kerr, but during the first year in Denver a deep, unexplained rift developed between the faculty and Dean Kerr. Apparently personal and professional issues contributed to the conflict, but the most basic issue was the distinct impression that Dr. Kerr was Pastor Bradford's nominee for president, and the faculty members feared the school would fall into the hands of the militants.[3]

Hoping to resolve their differences, Dr. Kerr and the faculty members drove to Fort Collins in January to meet with William

Whittemore. Their open and direct discussion seemed to resolve their differences. But in a short time this assumption proved wrong, and as the first academic year moved to a close the division seemed to widen.

This was the situation, then, when the board first met with Vernon in Buffalo, New York. Board members became aware of the conflict, some for the first time, even as they were considering inviting Vernon to teach Christian Apologetics. Only a month later, on July 18 and 19, a select but representative board of trustees met in Denver in an attempt to resolve the conflict within the school. During the morning of the first day, meeting in the French Room, the board heard a long list of charges, written by a young ally of Pastor Bradford, against acting president Whittemore and his ally, Pastor Spratt. After dinner that evening the board heard the other side of the controversy from two faculty members.

After listening to both sides describe their differences, the chairman of the board, I. Cedric Peterson, said to the young militant, "We find no solid evidence that these written charges are true. We are asking you, my brother, to apologize."

Instead of apologizing, the young pastor turned on his heels and walked out of the room to join a group of cohorts waiting outside on the front lawn.

Next day, the board searched for some sort of reconciliation. They brought together representatives of both parties, two men on each side of the imposing table in the French Room, and encouraged the four men to talk out their differences. They talked at length, but at the end of the day Chairman Peterson said, "If you fellows can't get together, we will have to close this school! Why don't you give it one more try?"

Early in the summer, Whittemore had called Vernon in New York to finalize the invitation to Denver, and in that call the acting president had told him that upon his arrival he might be made dean of the school. But Vernon had no idea how deeply the conflict had divided the seminary—until the evening of his welcome to Denver. Clearly, Denver Seminary was no Camelot, except perhaps in the minds of ten or twenty students.

Troubling Questions

Vernon and Ann went to bed that night after the picnic deeply troubled, knowing that the big Weicker van with all their furniture and five thousand books would be there to unpack the next morning.

"Oh, God," they found themselves praying, "what kind of horrible mistake have we made? Shall we stay or shall we turn the car around and head back home? We thought we were following you, Lord. Is this it? Is this what you wanted?"

When the early morning light slipped across the bedroom, Vernon prayed, "Lord, you have led us this far. We can't turn back now. We'll stay. I think!"

But even as they began unpacking and moving into their duplex on Ogden Street, troubling questions remained—and continued to concern them for weeks. On August 4, Vernon wrote a former student, commiserating with him as he struggled with a huge disappointment upon arriving in his new pastorate in the state of Washington.

> Our hearts went out to you. . . . How discouraging it is to travel all the way across the continent and then find that things are decidedly different from what you anticipated! Well, if it will hearten you any, let me tell you that we have been going through the same sort of experience. In fact, I have been definitely on the verge of packing up and going somewhere else, although there has been no other plan open. So we can pray appreciatively each for the other. . . . Denver itself is

a beautiful city, and I think we will enjoy living here. . . . My books . . . are still packed, although I hope—if we remain— to get settled next week. By that time we should positively know God's guidance in this whole matter.[4]

Despite their uneasiness about the situation at the school, Vernon and Ann could sense the strange excitement of a new venture of faith and a sacrificial spirit abroad in the rooms and hallways of the old mansion. This was the way of the cross and the cost of discipleship.

Vernon's office was on the second floor. Down the hallway, left and right, were several sizable rooms that had once been bedrooms. The seminary had converted them to classrooms where students now studied Christian theology. One of the first things Vernon looked for, of course, was the library, and he was told that students had to drive across the south side of town to use the Iliff Seminary library on the campus of Denver University. But the seminary had plans to shelve hundreds of books in the basement of the mansion. Helen Bonfils had been devoted to the theater, in New York as well as in Denver, so the lowest level of the mansion offered a tiny family theater complete with stage. On the north side of the theater the family had a bowling alley and a small swimming pool. Vernon at once saw the possibilities for shelving *thousands* of books in all this space.

Yet even as Vernon walked the halls of the mansion, worked in his office to prepare for the new term, and dreamed of a new library, he knew that the dean and faculty were at odds, the trustees were divided between militants and moderates, and so he couldn't decide what he wanted to do. One day he was ready to resign; the next day he felt constrained to stay.

Hour of Decision

Within weeks of Vernon's arrival in Denver, three leaders of the militant faction met him at the mansion and took him for a drive

—in a direct attempt to enlist his support. As they rode through the streets of east Denver, they began to build their case against Whittemore and Spratt. But when they reached Cheesman Park, Vernon Grounds had had enough.

"Please, stop the car and let me out. I'll walk back from here." He returned alone to the school, deeply disappointed in the attitude of the three men.

A few hours later he walked down the marble steps from his office and into Douglas Birk's office, a folded sheet of yellow paper sticking out of his white shirt pocket.

Before he could say a word, Birk said, "I know what's in that pocket. Did God lead you to Denver or not? Look, Vernon, I don't know about you, but Don, Ray, and I believe God called us to this school. And we are going to stay."

Vernon stood there for a minute in dead silence. Then he said, "Do you drink coffee?"

The two of them walked four blocks to a drugstore on the corner of Ninth and Downing. In the back, at a small table with a marble top and wrought-iron chairs, they sat and drank coffee together for the first time, talking at length about recent events at the seminary. And there, in two hours of conversation, Doug Birk and Vernon Grounds established an unusual bond of confidence and interdependence that would last for the next twenty-eight years. As they headed back to the school, a summer shower passed over them, and the resignation in Vernon's pocket got wet and smeared his handwriting. But it didn't matter now. He was staying.[5]

While Douglas Birk was instrumental in convincing Vernon Grounds to stay in Denver, he was also the person who introduced the Grounds family to Trinity Baptist Church.

Even before heading west, Vernon had written to the seminary, inquiring about churches. Since he often traveled to speak on weekends, he knew a church family was vitally important for Ann, Barbara, and Mrs. Barton. When they arrived in Denver, Doug told Vernon about a new fellowship he and his wife, Lucille, were attending not far from the seminary, a group of about two hundred believers called Trinity Baptist Church. The Grounds family attended one Sunday and immediately felt at home. Several men who had helped to remodel the Bonfils mansion for the seminary were members of the church, and many in the congregation had already contributed significantly to the support of the seminary. Ann was soon at the piano and Vernon was among friends.

After getting his books unpacked, his family settled in a church, and all of them feeling at home in the area, Vernon assumed his normally crowded schedule. He would later describe his feelings about his calling to friends and students when he wrote: "I suppose that some souls would dismiss my particular mode of existence as hopelessly boring. I don't hunt lions or explore Arctic wastes; I don't have a long string of famous dignitaries waiting to chat with me every day. Granted! I do nothing except teach, write, study, read, counsel people, preach, and entertain my friends when there is opportunity. Yet I doubt whether anybody derives more solid satisfaction from the fleeting days than I do. What better can one desire than the privilege of serving Him, thinking His thoughts after Him, and trying to communicate to people the thrill and wonder of the Gospel?"

Vernon Grounds brought two convictions about Calvary love to the Denver campus that applied directly to the school's mission. First, that the seminary students could love God deeply by studying hard. Jesus Himself had said that the first and greatest commandment was to love God with the whole heart and *the whole mind*. Second, that a Christian community like the seminary must be united by the expression and enjoyment of the "brotherly love" that the apostle Paul, in his letter to the Romans, spoke of as the hallmark of the Christian community. Students soon saw evidence of both these convictions in Vernon's life around the school. He was a servant scholar who taught by example.

One student, Jim Conway, was dreaming of graduating, but a few months before the big day he failed his English proficiency test. Somehow Vernon heard about the problem and called Jim into his office. Over the next few days Dean Grounds himself tutored this young man in the grammar he had missed in high school and college. The personal touch proved wonderfully successful; it enabled Jim to graduate.

When Jim Conway was ordained in his first full-time church in Newton, Kansas, it was Dean Grounds who "traveled by train through the night across eastern Colorado and most of Kansas in a raging blizzard" to preach at the ordination service. And Jim later recalled that Dr. Grounds refused to stay in a hotel and "chose instead to stay in our 75–year-old parsonage to suffer the cold January winds with us. I remember that our kitchen floor was so cold the milk in the cat's dish would freeze." During that weekend Dr. Grounds often thawed the cat's milk and dried the dishes.

By conviction and example, Vernon Grounds slowly assumed leadership and influence in the young seminary.

CHAPTER 5

Winds of Controversy

A fundamentalist. . . . holds tenaciously to doctrines like the plenary inspiration of the Bible, the virgin birth of Jesus Christ, His substitutionary atonement, His bodily resurrection and His literal return. And, hence, of course, we are fundamentalists theologically. But very frankly some of us do not like to be tagged fundamentalists. For fundamentalism in many quarters has degenerated into a quarrelsome bickering over incidentals . . . . Maybe as Christians, and especially as fundamentalists, we have been lacking in Calvary-love. Maybe we have wanted to vindicate the rightness of our position and we are persuaded, in truth, that the position we embrace is right. Maybe we have wanted to justify ourselves. Maybe we have wanted to add converts merely to strengthen our churches because they are *our* churches. What we need is to cry out for Calvary-love. If and when we do, the aftermath may prove astonishing.

– Vernon Grounds,
Is Love in the Fundamentalist Creed?

What Vernon saw upon his arrival in Denver was but a tiny glimpse of the significant new evangelical movement spreading within traditional American Christianity.

Since early in the century many fundamentalist believers had turned their backs on the major denominations, justifying the move by arguing that this was a clear mandate of Holy Scripture—a strict doctrine of "separation from unbelief." These separatists loved to quote "Come out from among them, and be ye separate," and they extended this doctrine to American society generally, including schools of higher learning. But some of the children of these fundamentalists had begun to question the extremes to which their parents had gone. Their questions generated restlessness, and restlessness soon gave birth to an inspiring dream of turning America back to God.

Then came young evangelist William Franklin Graham's great Los Angeles Crusade in 1948, followed by the Boston Crusade and the Carolina Crusade. Almost overnight "Billy" Graham became a household name, and many Christians began to ask, "Isn't it time for a return to the vibrant evangelical Christianity that shaped the nation before World War I and the Scopes trial? Isn't it time to return to an evangelical Christianity marked by academic excellence and a social conscience?"

The vast majority of those from traditional fundamentalism who were now rallying in support of Billy Graham had no serious objection to the original doctrines of fundamentalism. But they felt that the movement had veered sharply from its original course and stumbled into a mire of cranky pessimism.

Just two years after the end of World War II, when the new voice in conservative Christian circles was a mere whisper, Dr. Carl F. H. Henry in his book *The Uneasy Conscience of Modern Fundamentalism* made it clear that in chiding fundamentalism's lack of social concern he was not taking a slap at fundamental doctrines. "The 'uneasy conscience' of which I write is not one troubled about the great biblical verities, which I consider the only outlook capable of resolving our problems, but rather one distressed by the frequent failure to apply them effectively to crucial problems confronting the modern mind. It is an application of, not a revolt against, fundamentals of the faith, for which I plead."

Most of the young critics acknowledged that early fundamentalism had tried valiantly to guard revealed truth from the deadly grasp of modernistic unbelief. But as society changed, many fundamentalists failed to apply that Christian message to the social and intellectual life of twentieth-century America. And by the time Vernon Grounds walked the halls of the Conservative Baptist Theological Seminary in Denver, he had joined the chorus for change. (The legal name of the seminary was Conservative Baptist Theological Seminary [CBTS], although it is often shortened to Denver Seminary.)

From Dean to President

Vernon was not the only new face at the seminary in the late summer of 1951. The new acting president of the school, Dr. Carey Thomas, joined the administrative team a few weeks later.

Carey Thomas, a retired pastor who had strong roots in the Baptist tradition, was one of the seminary board members who had interviewed Vernon in Buffalo, New York. As a boy, Thomas had come to America from England where his father, William Thomas, had been a pastor and a student in Charles Haddon Spurgeon's "preachers' college." With their mutual interests in Christian ministry, Carey's parents and the Spurgeons became good friends. It was only a few months after Spurgeon's death that William Thomas and his family moved to America and settled in California, where William served several churches—first in Oakland, and later in Garden Grove. Carey would later follow his father's footsteps into the ministry, serving churches in New Jersey and Pennsylvania. He gained a reputation as a wise and trusted pastor and was awarded an honorary degree by Wheaton College, making him Dr. Carey Thomas.

In his final years in the pastorate, the highly respected Thomas joined a score of Baptist colleagues who shared the dream of a new conservative Baptist seminary in Denver. He served on the first board of trustees and, in spite of failing health, was willing to consider spending his retirement years bearing the burdens of the presidency of the young school. He thought that his retirement income might even enable him to serve with a minimal salary, which was a great benefit to the young school. So Dr. Thomas and his wife, Elizabeth, left their home in the East and arrived at the school shortly after Vernon and Ann.

In August, after Dr. Kerr decided to leave the seminary, Vernon accepted the position of dean. Thus, from the beginning, the new dean and the new president faced the conflict between moderates and militants together as they began preparing to lead the school in its vision of a graduate school that would provide theological education for a wide spectrum of evangelical Christians.

Dr. Thomas handled many of the public relations problems, leaving Vernon free to teach, speak, and write. But as Thomas's health continued to decline in the following years, the board intensified its search for a willing candidate to move into the president's office permanently. Vernon wrote several of these letters inviting potential candidates to consider the presidency. After three years of halfhearted effort the board extended an invitation to Dr. Torrey Johnson, who had been associated with Billy Graham and Youth for

Christ, to become the new president. Vernon broke the news in his letter to the alumni: "We are hoping that before long we may be able to announce his acceptance. Without any question Dr. Torrey could give us very aggressive and able leadership, enabling the seminary to get on its feet financially and become the kind of institution we all want it to be."

But it was not to be. A few months later Johnson refused the invitation, and the board of trustees asked three of its members, Dr. Ted Taylor, Claude Moffitt, and Russell Pavy, to bring in recommendations for a new president. Over the course of more than a year, the committee approached several prospects, but all respectfully declined. Finally, one of the faculty members, Dr. Ray McLaughlin, suggested to Dr. Thomas that the search committee seriously consider their own dean, Dr. Vernon Grounds. The idea was not entirely new. Dr. Thomas, at least, had considered it. But he and the board had hesitated to pursue the matter because they were concerned about his ability to administer the school and about his lack of passion for such an office. On the positive side, however, they were well aware of how much a part of the school Vernon had become, and especially the way he was endearing himself to students and friends of the school.

To make the proposal more feasible, Dr. Thomas created a new administrative plan and took it to the search committee. The plan called for Vernon to be elevated to the presidency and serve as the public representative of the seminary; Douglas Birk to assume the new post of executive vice-president to handle the administrative chores within the school; and the board would then invite Dr. Earl Kalland from Western Conservative Baptist Seminary in Portland, Oregon, to assume the deanship.

Only one committee member withheld his support of the plan. When Dr. Thomas learned that Russell Pavy, a pastor in Fresno, California, was resisting the decision, he flew to Fresno to talk to him. After exchanging greetings in the church office, Dr. Thomas made a strange request. "Mr. Pavy," he said, "I've never seen a California orange grove. Will you show me one?"

According to Pavy's story, he was happy to do that, but once they had driven out to a grove he realized that Dr. Thomas had no interest whatsoever in oranges. As they stood there surrounded by fruit trees, the highly respected leader from Denver pulled out a chart and said, "Now, Mr. Pavy, on this chart I have Vernon for president, Doug for vice-president, and Earl for dean. Don't you think this is a great team?"

When Carey Thomas said "Mister," no one was inclined to disagree. Nor was Russell Pavy. Vernon Grounds, Pavy would later say, "became president of Denver Seminary right there—in a California orange grove."[1]

In the January-March 1956 edition of the *Conservative Seminarian*, the school's tiny publication, Vernon wrote: "With poignant regret the Board of Trustees has accepted the resignation of Dr. Carey S. Thomas. . . . He has gallantly borne the heavy demands and responsibilities of this office. . . . But the change in administration will bring with it no change in our program and purpose. For this Seminary is centered in Jesus Christ . . . He is its Foundation, its sole Reason for existence, indeed, its very Life."

In 1955, on the very day of his official retirement, Carey Thomas entered the hospital. A week later, he moved on to the land of endless days . . . no night and no pain. God's providence had, once again, proven both timely and merciful.

———

During the years of the Cold War, this new administrative team of Grounds, Birk, and Kalland was often called "the troika" within the seminary family, named after a similar arrangement adopted in the Soviet Union. The plan called for Vernon to "give himself to a larger public ministry" while maintaining his "contacts" in the class-room. This allowed him to pursue his academic, preaching, and counseling interests, but it also placed on him the heavy burden of raising funds for salaries. When it came to fund-raising, Vernon felt woefully inadequate. To lighten his load, he decided that he would accept his own paycheck only after others received theirs, and that he would travel constantly to win new friends for the school.[2]

When the board of trustees chose Vernon Grounds to be the second president of Denver Seminary they knew his strengths and his weaknesses and his servant heart, but they had no idea how deeply or how quickly this man would stamp his image on the insti-tution. For Vernon, the weight of the large presidential medallion placed around his neck at his inauguration set the tone for his new role, with its cross and covenant, "Set for the defense of the gospel." He was already widely known as a Christian apologist, and that rep-utation gained him entrance to many schools for lectures and stu-dent recruitment. But Vernon was only beginning to understand the implications of the cross for his life and ministry. He had made love the theme of his life, but that guiding principle would soon face severe challenges.

With the faculty and the local moderates on the board now in a position of strength, the militant minority of board members slowly withdrew their support from the school. Years later, Vernon revealed his own impressions of that time: "I was caught up in a rather ugly situation which threatened to destroy a school at which I had begun to teach. Under extraordinary pressure, I kept praying for some reassuring indication of God's guidance. What was I to do, a wholly innocent bystander who had been forced willy-nilly to become a participant in a distressing controversy?

"Should I resign or should I stay and struggle to set right things that were in my opinion wretchedly wrong? I distinctly remember the time of day and the very spot on the street where, as I was walking and subvocally praying, confusion abruptly clarified, uncertainty gave way to calm decisiveness and a sense of God's sustaining strength took possession of me.

"It would not be truthful to assert that 'heaven came down and glory filled my soul.' Neither do I think that with integrity I can testify God spoke to me. Yet as I analyze what took place there on that street I must declare that God ministered to me as directly and definitely as if He had spoken audibly."[3]

Without rancor or rage Vernon took his stand, first as dean and then as president, slowly becoming a significant influence in the evangelical renewal underway in American fundamentalism. It was Vernon Grounds who raised the flag and called both faculty and students to join the great venture. Still, it was not easy. Many felt that theirs was a great cause, but every month leaders of the school struggled to raise enough funds to meet the modest budget. Payment of salaries was often delayed, sometimes for as much as two months. Faculty contracts specified that professors were to represent the school in public relations and fund-raising, and many of them took weekend ministries to supplement their income of a few thousand dollars a year.

Many years later Dr. Ray McLaughlin, who taught pastoral theology at the school, recalled Vernon Grounds's initial impact upon the school: "When [he] came to join us here at the Seminary, we saw in [him] a welcome breadth of scholarship, a tolerant but firm faith, and above all a kind and loving spirit. These qualities opened the doors of freedom of thought and action for us. We have never wanted to return to our former brittle life."[4]

Periodically the faculty gathered for potluck dinners, and during these gatherings Vernon often stood beneath the gold leaf ceiling of the chapel to tell the men and their wives of some new charge from the militant separatists and to speak of the latest financial bind. Then he would recall some encouraging text from the

Scriptures, such as the apostle Paul's assurance to the Ephesian elders: "None of these things move me." They would conclude the
evening together in prayer, thanking the Lord for the privilege of
serving Him.

Faculty and students united not only for days of prayer, but days
of work. Criticism from the outside only intensified the loyalty on
the inside. Through the years, the school had relatively few full-time
faculty members leave for any reason whatsoever; and every full-time
faculty member who survived the crisis of the1950s either retired
from Denver Seminary or died before they reached retirement age.
By the late 1950s the school had grown to nearly one hundred, and
other younger members were added to the faculty.

Loveless Faith

In 1954, Vernon sent an article to his old friends at *Eternity*
magazine back east in Philadelphia. In the article he raised what he
considered a most crucial question: "Is Love in the Fundamentalist Creed?" The article rather clearly spoke to what he and the
school were experiencing—along with many others in the new
evangelical movement.

"We are fundamentalists theologically, but very frankly some of
us do not like to be tagged fundamentalists," he wrote. In many
quarters, fundamentalism "has degenerated into quarrelsome bickering over incidentals; indeed, it is incidentalism rather than fundamentalism."

To describe fundamentalism's behavior he resorted to uncharacteristically stinging criticism, calling it "legalistic Phariseeism,
hard, frigid, ineffective, unethical and loveless." This was the heart
of his indictment—not doctrine, but life.[5]

In another *Eternity* article two years later, Vernon quoted the
jibe he had heard first at Faith Seminary: "Fundamentalism is too
much fun, too much damn, and too little mental!" This threw

even more gasoline on the mounting flames of criticism from militant fundamentalists.

Somehow surprised by the resulting furor, Vernon felt compelled to write to alumni. "Perhaps you have read some of the criticism which lately has been directed against me, criticism which is simply a perverse misinterpretation of some articles which I published earlier this year. By God's enablement I am endeavoring to live out those words of Paul, 'None of these things move me.' The petty criticisms to which we are subjected fade into nothingness when we recall the humiliation to which our Lord was subjected— buffeted by Roman soldiers, spat upon, lied about, forsaken even by His disciples, and all of that a prelude to agonizing crucifixion! What right have we to complain regarding our light affliction?"

Some might easily dismiss such a remark as some sort of vague rationalization, but it was far from that. For years Vernon had been exploring the depths of Christian love. But only after his move to Denver and his firsthand experience with the school's crisis was he ready to apply Calvary love so boldly. "Is Love in the Fundamentalist Creed?" may be the most revealing article Vernon Grounds ever wrote. It demonstrates not only his deep feelings about fundamentalism's critical flaw, but also how much he had learned about Calvary.

"Neighbor-love," he wrote, "is the royal law, a duty which should reign supreme in Christian behavior. If I love my neighbor, I will do my utmost to, as Paul puts it, cherish him. I will long for him to get the best which life has to give. And what is the best which life has to give? Unquestionably it is God's salvation through faith in Jesus Christ."

Another Storm

Nothing compares with Denver's awesome view of the majestic Rocky Mountain peaks to the west, sparkling white in winter and deep purple in summer. But nature's beauty often veils peril. Winter's snow can bring a mountain avalanche, and summer's heat can trigger sudden rain and flash floods. Vernon and Ann Grounds learned this personally and painfully in the summer of 1956.

Upon their arrival in Denver, Vernon, Ann, Barbara, and Mrs. Barton had moved into a tan brick duplex ten blocks from the Bonfils mansion. This was convenient for a time, but as soon as they could afford to, they moved to a new and larger, more comfortable house on South Corona Street. It was a red and tan brick home, with stairs leading to the front door and a porch marked by a little iron fence about it. The living room, kitchen, and two bedrooms were upstairs. Downstairs, a garden level provided a large room for Ann's grand piano and shelves for hundreds of Vernon's books.

Unfortunately, the land around their new home was low and had a drainage ditch cutting west toward Harvard Gulch a block away. On a Monday in early July 1956, Ann watched dark afternoon clouds roll off the mountains to the west and heavy rain start to fall. Fear swelled up within her as the little trickle of water flowing through the nearby gulch quickly grew into a raging torrent.

Ann, Barbara, and Mrs. Barton took refuge in a neighbor's house where Ann called Vernon, who was seventy miles away in Colorado Springs, teaching at Young Life Institute. "We are having a terrible storm," she told him. "The water is up to our steps." Before the rain stopped, water had seeped through the windows and gushed into the downstairs rooms, threatening Ann's piano and Vernon's books.

Vernon left the seminar as soon as he could and rushed back to Denver, arriving early on Tuesday morning. With the help of some kind women from their church, Vernon and Ann were able to clean out the debris and even shine the windows!

Around six that evening, Vernon left to return to Colorado Springs. As he drove south, the rain began to fall in torrents. He pulled off the highway at a service station and tried to phone Ann, but with phone lines apparently down, he had no way of getting through to her. He called again when he reached Colorado Springs and this time got through. The news he heard was not good.

Water had risen against the downstairs windows, and suddenly, without warning, one window cracked and broke into tiny chips, and water surged through the opening and into the rooms below. The lower level of their home had become a swimming pool, with water up to within eighteen inches of the ceiling! Ann, Barbara, and Mrs. Barton had once again taken refuge with neighbors.

Vernon turned his car around and headed back through the rain, over roads that were quickly becoming impassable. He made it safely to Denver, but it was pitch black when he arrived. His headlights caught what looked like a lake spreading out before him. Then he saw an amazing sight.

Doug Birk had called seminary students and church friends from around the city. Some of the students were half walking, half swimming, in water up to their necks in the middle of the street, trying to carry an electric cord to the house so the water could be pumped from the flooded rooms. Other volunteers were operating a motorboat to move people and goods in the darkness, so Vernon climbed on board and rode up to the darkened house where he joined the bucket brigade and led the workers in a few choruses of praise. By four the next morning, the faithful crew had managed to pump all the water from the house.[6]

But, oh, how disheartening!

Ann's grand piano was ruined and the furnace was not working. The deep-freeze had been turned on its side and all its contents had floated out. The lower bedroom furniture was ruined. And with daylight Vernon found that his lifelong collection of lecture and sermon notes, scattered about, faded and wet, were a total loss.

It took weeks to repair and restore order to the lower floor of the house. And the shocking events set Vernon and Ann thinking about "where your treasure is" and counting the costs of a move to higher ground.

In his next letter to alumni, Vernon, typically, found a bright lining to their dark cloud. "Disaster," he said, "brings out friends as night brings out the stars." Students, faculty, and fellow Christians from all over Denver—even neighbors and strangers—had cleared out the broken glass and damaged furniture; then, as the house slowly dried out, they also repaired and repainted it. "Through the amazing liberality of friends and churches," he wrote, "we were able to refurnish our home. So while we suffered some losses, we also learned some valuable lessons.

"The *Daily Light* portion for August 4, which Ann and I came upon one night when our spirits were a trifle low, says: 'When thou passest through the waters, I will be with thee; and through the rivers, they shall not overflow thee' (Isaiah 43:2 KJV)."

The violent summer storm of 1956 was typical of the Grounds's first decade in Denver. Fear, shock, and disappointment had swept over them, but in the end they also discovered the blessing of students and friends who rushed to their rescue. Such storms, both from the skies and from human adversaries, strengthened Vernon and Ann's ties to their faith communities in their church and at the seminary.

President Grounds

It was now clear who was leading Denver Seminary, but the struggle between militants and moderates continued. Militants gained several strongholds, especially in some Conservative Baptist churches in the Midwest and the San Francisco area; and here and there some assembly would pass a resolution condemning the "unbelief" or compromises of the seminary. The board attempted to respond positively to these resolutions, but it was Vernon who best articulated the school's position.[7]

Within his soul, Vernon Grounds abhorred conflict. He was never sure why, but his inclination was always toward peace, almost at any price. Much had changed about him since his early days at Rutgers, but temperamentally he was still a pacifist. Yet here he was in a storm of controversy.

It was during these days that Vernon penned the lines that appeared for decades in the Denver Seminary catalogue:

> Here is no unanchored liberalism—
> > freedom to think without commitment
> Here is no encrusted dogmatism—
> > commitment without freedom to think
> Here is vibrant evangelicalism—
> > commitment with freedom to think
> > within the limits laid down in Scripture.

To counter so many false charges against the school, the seminary sponsored a series of banquets in conjunction with the large annual meetings held by Conservative Baptist churches. Here Vernon, as president of the seminary, had a platform for interpreting for a nationwide audience the philosophy and politics of the Conservative Baptist movement as well as the mission of Denver Seminary. For years these banquets were for many the highlight of the Conservative Baptist annual meetings because Vernon Grounds had a rare ability to lift their eyes above the petty struggles to a higher level of significance by showing the hidden ethical or spiritual truth for life and ministry.

At one of these banquets in the late 1950s he told the crowd, "People, according to Schopenhauer, the German philosopher, are like a pack of porcupines on a freezing winter night. The sub-zero temperature forces them together for warmth. But as soon as they press very close, they jab and hurt one another. So they separate again, only to attempt in vain over and over again to huddle together.

"What a sad, semi-humorous picture of humanity that is! But why are people like porcupines? It is simply this. While we have been made by God to live together, apart from Jesus Christ we do not and we cannot live in fellowship. . . .

"Why is it impossible to achieve fellowship without Jesus Christ? Why is it that, instead of finding joyful fulfillment in relationship with people, we often experience agonizing frustration? The Bible gives a simple answer. Sin has fractured human fellowship, and sin keeps on fracturing it. Sin splinters relationships even among old friends, even within families, even between husband and wife."[8]

The often-vicious criticism of the seminary from the militant churches continued well into the 1960s. On May 8, 1962, the Colorado state association of churches held its annual meeting at Beth Eden Baptist Church, where Sam Bradford had just resigned. The council of the association, led by the state director and a long-time Bradford ally, was now directing the militants, many of whom were graduates or supporters of Bob Jones University. The council introduced a resolution at the meeting calling for the repudiation of Denver Seminary for its doctrinal deviance and its interference in the churches.[9]

Vernon had written two lengthy papers defending the position of the school, but when he sensed the hostility of the opposition, he made only a few brief remarks and sat down.[10] In that atmosphere, any defense of the school or affirmation of faith was an exercise in futility. Shouts and angry charges continued until the militants, clearly dominant in this meeting, voted to repudiate the seminary they had voted to establish only twelve years earlier. It was clearly a political move designed to break up the association, and their objective became obvious within the year. On Tuesday, October 2, 1962, at the semiannual meeting of the Conservative Baptist Association of Colorado, the assembly voted by slightly more than the required two-thirds vote to let the present association quietly die.

"It could so easily have been avoided," Vernon explained to alumni, "if only common sense and judgment had prevailed. In another sense, however, after the result of the balloting was announced, I silently exclaimed 'Hallelujah!' Now each of the two groups will undoubtedly reorganize and do its own distinctive job for our Lord. [Two groups were formed, and some went entirely independent.] Previously we were like two cats tied together by their tails dangling over a back fence and simply causing misery to each other while we disturbed the serenity of our little ecclesiastical world by frantic howling."

Ever the optimist, Vernon told the board that this eruption of hostility between the seminary and the militant wing could well prove to be a positive development since it would make the differences between the militants and moderates clear to everyone. He couldn't escape the apostle Paul's words to the Philippians: "Some . . . preach Christ . . . of envy and strife. . . . What then? . . . Christ is preached; and I therein do rejoice . . . and will rejoice."

For seminary students the conflict proved to be a life-changing lesson in godly leadership. One graduate, who had been serving a church in Colorado at the time and attended a meeting where he heard the wild and unfair charges fired at Dr. Grounds, later wrote to Vernon to thank him. "You showed the love of Christ in not retaliating in kind toward those who are unkind and you convinced me through your loving response that I must stand with those who are loving and kind, not with those who criticize fellow-Christians who disagree with them."[11]

By 1962 the worst of the ecclesiastical storms had passed, and as he had with the storm and flood in the summer of 1956, Vernon would look back and trace the silver lining, the love and support of new friends. It was Henri Talon, John Bunyan's biographer, who once said, "It is not books that copy books, but souls that copy souls." And so it proved true in Vernon Grounds's life.

CHAPTER 6

A Chance to Serve

Study and ponder the truth you have, lost in wonder and worship, overwhelmed by the goodness of God and the glory of the Gospel. . . . Appropriate more and more fully the truth you already possess. You come to the task as a Christian committed and convinced. You do not come with complete neutrality and cool detachment analyzing Scripture with the attitude of a zoologist who indifferently dissects a worm. Not in the least. You come as one who has first been to Calvary. . . . But commitment to the truth is not enough. It may become simply an academic matter, an impersonal and painless subscription to a set of dogmas. But God wants more than that from you. Listen to Jesus: "If any man will come after me, let him deny himself, take up his cross daily and follow me."

— VERNON GROUNDS,
Check Up on Your Commitment

Vernon Grounds had been traveling on weekends since his days in New Jersey with the Harmony Gospel Quartet. Through the years he had maintained this pattern for one reason: he lived to serve. Books could be filled with the experiences he had and the people he met. Few who encountered Vernon, either as speaker, guest, or friend, ever forgot him—nor did he forget them.

On one of these weekends in the 1960s, Vernon had flown across the country to speak at a church missionary conference in Manchester, New Hampshire. Al Melton, who had invited him to have dinner with them, met Vernon at the airport.

The Meltons had never before had the president of a seminary as a guest in their home, and they were more than a little nervous. It seemed a little like having Moses or Elijah come for dinner. They were honored, but Al and his wife prayed for no embarrassing disruptions. They "laid down the law" to the children: "No goofing off. Be on your best behavior (or else). Speak politely. Please! Please!" and so on.

When Al walked into the house with Dr. Grounds, he was on edge, not knowing how the children might greet him. But he didn't have to be anxious for long. Four children lined up on the stairs to greet their guest, as excited and nervous as their parents to meet "this great man of God."

From the moment Vernon walked through the door, he won the children's hearts. He greeted them warmly and asked their names—and remembered them! Then he bypassed the living room and went straight to the kitchen, inquired about dinner cooking on the stove, and captured the heart of Mrs. Melton's mother with his open-hearted manner! In less than thirty seconds Vernon had put the whole family at ease, and at dinner he even succeeded in getting one of the children to eat his carrots![1]

The president of Denver Seminary was seldom what people expected. Though not a tall man, Vernon Grounds was a most impressive man, in voice and manner. Dignified, though never artificial or pompous, with prematurely gray hair and strong, broad shoulders, he had a way of putting his hand on a man's shoulder, looking him in the eye and making him feel important. As a result, he made friends for himself and the school almost by impulse.

But what was his secret? Probably the two things that contributed most to his ability to connect so unerringly with everyone he met were his genuine humility and his authentic love for people.

Sadly, the militant pastors in Colorado never got close enough to Vernon to see him as he truly was. They believed what they read in fundamentalist publications, and that was bad. But even as they plotted to make him a public disgrace, hundreds upon hundreds of people across the country, like the Meltons, were getting distinctly different impressions. In effect they were thinking, *If this is leadership, it is a strange type, unlike any that I have seen before. This man is like one of the family.*

In the midst of the ecclesiastical war in Colorado Vernon sent another article to *Eternity* magazine that clearly captures the essence of his life. In "Check Up on Your Commitment" he wrote that when Jesus gave the great commandment, "Love God with all your heart and with all your mind and with all your life," He was demanding that we love the Lord so completely that all we want is "a chance to serve Him."

"This is not an optional request," Vernon wrote. "It is a totalitarian demand. It is a call for a Christian commitment which acknowledges God's sovereignty in every dimension of your experience, enthroning Him as Lord of your heart, Lord of your mind, and Lord of your life."

Scholarly studies and popular books on leadership were rare at the time. Robert K. Greenleaf's pioneering work, *Servant Leadership,* wasn't published until 1977, and James McGregor Burns's classic and highly influential *Leadership*, stressing leadership as essentially relational, appeared in 1978. The term and concept of *servant leadership* had not yet appeared, but that was Vernon's vision for and view of his presidency at Denver Seminary. He didn't define it or explain it in those terms, but that is what he was thinking—and that is what he was doing. His vision of servant leadership was a result of his ceaseless meditation on Calvary, the love Jesus revealed there, and the consequences of that love in human hearts.

Remembering how his father had neglected his health and sensing that regular exercise was vital to maintain his pace, Vernon had established a fitness routine early in his ministry. As part of his this routine, he usually walked in the early evening. One day in the fall of 1963, after the family had moved from the home on Corona to a new place on the corner of Garrison and Fifth Avenue in Lakewood, Vernon headed out the door for a walk. He was enjoying the November evening when suddenly, out of nowhere, a car roared at him. The impact knocked him some distance up the shoulder of the road where he landed on the right side of his head and face.

Someone rushed up and shouted to people from a house nearby, "Call an ambulance!"

Within minutes the ambulance arrived and rushed him to the hospital. There sometime during his first foggy night as he drifted in and out of consciousness, Vernon received a distinct promise: "I will not die but live, and will proclaim what the LORD has done" (Psalm 118:17 NIV).

After several days in the hospital, and a week at home recuperating from the concussion and dizziness, Vernon was able to resume his busy schedule and his regular trips to the gym.

No single incident can create humility in the soul, but this near-death experience certainly served as a powerful reminder to Vernon of the Lord's call in his life.[2]

Book Bag and Flight Number

During the 1960s, the years of evangelical renewal, Vernon Grounds was something of an ambassador-at-large; and for him the larger, the better. His friend Dr. Bernard Ramm, philosopher and apologist who taught at the American Baptist Seminary of the West, once compared Vernon Grounds with John Wesley and his ceaseless travel. There was a striking similarity. Both men had the rare ability to read, write, and think on the move, something not everyone can do.

Vernon's life consisted of teaching classes during the week and then flying off on weekends to speak somewhere in the U.S. Come Friday noon, he rushed from his office with a big book bag in one hand and his coat and luggage in the other. He met the student-maintenance man at the back door of the mansion, climbed into the car, and headed out east 32nd Avenue on Denver's east side to Stapleton Airport.

Once at the airport waiting for check-in, or on the plane at 28,000 feet, he would open the book bag, pull out a yellow legal-size pad of paper, and begin outlining and writing an article in progress or his message for the weekend. The books he carried often had little slips of paper between pages marking the quotation or illustration that he wanted to insert into his sermon or lecture. For Vernon Grounds, travel time was study time.

Some friend or soon-to-be friend would be waiting at the airport in Chicago or Minneapolis or whatever his destination was, and he would be whisked away to dinner or a meeting at the church. After the meeting the pastor or another host would bring him home to spend the night and have breakfast the next morning.

Saturday might include a men's breakfast or youth conference and a Saturday night meeting of some type. Then on Sunday Vernon would preach both morning and evening, usually in two different churches. On Sunday evenings he often took some old or new friends out to a restaurant for light refreshments.

On Monday morning he often met with local ministers or spoke in chapel at a nearby college in order to talk to prospective students about the seminary. If he lectured at the college, his stay would be extended two or three days.

In one three-month period, from September to December in 1967, Vernon spoke in chapel at ten Christian colleges, from Westmont in Santa Barbara, California, to Gordon College north of Boston. His schedule always hinged upon a local church in an area inviting him for a Bible, missionary, or spiritual life conference. This gave him the opportunity to visit nearby colleges and gain access to students' lives. His wide reading made him knowledgeable on a whole range of subjects currently under discussion on campus, and colleges eagerly called upon him for special lectures and commencement weekends.

In a typical weekend of ministry Vernon talked and listened intently to scores of people. And when the plane touched down in Denver, he had more names, addresses, and birthdays to add to his personal mailing list for birthday and sympathy cards, books, and Christmas letters. By the 1970s this personal mailing list had reached 1,700 names.

In 1962 alone, Vernon estimated that he traveled 75,000 miles! That is three times around the earth! And that is how the man lived for over half a century—and how he built Denver Seminary and helped change the face of evangelical Christianity in America.

But always he sensed his life's mission in his airtight schedule. "I have been busy to the point of giddiness and as happy as I have been busy," Vernon said in 1965. "I must invest my time in sharing the reality and sufficiency of God's love in Jesus Christ. Ultimately, what matters but to experience and communicate the wonders of redeeming love?"

Risks Along the Way

The safety record of the airlines was good, but when you travel hundreds of thousands of miles, sooner or later you are likely to encounter an "incident." Vernon had his encounter on Monday, November 18, 1968. After lecturing at San Diego State College, he flew to Los Angeles and waited there for an after-midnight connection to Denver. Fog closed in, however, and the flight was delayed and eventually canceled.

The next morning at eight o'clock the replacement flight was soaring toward Denver when there was a jarring, a muffled explosion toward the tail of the plane, and smoke began filling the cabin. A flight attendant rushed to the rear of the plane with a fire extinguisher, and within minutes she had doused the flames. While the smoke gradually cleared, Vernon and the other passengers breathed with the help of the oxygen masks. Once the plane was on the ground in Denver, the FBI rushed on board and arrested the saboteur who had tried to detonate a bomb to destroy himself and everyone on board.Reflecting on the mystery of God's ways, Vernon mused, "Suppose there had been no fog in Los Angeles the previous night when the suspect boarded the plane? Had the passengers been asleep and the crew less alert, the fire might not have been put out in time."

But it was! Everyone on board was saved from flaming horror and certain death.

Vernon put his grateful testimony in the psalmist's words: "Be at rest once more, O my soul, for the LORD has been good to you.

For you, O LORD, have delivered my soul from death, my eyes from tears, my feet from stumbling, that I may walk before the LORD in the land of the living" (Psalm 116:7–9 NIV).[3]

Another danger in an itinerating ministry is the neglect that can result when a man leaves behind his wife and family and his family responsibilities. The families of many great spiritual leaders have suffered from neglect. Wives have sought and found separation or divorce. Children have grown up critical of their father and his faith. Vernon was not unmindful of these risks, and he always tried to deal with them. Ann frequently joined him for anniversaries in the East, and he traveled hundreds of miles, at times, to see Barbara.

In his book *Radical Commitment*, written later in his life (1984), Vernon opened a window onto this private world with a touch of his wry humor: "I arise early and am off almost every morning for breakfast with a friend or a Christian group. Then usually I return home after six o'clock—unless it is a weekend and I am away from Denver, and as a rule I am. We have supper, spending an hour or an hour and a half together. After that, I go to my study, leaving my deserted wife by herself. Oh, once in a while, exercising great condescension, I bring my work into the family room and continue to do it there, provided my wife refrains from interrupting me. With even greater condescension I may even reach out and touch her, or I may grunt some greeting. But she assures me that I do not even have to be in the same room with her all the time and I do not have to talk to her. The awareness of my presence transforms the home."[4]

For her part Ann, when asked about Vernon's constant travel, simply said, "I'd rather have Vernon Grounds 10 percent of the time than any other man 100 percent." And she was certainly not sitting around waiting or moping. Ann had her own creative challenges with her music and her piano students, and she led an active life with her daughter and mother. All three women in Vernon's life had close friends at Trinity Baptist Church.

"Mom and Dad did so much entertaining that a revolving front door would not have been amiss," says their daughter, Barbara. "When company was coming, we all pitched in. Mom bought, prepared, and served the food. Grandma manned the kitchen thoroughly if not too quietly. I ran back and forth following orders, and Dad held forth with the guests. . . . Even when Dad was away—which was often—Mom entertained. Sometimes it was a group of single ladies, sometimes faculty wives, and sometimes just one woman in need of encouragement. Everyone is aware of Dad's counseling ministry, but Mom also spent hours listening and advising. . . . Grandma and I were never excluded from joining the guests, even though a messy kid and a widowed woman who never hesitated to express her opinions undoubtedly complicated things at times. And no matter who was in the house, when it came time for me to go to bed, Mom always left her place as hostess in order to pray with me before I went to sleep."[5]

Vernon's reading and writing on the weekend flights proved useful in his classrooms, giving his lectures and discussions a contemporary edge. He habitually arrived in class with eight or ten books under his arm and seemed to know about everything going on in the world—all the current issues, hottest topics, and big ideas. But like most scholars, Vernon had had little training in the dynamics of classroom learning, and students, on occasion, found his sessions stimulating but disorganized, especially when he had just arrived on campus from the airport. There were also stories on campus, always told with a smile, about Dr. Grounds's notorious practice of handing in his grades late—sometimes weeks late.

Yet these somewhat negative reports were puny indeed compared to the number of students who spoke of personal conversations with Dr. Grounds after class, or invitations to an early-morning breakfast with him. Many students learned some of their greatest lessons during these personal conversations and interactions.

Return to Drew

Perhaps the greatest conflict created by Vernon's constant travel, at least in his own soul, came in finding time to write. When he first accepted the presidency of the seminary, he had just received the shattering news that his eight-hundred page doctoral dissertation had been rejected by his committee at Drew and would require a total rewrite. His mentor told him he had tried to cover too many fields: psychology, philosophy, and theology. But he had spent so much time, so many valuable hours, researching and writing. How could he possibly find time now to write a second dissertation? Yet if he did not, how could he, with integrity, teach graduate students in a theological seminary?

Now the conflict Vernon disliked so much was within his own soul! He put the dissertation aside for two years.

Then came the letter from his friend David Hubbard, who was studying in St. Andrews, Scotland. He had just found a volume of Sigmund Freud's works in an English translation and thought Vernon might be interested. "I can mail each volume to you as they come off the press," he said. Encouraged by this prospect, Vernon made time in his crowded schedule and turned once again to working on his dissertation.

He wrote an almost totally new manuscript of nearly five hundred pages on "The Concept of Love in the Psychology of Sigmund Freud," and resubmitted what he hoped would be the final draft. In early May of 1960 the registrar at Drew phoned to say that his dissertation—after ten long years—wonder of wonders!—had finally been approved! Only one last hurdle remained: the oral examination and defense. Since Vernon was scheduled to be in the

East for a Bible conference at the end of May, he arranged to meet with his committee on Saturday afternoon, May 28.

That afternoon, he turned off Madison Avenue and drove through the stone archway entrance to the Drew campus for the first time in nearly ten years. But before he went to the meeting room in Bowne Hall, he had to stop by the registrar's office. He had no idea why but had been instructed to do so. To the best of his knowledge he had no bills outstanding, so he assumed that he might owe a few dollars incidental to graduation, should he pass the oral exam. But upon arriving at the registrar's office he was handed a bill for $800!

"Why $800?" he asked the woman at the desk.

"The Graduate School charges a full year's tuition when a thesis is accepted and a doctorate granted. And accounts must be paid in full before Commencement."

As Vernon walked across the campus to Bowne Hall, he was disturbed, and ill-prepared for a two- or three-hour oral examination. But he turned to God and committed his need to the One who is able "to do immeasurably more than all we ask or imagine," and before he entered Bowne Hall and faced his interrogators, he knew that somehow he would be able to get the money by Monday.

Vernon's oral examination was given by three professors. Two were rather well-known: Dr. Carl Michalson, who had served as the chairman of his doctoral committee for years, and Dr. Will Herberg, the popular author and sociologist. It had been some time since Vernon had written much of the dissertation, and he worried that Herberg might focus on the meaning of some of the more extended quotations—one in particular.

The questioning and discussion went well until Dr. Herberg zeroed in on the one quotation—out of hundreds in the dissertation—that had caused Vernon such anxiety. "Mr. Grounds, in your dissertation on page 190 you quote: 'Freud must construe love hedonistically as the ego's relationship to the sources of its pleasure.'

Later, on page 251, you say that for Freud love is also a 'cosmological principle.' It is 'a key which unlocks the mysteries of culture with all its amazing triumphs and all its appalling ambiguities.' Could you speak to the meaning of this?"

Vernon searched his memory and responded with some kind of answer (which he later could not even recall). Apparently it was adequate, for after two-and-a-half hours of questions, answers, and discussion, the committee gave final approval for the degree. Dr. Michalson capped the afternoon by conceding, "Not bad, for a fundamentalist."[6]

Now there was only the matter of that $800. Ann had traveled to New Jersey with him, and three days later when they were visiting in the home of their dear friends Jacob and Deane Stam, the telephone suddenly rang at about 11:15 at night. Jacob returned from taking the call and announced to Vernon and Ann that someone who wanted to remain anonymous would be providing the $800 for the graduate school. (Vernon would later learn that Jake had engineered the gift.) "I was flabbergasted," Vernon said, "and hardly able to sleep for joy and gratitude. Great is His faithfulness!"

With light hearts, he and Ann finished out their days in New Jersey, speaking and meeting old friends from the Harmony Gospel Quartet days and visiting his sister, Mildred, in Clifton.[7] Ann played, the quartet sang, and Vernon confessed to "occasional twinges of nostalgia, an undercurrent of sadness, as I reflected on the transience of life; and yet the dominant mood was the joy which springs from faith in an eternal Savior who stands triumphant over change and decay."

New Evangelicals

Personal salvation had always been the hallmark of evangelical Christianity, and that was certainly true in the 1960s when Billy Graham often topped the list of "America's Most Admired People."

Though preaching in crusade after crusade, "You must be born again," he was extremely popular and sought by national politicians of both parties.

In 1956, after ten years of revival crusades, Graham and his father-in-law, Dr. Nelson Bell, had founded *Christianity Today* magazine in hopes of its becoming the leading voice for the new evangelical coalition forming around the Graham renewal movement. Dr. Carl F. H. Henry had been called from his classroom at Fuller Seminary in California to serve as the magazine's editor, and he had enlisted scores of evangelical scholars to write for the journal, including his ally in the renewal, Vernon Grounds.

Throughout the 1960s Vernon produced a steady stream of articles. They poured from his pen and pad like a mountain creek nearing flood stage. Many of his writings were mimeographed papers or position papers responding to the issues of the day and to criticisms aimed at the seminary; but many others were written specifically for the newly created evangelical publications. Vernon wrote a monthly report and theological critique of the Second Vatican Council for the *Christian Heritage* magazine and continued to write from time to time for *Christianity Today*.

By now Vernon's case for Christianity and his message harmonizing human relationships with the supreme personal relationship with the Lord Jesus Christ carried a fresh new sound and a deep ethical quality. But none of his articles was more revealing than one he had written in 1960 for *Eternity* magazine, "Check Up on Your Commitment."

> "When you love Jesus Christ with all of your heart," he wrote, "your human loves are strengthened and purified. Yet Jesus said, 'He that loveth father or mother more than me is not worthy of me: and he that loveth son or daughter more than me is not worthy of me' (Matthew 10:37 KJV).

"When you make Him the Lord of your heart, your love for Him must have unconditional priority. And you do this gratefully. It is not done under pressure, nor is it motivated by a subtle fear. You do this because you love Jesus Christ supremely.

"Why? Because you have been to Calvary. You have seen Him dying for your sins. You have knelt in adoration and amazement before your Creator as He agonized to become your Savior. And now your heart belongs to Jesus Christ.

"With Simon Peter you cry out: 'Thou knowest all things. Thou knowest that I love thee.'"

Vernon Grounds was a man who obviously loved ideas and books and words. That is what made him a scholar, a professor, and a sought-after public speaker. But he was a most unusual scholar in that he loved people more than he loved his studies and his books. In some strange way he read words but saw human faces. He explored the life of the mind but focused on the life of the soul, and he saw his high calling as "the cure of the soul." He had heard Jesus' command, "Love your neighbor as yourself" and he remembered that nameless woman at the well, Zacchaeus in the tree, and Levi at the tax table, all individuals on the fringe of acceptable society who met Christ and went home changed.

⌐────⌐

Vernon's travel schedule had become increasingly crowded. His speaking beyond the school was his way of stooping like an Olympic weight lifter, taking a firm grip on the young seminary, and muscling it gently above his head. He invited George Beverly Shea to sing to 850 seminary friends at the 1962 Layman's Banquet, and later the same year Vernon attended his first Graham crusade. By 1965 when Billy Graham arrived in Denver for a crusade, the name Vernon Grounds was synonymous with Denver Seminary. He had made it so by his ceaseless travel.

He was committed to giving his life away, trying to change the world by listening to people and their problems, one person at a time, until he had literally touched thousands in Jesus' name. "The first overture of love is a listening ear," he said. This was, in his words, "the Jesus way."

During the social revolution of the 1960s, when students left his office they could not miss a bit of philosophy taped to the president's outer office door. In the background of a poster was an urban skyline and in the foreground was a bold message, a Campus Crusade for Christ slogan Vernon had picked up at some student rally: "Changing the world, one person at a time." Vernon Grounds believed it deeply and embraced the slogan as his own.

Because he did, he had a unique way of creating and nurturing friendship. When he met someone for the first time, he would mention some common interest. "I understand that we both have an interest in psychology." Or, "I have wanted to meet you. I understand you know my friend, Stan Clarkson." He had mastered Dale Carnegie's *How to Win Friends and Influence People* and recommended it to others.

On one of his many trips Vernon flew to Logan Airport in Boston where Pastor Nathan Goff met him for ministry at Grace Chapel in Lexington. Goff and his wife, Ruth Marie, and their family of five children had no room for Vernon to spend the night, so their next-door neighbors, new Christians at Grace Chapel, welcomed Vernon to spend the night with them.

Before finding faith, the man of the house had been a captain in the Marine Corps, an avid poker player, and rather skilled in abusive language. Over the following years Vernon stayed with this couple at least a dozen times—often enough for this ex-Marine to eventually attribute his early Christian growth to Vernon's weekends in his home.

On these visits Vernon would usually have breakfast with the couple and then cross the lawn to the Goff family's back door, sometimes entering a steamy kitchen. There, he would find the children having oatmeal around the table and the room filled with noise and confusion: "Drink your orange juice." "Do you have your books?" But Vernon would sit down with the children and engage them in conversation, as though he were a member of the family.

Once when Debbie, the youngest, was five or six, Vernon spoke at Grace Chapel and needed a ride to Logan Airport after the Sunday evening service. Her father asked Debbie if she wanted to go to the airport with him, so she climbed into the back seat of the car. Vernon sat in the front seat, but when they came to the bridge over the Charles River and drove alongside the river, he turned to her and, in a falsetto voice, started talking to her as though he were the river. He spun out a captivating tale for the little girl about the winds and waves. Years later Debbie said to her father, "Dad, do you remember when Dr. Grounds was the Charles River on our trip to the airport?"[8]

Vernon also traveled, whenever possible, to the ordination services of Denver Seminary graduates. These were often in small towns, where attendance was fewer than fifty people. Still he went willingly to these distant places—like northern Maine in January when many roads were impassable—and sometimes spent the night in a home with "outside plumbing." He gave his love and his time and his wisdom to people whom many speakers and teachers would ignore as "too few" or "too out-of-the-way." In word and deed, Vernon Grounds had grown into a servant leader.

CHAPTER 7

The With'ring Leaves of Time

The new morality is actually not quite so new as its propagandists claim, at least in their unguarded outbursts of enthusiasm. . . . All through the centuries, from Paul on down to modern times, Christian ethicists have taught that the law of love is the central and commanding principle of morality. . . . The new morality leaves us floundering in a semantic fog. In a desert of ambiguity it bids us to plot our course by the pursuit of tantalizing mirages. . . . fundamentally the new morality is a species of impractical idealism built upon a defective view of human nature.

– VERNON GROUNDS, *The New Morality?*

One afternoon in the summer of 1969 while at the Canadian Keswick Conference, Vernon Grounds found himself free to sit, relax, and reflect as he looked out upon lovely, tranquil Lake Rousseau. It was not yet mid-August, but traces of red and yellow and brown already dotted the trees, and the changing leaves stirred thoughts about age, death, and the passage of time.

An inner Vernon Grounds and an outer Vernon Grounds always existed. He was fully conscious that life around him moved on in a steady course; at the same time he was deeply concerned that the person within him also move on to maturity. In the early 1950s he had begun to write annual or semiannual letters to the seminary family and his many far-flung friends, and in these letters he often reflected his deepest thoughts about his inner and outer life.

"I refuse to call melancholy or morbid my reaction to autumn's advent," he wrote on the shore of Lake Rousseau. "I view it, rather, as biblically realistic. Green foliage turning to yellow or red or brown reminds me of that text in Isaiah 64:6, 'We all do fade as a leaf.'

"Summer still seems to be at its height, yet the year is pressing relentlessly along the grooves of time, and within a few months snow will blanket the earth, here in the North, and nature's immemorial cycle will again have run its course.

"After one has celebrated his 55th birthday, as I did on July 19, such somber reflections seem more justified. But I have been host to the same reflections as far back as I can remember; the oncoming of life's late afternoon merely accentuates them. And as I grow older, my human environment is steadily diminished by the inroads of death. So the words of Thomas Moore's 'Oft in the Stilly Night' become personally meaningful:

> 'Then I remember all the friends once linked together
> I've seen around me fall like leaves in Wintry weather.'"

Vernon does not recall exactly when he first read Erik Erikson's book *Childhood and Society* and began thinking deeply about his own eight stages of life. But whenever it was, he started to look at his life in phases and to take a periodic check of his progress.

"At fifty-five," he wrote, "I am poignantly aware that I must make the hours count. 'We all do fade as a leaf.' Human beings have zoomed to the moon and back, and maybe they will eventually explore one of the planets, but the realities of sin and guilt, pain and wonder, hope and despair, aging and death, heaven and hell and God remain untouched by technological achievements.

"We mustn't forget those realities which can't fade. At the beginning of his first letter, Peter speaks about 'an inheritance incorruptible, undefiled, and that fadeth not away.' So as the leaves fall and the seasons change, the Christian pilgrim must keep his eye on the land that never fades."

His thoughts then shifted to the twentieth anniversary of the seminary, only a few months away, and he recalled the years of struggle with ecclesiastical and financial difficulties, years in the center of unsolicited controversy, but also years of stimulating fellowship, years of growth and progress, and years of remarkable victories.

"Here at Canadian Keswick, which perpetuates much of British evangelicalism in its heyday," he wrote, "the hymns come from a huge collection compiled by Ira Sankey, *Sacred Songs and Solos*. I purchased a copy for my wife and have been reading it through. The hymns repeatedly strike the authentic New Testament note. Thus after one of my daily walks during which I observed autumnal tints beginning to dye the leaves, I came across Horatius Bonar's lines on future glory:

> 'Where the love that here we lavish
> On the with'ring leaves of time
> Shall have fadeless flowers to fix on
> In an ever spring-bright clime;
> Where we find the joy of loving
> As we never loved before.
> Loving on, unchilled, unhindered,
> Loving once and evermore.'"[1]

Vernon Grounds was a multi-gifted man. He always, with true humility, professed his ignorance and clearly knew his limitations, but in reality he was a man with an amazing grasp of psychology, philosophy, literature, and the history of Western thought. He knew that scholars spoke of the *mind* of an age and that his, like the leaves, was changing. There was a medieval mind, a modern mind, and clear signs of a postmodern mind. The apostle Paul had long ago recognized the *spirit* of his age, and Vernon often meditated on the changing colors and texture of his own.

As the leaves and the calendar changed that fall, he sensed the change in his soul. At fifty-five he felt deeply the fragile texture of life and death, time and eternity; and he yearned for a fresh touch of abiding love. He longed to see the power of *agape* at work in his own heart and in the hearts of those at the seminary, on America's campuses and in her inner cities.

The Social Revolution

Between 1965 and 1975, American society was transformed. In one short decade Americans experienced nothing less than a psychological revolution as a new popular culture turned its back on the traditional vision of faith, love, and truth. The ethic of self-denial was replaced by the bright, appealing ethic of self-expression.

The 1960s started on a bright tone of optimism, with the election of a young, handsome, and vigorous president, John F. Kennedy, promising a heroic new age. But the decade ended and moved into the 1970s in a mood of pessimism and doubt. In 1963 President Kennedy was assassinated in Dallas; civil rights marches spread throughout the South; and Martin Luther King Jr. was assassinated in Memphis. The national gloom deepened with the tragic, relentless war in Vietnam and the racial strife in America's streets. This affected every major institution in American society, the university and business, the church and family. Across the country people were caught up in the vast questions about the meaning of life. Nationally known columnist James Reston wrote, "There was scarcely a man or woman who felt confident about where the nation was going." And Gunnar Myrdal, the Swedish scholar, said after the election of 1968 that America faced the worst national crisis since the Civil War. "America is now in a real crisis and only God knows how she will get out of it."

Civil disobedience by young antiwar demonstrators broke out on university campuses, and it was condoned and encouraged by influential religious leaders such as civil rights leader Martin Luther King Jr. and William Sloane Coffin, chaplain of Yale University. By the end of 1967 President Lyndon Johnson could not go freely into any great city of the nation without being picketed by his antiwar critics. "Today," said John Gardner, Secretary of Health, Education and Welfare, "all seemed caught up in mutual recriminations—Negro and White, rich and poor, conservative and liberal ... young and old."[2]

Cascading events produced a "mood of questioning, doubt, and frustration in America." Young militant blacks threatened to use violence—"Black Power" as they called it—to bring equal opportunities for the oppressed, and racial riots burned in the streets of Chicago, Los Angeles, San Francisco, Detroit, and many smaller cities.

In this atmosphere of disillusionment and defiance a youth-led counterculture arose, using music as the primary medium for expressing its thoughts and feelings. Crowds swayed to the sounds of guitars and protest songs, their arms locked in understanding and agreement. In this age of uncertainty, anger, protest, and melancholy, this totally new social class, symbolized by the "hippies," experimented with psychedelic drugs, expanded their consciousness with Eastern religions, and opposed established social institutions, including the church. These counterculture "flower children" valued subjectivity and experience, depreciated history, and reacted against the technology of Western society. In pursuit of happiness these young revolutionaries adopted the motif of the Age of Aquarius, painted flowers on their VW vans, sang about their destiny in the stars, and preached, "Make love, not war."

Out of this strange countercultural world came something else: a new spirituality called "the Jesus people movement." These young Christians were sometimes labeled "Jesus freaks" because of their former life on the streets and in the drug culture. But many also came from mainstream Christian churches where they claimed they had found only a form of godliness without a hint of life or power.[3]

The "Jesus people movement" consisted of a number of diverse subgroups united only by common concerns. Their slogan "One Way!" could be heard and seen everywhere, and events like beach baptisms and Jesus concerts gained them wide media coverage. These followers typically carried huge Bibles and wore long hair and unconventional clothes. Their Jesus coffee houses, Jesus newspapers, and Jesus bumper stickers proclaimed, "Have a Nice Forever."

 The music of the movement—"Jesus rock"—expressed youthful frustration with traditional religious forms. Many, though not

all, in the Jesus movement were charismatic Christians; their services were intense, emotional, and infused with evangelistic zeal and
apocalyptic fervor. Experience and emotion far outweighed Christian doctrine.

After a few years, however, the faddish elements and excessive
emotionalism of the movement faded. When they reached adult-
hood, Jesus freaks tended to drift off into one of two general direc-
tions. One stream, consisting of groups such as the Children of
God and The Way, became increasingly authoritarian and assumed
cultic characteristics. Another stream moved toward more mainstream evangelical Christianity and helped to revitalize the movement through its music and informal worship.

———

Vernon Grounds was well aware of the changing culture. In his
1968 midyear letter to friends he told about a recent personal experience: "A few weeks ago I was having breakfast with my friend,
Keith Fredrickson, who in 1961 engineered for me the purchase of
a 1952 Chevrolet. Jokingly he asked if I was still driving that rather
decrepit wreck. I was. Why not? It was functioning efficiently in
spite of its none too elegant appearance. I told him, though, that
in the fall I might buy a second-hand Volkswagen. He said nothing very much about the matter. But three days later a 1966 Volkswagen, freshly painted a bright red, was standing in my driveway,
donated anonymously to the seminary for its president's use. So I
now have 'four on the floor' and thus, belying my 54 years, I can
lay claim to membership in the young-in-heart fraternity."

Then, significantly, the poet in him came out as he added
Henry Van Dyke's prayer:

> Let me but live my life from year to year,
> With forward face and unreluctant soul,

Not hastening to, nor turning from the goal;
Not mourning for the things that disappear
In the dim past, nor holding back in fear
From what the future veils; but with a whole
And happy heart, that pays its toll
To youth and age, and travels on with cheer.

Many of the students coming to Denver Seminary in the early 1970s drove their own VW "bugs." Some were from universities caught up in the spirit of the age, and some had found new faith in Christ as members of the "Jesus people." Many were from California, where they had come of age singing, "Put your hand in the hand of the man from Galilee." Some from northern California had been converted to faith or nurtured in the faith by Ray Stedman's ministry at Peninsula Bible Church or the Christian World Liberation Front in Berkeley led by Jack Sparks, a professor who had left his classroom to reach young people on the streets. Both groups had major ministries to the counterculture world.

Change in Denver

By the late 1960s the neighborhood around the old mansion on Capital Hill was showing many of the signs of the drug culture, but Humbolt Street on the west side of Cheesman Park had become a choice location for high-rise apartments with an awesome view of the Rockies. The school needed to expand, and as it moved toward accreditation, the addition of a library was becoming essential. Douglas Birk and a committee of board members spent long hours searching for additional property, but several attempts to secure property near the mansion proved futile. No library meant no accreditation! They were on the edge of despair when the possibility of moving south near Denver University came out of nowhere.

In the summer of 1967, Douglas Birk, while talking with a real estate friend, discovered that the Kent School for Girls was soon to be up for sale. The Kent School was a prep school located on twelve acres of land on the northwest corner of University Boulevard and Hampden Avenue. On the south side of Hampden was the prestigious Cherry Hills Country Club community and a mile north on University was Denver University. The property had a two-story academic building with a series of classrooms on an east wing, a gymnasium that could be easily converted to a library, and a red-brick residence on the northeast corner of the land. The remainder of the property was mostly tall native grass except for the girls' well-kept soccer field.

Then, in just a matter of days, "some benefactor"—to use Vernon's term—upon hearing the possibilities of the new campus, offered the seminary an initial matching-grant of $100,000.

Suddenly everything was on the fast track. If they were to secure the purchase, the school had to raise the matching funds of $100,000 in a matter of weeks. Vernon wrote to friends and alumnae, "We are thrilled as we envision a campus which will enable your *alma mater* to offer its students a top-drawer theological education."

But it wasn't just a matter of getting the money and the property. In two short months, over the summer of 1968, they would have to renovate buildings, transfer all the equipment from the mansion, including the libraries, and be ready for the opening of classes the first week of September!

"We face this task," Vernon wrote, "not as a backbreaking chore; we face it, instead, as a blessed challenge." Then he explained to alumnae that "Mr. Birk will be carrying the heaviest burden of responsibility in this complicated transition." He, himself, was scheduled for a month of teaching and counseling at the Winona Lake School of Theology, with weekend engagements in Detroit, New York, Chicago, and Oklahoma City. He would be returning to Denver just in time to move his office and library to the new campus.

Thanks in large part to longtime friends of the school, Harold and Virginia Simpson, the Kent School properties were transformed in a matter of months. The Simpson Construction Company converted the gymnasium into a library and the junior high classrooms into adult classrooms. Classes resumed in September.

The Case for Activism

The social revolution of the late 1960s and early 1970s constituted a major challenge for Christian ethicists, and none felt the burden more deeply than Vernon Grounds. He tended to identify more and more with the countercultural message, although he was well aware that few of the seminary's supporters shared his views. During the Vietnam War he understood the "peaceniks'" protest, though he was never much of a marcher and wanted no part of violence; and privately, he applauded Republican Senator Mark Hatfield's stand against the war. He also welcomed the countercultural collegians from California and speakers who were invited to minister to them on campus, such as John Howard Yoder, the Mennonite scholar; Foy Valentine, the Southern Baptist activist; Jack Sparks; and Jim Wallis. Vernon himself began to write a few articles for Wallis's cutting-edge publication, *The Other Side*.

In November 1967, just before the move to the new campus, Vernon flew back east for a series of lectures at the Evangelicals in Social Action Peace Witness Seminar meeting on the campus of Eastern Mennonite College in Harrisonburg, Virginia. Drawing upon the writings of Princeton University's Paul Ramsey, John Howard Yoder, and Foy Valentine, he made his best case for evangelical activism in American society.[4]

The New Testament, he said, views man as "inextricably enmeshed in the processes of nature, the movements of history, and the structures of culture." When men and women become Christian believers, they are not somehow abstracted from the world with its organizations and its obligations. No, they, too, remain enmeshed in the structures of society. They can no more escape participation in politics than they can divest themselves of their "own epidermis." They are not "abstracted," he said; they are, rather, "realigned to the world."

Vernon assured his audience that the Word of God guides believers in fashioning and following a social ethic, laying down certain evangelical affirmations. "While Christians are blessed with divine revelation, we do not have many of the answers to the problems of society. But we must refuse to be intimidated into passivity by our ignorance." The church, he stressed, is a supernatural fellowship living under the law of holy love. "We are obligated to maximize love by maximizing justice. We recognize the limits of individual concern and private charity. But let us be honest about the impact these regenerate citizens have made and are likely to make on society.

"Some problems today in our technological, urbanized, more and more depersonalized society are so complicated, so far-reaching, so deep-rooted, so massive that they baffle the resources of individual action and private charity. They require governmental intervention on a mammoth scale; and this means the use of legislative and administrative apparatus."

Then came the statement that reveals how far he had moved personally from the fundamentalism of his early days at Faith Seminary and Johnson City. "The church," he said, "has the responsibility of nurturing and judging the ethos of our political and economic life. Its responsibility is that of improving the moral climate of society, elevating standards and sensitizing consciences. Certain factors render political action imperative. We recognize the necessity of Christian political action. We must instruct and inspire regenerate citizens."

The New Testament does warn against utopianism, he said— against any romantic illusions about sweeping and permanent reforms. Christian activists, being human beings, are also infested with sinful self-interest, and social structures will be more or less corrupt until the end of history. But the church "is that community which prayerfully struggles to translate Paul's eulogy of love in 1 Corinthians 13 from poetry into practice. It is that community which prayerfully struggles to function as light and salt and yeast in the midst of society, bringing individuals into the life and likeness of holy love."

"A Christian believer," he argued, "owes the state the *duties of honor, prayer, taxes* legally demanded, *service* in the sense of the glad performance of every ministry which a Christian can conscientiously render, and, finally, *obedience,* a hearty compliance with the laws. But civil obedience has its limits. It is by no means unqualified. What if the state does not fulfill its function? What if, instead of being a minister of God, it becomes unmistakably a tool of the devil?"

How should Christians register their disapproval of constituted authority? By passive obedience? Acts of nonviolence? Or even bloody revolution? These questions he left unanswered.

The New Morality

About the same time—in the late 1960s—*His* magazine, the publication of InterVarsity Christian Fellowship, invited Vernon to speak to the highly publicized "New Morality" doctrine advanced by Anglican Bishop John Robinson and the ethicist Joseph Fletcher. Vernon wrote five articles addressing the ethical dilemma that collegians faced on their campuses.[5]

"We are living in a revolutionary era," he wrote, "exciting of course, but as perplexing as it is exciting. A theological revolution is in process, and it is furthering a moral revolution; this in turn is furthering, and being furthered by a sexual revolution. Since 1914 vast cultural forces have been at work, undermining the old order of things . . . emancipating women, providing contraceptive methods which are inexpensive and almost foolproof, creating the mass media that evoked Hollywood and *Playboy,* allowing Sigmund Freud and Alfred Kinsey to gain prophetic status. Our world consequently is in a state of ethical ferment. As Rabbi Richard Rubenstein sums up the situation: 'We are experiencing a new sense of personal freedom. We now ask, "Is this right for me?" We no longer ask, "How do I comply with a set of inherited commandments from my religious tradition?" We enjoy a degree of freedom today that people have never experienced before.'

"Pity, then," continued Vernon, "the collegian who, a sexed creature, finds himself on the one hand enticed by high voltage impulses and, on the other, unsure as to which guidelines merit his allegiance. If only he could be sure that the old principles have no validity! If only he could be sure that the new ethicists are right about wrong! If only he could be sure that his anxiety and guilt are products of social conditioning rather than evidences of a transcendental relationship! If only he were an amoral animal instead of being a man who seems destined to live perpetually in a condition of civil war!"

Then, argument by argument, Vernon stripped the "New Morality" of its aura and showed that it left the student in a "semantic fog." In a "desert of ambiguity [the New Morality] bids us to plot our course by the pursuit of tantalizing mirages." The ethic, he insisted, is built entirely upon a defective view of human nature. Far better to trust the Bible's affirmations "all have sinned" and "God is love" and believe that He has taught us all to live wholly and ethically by the power of Calvary-love.

Changes and Challenges
By 1975, which marked the seminary's twenty-fifth anniversary, the Vietnam War had ended and the anger of the youth cul-

ture had subsided. Only the "expressive individual" remained. "Success" now meant a life rich in strong, sensual experiences and self-expression. "Freedom" had become the freedom to express one-self against society's constraints and traditions. And everyone, it seemed, was "into happiness," even the workplace. Delta Airline's slogan—"We love to fly and it shows"—was typical. Corporate America had discovered that "good feelings" sold more airline tick-ets, automobiles, and electric shavers than did safety or quality.

In two short decades the traditional image of the noble Amer-ican as a self-reliant, take-charge individual who on occasion must turn his back on the larger community in order to do what is right and good was transformed into the liberated, expressive baby boomer who was "free to be myself." Since the "real self" was, in effect, an indefinable entity, this discovery was destined to be an unending search.

Earlier generations of Americans had turned to family, home-town communities, the government, the church, or God Himself during difficult times. Many baby boomers, however, had nowhere to turn. The concepts of duty, self-denial, self-restraint, all previ-ously considered virtues, were no longer viewed as valuable. Now the focus was on rights and opportunities. By stressing the libera-tion of the self, "expressive" Americans came to treat every com-mitment—from marriage and work to politics and religion—not as a moral obligation but as a mere instrument of personal happi-ness. And millions "caught the spirit."

In this sacred status of the self, sexuality filled a particularly crit-ical function. The hippies had preached "Make love, not war!" Now, with the war a thing of the past, only lovemaking remained, and it was widely considered the primary source of "ultimate" sig-nificance for the soul. The liberation of sexuality from social con-trol became a pervasive social cause. Boundaries, and the security they provide, were all but gone.

This rise of the "culture of narcissism"—to borrow Christopher Lasch's term for it—set American against American. Two parties, liberationists and traditionalists, struggled for the nation's soul in a not-so-civil war. This war was the most obvious sign that Americans no longer shared the same code of morality. One half of the country—America's academic, artistic, and media elite—considered "alternative lifestyles" as great advances for human freedom and dignity. The other half of the nation tended to see this as moral decadence and social degeneration.

These social forces would slowly redefine Vernon Grounds's career and the future of the Denver Seminary.

CHAPTER 8

Lifting Up the Fallen

Because he is a sinner, man has a tendency to love things inordinately and use persons instrumentally. In so doing he not only hurts others but he also hurts himself. Made in love, he can experience self-fulfillment only as he lives in love. This means that he must love persons supremely and use things solely in order that person-love may be enhanced and augmented. Hence when he loves things inordinately and uses persons instrumentally in order to obtain more things for himself, he lives in frustration, estranged from his neighbor. And our human tragedy lies precisely at this point: everybody is guilty of loving things inordinately and using people instrumentally, and thus the tangle of estrangement becomes more and more knotted.

— VERNON GROUNDS,
A Theology of Interpersonal Relations

In the late 1970s a young seminary graduate and his wife, serving their first church, were swept up in one of those painful feuds that often erupt in small rural churches. Nearing the breaking point after months of hostility and hate, they slipped into their car one morning and drove several hundred miles from Wyoming to Denver to meet with Dr. Grounds and tell him all their troubles.

The young wife later wrote to Vernon, expressing their gratitude. "You were there for us, waiting to help put back together the shattered pieces of our broken and bruised lives. I remember that I was so scared and hurt that I had withdrawn into a shell so thick I didn't think God Himself could get through, but there you were, ointment and bandage in hand, strong, yet gentle enough to let the scared, hurt, little child in me come out and sit down beside you. You loved me back into living, and for all that, and so many other reasons, I shall always love you."[1]

Perhaps Vernon Grounds's most significant contribution to the renewal of evangelical Christianity was his understanding and practice of *agape* love, especially its application to pastoral care and the cure of souls. He realized that the mainspring of Christian ministry —and especially Christian counseling—is the love of God. Literally thousands were healed spiritually and emotionally, at least in some measure, by his touch. Care was his greatest gift. He was almost supernaturally adept at it. He preached the gospel. He read and understood psychology. He taught crisis counseling. But he lived pastoral care.

For more than three decades, Vernon's daily schedule at the seminary was sprinkled with counseling appointments. Someone always seemed to be waiting in his secretary's office to follow him into his own office and sit down in one of the well-padded chairs at the round table. His caring heart and his wise, professional counsel were legendary.

On one occasion a Denver attorney sought his help. Vernon had met this man at the gym where they shared an interest in weight lifting and often compared their bench-pressing abilities. The two men had become friends, so when the lawyer's marriage began to crumble rapidly and his wife wanted a divorce, he called his friend Vernon, the pastor-professor-seminary president who lifted weights.

One day, as the two of them were discussing the man's problem, Vernon had him draw up a list of options on a piece of paper. He listed:

1. stay in the marriage
2. separate
3. divorce

Then, since some rather desperate events had driven the man to consult him, Vernon urged him to list a fourth option:

4. suicide

Then Vernon said matter-of-factly, "And, of course, there is murder."

Not many things can shock a practicing trial lawyer, but this snapped Vernon's friend into focus. He began to object, "Such a choice never entered my mind."

Vernon brushed the response aside and said, "Come now. You mean to tell me that a lawyer who has spent as much time in the courts as you have, doing everything including criminal defense, does not know someone who will kill for money? Surely, the thought has crossed your mind."

"Vernon may as well have clubbed me with a large baseball bat," the man said later. "He was right—the name of such a person was instantly in my mind. The thought had surely been present at least for a moment. I could not respond."

"Write it down," came the voice from across the table.

As the man tried to compose himself, Vernon took the list and said, "Can we agree that as Christians murder is not a viable choice?"

The lawyer nodded in the affirmative as he struck the word from the list.

Pressing onward, Vernon said, "Can we also agree as Christians that self-murder—suicide—is not a viable choice?"

The whole exchange was so shocking that the man never forgot it. A decade later he reflected, "Some might think this a rather bizarre approach to counseling. But it demonstrates the absolutely unbelievable insight God has given this man. I was in dire need of a serious dose of reality, and Vernon knew exactly how to deliver that reality dose so that I could focus upon the other choices in the manner necessary to get through those times—particularly without ever again considering suicide as a choice."[2]

The Cure of Souls

Counseling was rapidly becoming Vernon's second career. He always thought of his busy life as ministry, but it had, in fact, become two callings—ministry and counseling. During the week his life was like a beautiful string of beads, with faces of individuals neatly spaced throughout the day. First thing in the morning he met with some small group over breakfast, and throughout the morning and afternoon he saw individuals between classes and meetings.

Vernon's counseling career grew during the very decades when psychology and psychotherapy were spreading like spring pollen over the social landscape. The secular psychologies of Freud, Adler, Jung, and others appeared not only on university campuses but in theological seminaries, where theologians had begun to explore the interplay between theology and psychology. Counseling courses multiplied, and a new movement emerged: Clinical Pastoral Education.

Therapy was a new way of looking at reality. As Christians responded to the therapeutic culture, some simply assimilated the secular psychologies while others tried to exclude themselves completely. And some tried, in various ways, to integrate them into specifically Christian practices.

One pioneer who gained a large following in American evangelical circles in the 1960s was Dr. Paul Tournier, a Swiss physician who had grown up as a lonely orphan. In 1932 Tournier's career as a general practitioner had taken a surprising turn when he became involved in a Christian group called the Oxford Group in Geneva. This experience gave him new interest in the spiritual life and a deeper awareness of human needs. Soon Tournier was spending more time listening to his patients' problems and less time attending to their routine medical needs. Slowly he developed his own counseling skills, and in 1940 he wrote a book about this counseling, *The Healing of Persons*.

Vernon Grounds had a similar experience, but as a pastor rather than a physician. As a young pastor in New Jersey, he had felt drawn to people and seemed to have a natural gift for making friends—deep, abiding, lifelong friends. At the same time, he caught a glimpse of a loving pastor's power to heal. Thus, he moved more and more from tent-meeting evangelism toward that longstanding tradition in Christianity called "pastoral care."

After he had entered Drew University and during his years in Johnson City, Vernon began to read psychology and came to focus on the power of Christian love. It was in Johnson City that Vernon began to understand how radical Christian love is, how much like God's heart and how much unlike the unchanged human heart. He learned to blend his counseling and his teaching, and in doing so he took a personal interest in every student at Baptist Bible Seminary. As both dean and friend he mentored many of them in Christian service. Vernon's counseling of troubled souls and his relationship with individual students was what Søren Kiekegaard once called "works of love."

"He helped us identify talents we scarcely knew we possessed," said one former student years later. When he was a freshman with an inferiority complex, he had been recruited by "Dean Grounds" to play in a trumpet quartet that traveled with Vernon and Ann to minister in churches around the Binghamton area. Under Vernon's inspiration, the young man's self-confidence began to grow, his academic performance improved, and he began to catch a vision of his future. This once-shy freshman, with deep feelings of inferiority, went on to earn his Ph.D. and D.Min. degrees—and throughout his life he considered Vernon and Ann Grounds his dearest friends. Vernon had taught him to think critically, he said, and to allow his faith to be "strong enough to tolerate doubt, and deep enough to withstand the superficiality of a materialistic world."[3]

In 1953 the English translation of Anders Nygren's influential book *Agape and Eros* became a part of Vernon's reading for his doctoral work at Drew. In the book Nygren fashions the biblical concept of love like a master diamond cutter, bringing out the sparkle of every facet of biblical truth. He cuts a sharp distinction between self-obsessed *eros* and self-sacrificial *agape*. Then, by concentrating on the apostle Paul's use of *agape*, he identifies a cluster of its major characteristics:

First, he says, *agape* love is primarily God's love for humanity and only secondarily the Christian's love for others.

Second, *agape* is not motivated by any value in the object of love. It is spontaneous, driven from within by its own unique nature.

Third, *agape* is "indifferent to value" in the object of love; it creates the value in the object of love. It is never earned; it is a gift from God.

And fourth, *agape* initiates fellowship with God. Because the human response to God's love is always motivated by the supreme value of God's love, the apostle Paul speaks of this response to God's love as "faith." Christian faith, then, or *agape* love in the believer, is always traceable to God's gift of love. To live by faith is to live by love.

After his move to Denver, Vernon began to speak more and more of this Calvary love. After three years he had a dozen or so messages that he turned into articles and published in the fledgling Conservative Baptist magazine, *The National Voice*.[4] Encouraged by the response to the articles, he then put the messages together into a short manuscript called *The Lord and Life of Love*. Over a three-year period he contacted four publishers with the manuscript and was deeply disappointed when none seemed interested in publishing it.

The fourth publisher postponed a decision for a year and then suggested in a letter that the material might need some editing. Vernon responded in an unusual but revealing few lines. "No manuscript," he wrote, "least of all anything I write, is sacrosanct, but when a man is head over heels in work he hates to re-tackle some stale material." His schedule was full, and the book was never published.

Integration

By 1956, the year that Vernon became president of Denver Seminary, he had come to believe that psychotherapy and pastoral care might well be integrated. That same year he wrote an article for

Eternity magazine in which he gave a number of clues as to what that integration might look like. His article, "Has Freud Anything for Christians?" was a detailed review of Ernest White's new book, *Christian Life and the Unconscious.*

Vernon did not hesitate to fault Freud's explanation of religion, but he praised Dr. White, an English therapist, for his bold attempt to integrate psychotherapy and the Christian faith. White showed how psychology could serve as an oxygen tank, equipping the thoughtful Christian to plunge into the depths of the believing soul. He acknowledged the large area of the mind below the level of consciousness but maintained that this is not an entity in itself. It is, rather, a descriptive term applied to a particular functioning of the mind; it is the mind when viewed from a distinctive angle.

White then described Christian regeneration and conversion in psychological terms. The Christian, he said, may be unaware of regenerative change except as he recognizes three new desires within his inner life: the desire to pray, the desire to witness, and the desire to fellowship. Conversion, however, is a conscious change involving conflict and crisis. Centrally it involves the will, and it has a whole range of manifestations, nearly always with a new emotional quality and a deep-rooted direction in life. Christian redemption, he said, is not merely a split-second transaction; it is also a process. Because of this, Christians can never expect a life free of conflicts or struggles. Sin remains a fact of life.

"It is an axiom of psychotherapy," Dr. Grounds concluded in his review, "that interpersonal relationship is the primary factor in molding human character. Indeed, as Lewis Joseph Sherrill sums it up, we are formed by interpersonal relationships, deformed by them, and only by them can we be transformed.

"Thus, all White does is translate the language of Paul and John into more modern terms, showing the profound compatibility between psychiatric insight and New Testament truth."

The years passed, and Vernon still had not written his book revealing his theology and practices of Christian love. He had, however, written many articles. In 1971, his article for *Christianity Today,* "Therapist and Theologian Look at Love," once again magnified *agape* love and gave an abbreviated version of his integration of psychology and the Christian faith.

The "therapist" Vernon refers to in this article is primarily Erich Fromm, who was raised an orthodox Jew but later in life renounced his faith and became an internationally known psychoanalyst. In the mid-1950s Fromm published two books, *The Sane Society* and *The Art of Love*, in which he explored the relationship of love to Western society and human personality.

The "theologian" in the article is primarily Dr. Vernon Carl Grounds, after having read Sartorius, Kiekegaard, and Nygren. "Psychotherapy," he writes, "is a discipline concerned with understanding and treating personality disorders. . . . Any discipline that can help to release human beings from a self-centered love, that inverted love which prevents a true self-acceptance and a true self-understanding, ought to be Christianity's welcomed ally."

Although the theologian may be deeply appreciative of psychotherapy, if it is based on "reductive naturalism, it holds a defective and ultimately frustrating wisdom about man. It fails to realize that to experience the highest form of health, healing, and happiness, human beings need a cosmic environment of love—divine love. This love supplies redemptive meaning and hope, and through the Church even the hope of community in a splintered world."

Listening to Erich Fromm, the "theologian" agrees that if man is to experience fulfillment, he must live rationally, productively, and above all lovingly. "He also agrees that human beings are frustrated precisely at this point: they are unable to live in free, outgoing, creative love . . . And he agrees that something must be done to help frustrated people gain or regain the capacity to love."

But psychotherapy, says Dr. Grounds, "while it may indeed be healing and liberating, cannot penetrate to the bottom of the frustration and failure people experience in their relations with others if it ignores the one all-determinative interpersonal relationship—that between God and man. This concept of the human predicament differs radically from the psychotherapist's. Assume that in self-love . . . man chooses to make himself the center of things, shouldering God aside . . . Assume, consequently, a malignant relationship between the creature and his Creator. . . . Then what? In this predicament a therapy far more radical than psychotherapy is required. What man needs is something that only God's forgiving grace can provide: the therapy of divine love."

The major components of this therapy, according to Dr. Grounds, are the atonement made by Jesus Christ and the ministry of the Holy Spirit. The gospel announces that in the miracle of the atonement "God died *for* man and *with* man in order that he and man, dying 'jointly to an old life,' might 'jointly rise to a "new one."' In the Cross man beholds the consummate evidence of love. This revelation of sin-bearing love breaks the bondage of self-love and sets man free to live according to the law of love."

In this process of redemption, this metamorphosis of self-love, there is another "mind-staggering aspect of the Gospel. The indwelling Spirit of God, who is the Spirit of Jesus Christ, comes to fill the love-conquered heart with the love of God, changing the personality more and more into the likeness of incarnate Love.

"God, the moving Spirit of the universe, is an aggressive lover who by the miracles of incarnation, atonement, and resurrection, together with the powerful operation of the Holy Spirit, cracks through the sinner's imprisoning egocentricity and elicits love. . . . The vision of Calvary, where Love died, is brought home to the conscience with ego-penetrating power by the Holy Spirit, winning the response that produces love for God and man."

This may well have been Vernon Grounds's finest statement of his lifelong vision.

Passing the Torch

For years Vernon had dreamed of multiplying his counseling ministry based on this faith in the power of *agape* love. He had lectured to students on campuses around the country and in medical schools in the greater Denver area. These lectures often served to challenge Christian young people to pursue a career in psychology or in Christian counseling.

Sometime during the 1970s one Christian psychiatrist looked back to his first days as a young intern at Denver General Hospital in the early 1960s and to his first encounter with Dr. Grounds at a Christian medical society meeting, where Dr. Grounds spoke of Freud. The intern had a strong interest in psychiatry and a smattering of knowledge about Freud, so he was deeply interested in hearing Dr. Grounds's point of view. He was not disappointed. Later he wrote, "As a young intern I was greatly impressed with your depth of knowledge about the man personally as well as about his contributions to the field of psychotherapy.

"I was particularly impressed by the fact that a theologian would have that amount of knowledge concerning a man whose philosophy the Christian community saw as rather threatening. As a young man and relatively young Christian, I had some concerns myself about integrating my Christianity with the psychoanalytic concepts.

"You gave me courage that night as well as a conviction that a Christian does not need to be threatened by man's limited understanding about himself or about his fellow man. It was reassuring to have you affirm for me, once again, that the Bible gives a much better understanding of man, his meaning and purpose of life than any other philosophy can provide."[5]

The young intern's experience was not untypical. A growing number of teachers in Christian schools and counselors in practice were now testifying of Vernon Grounds's influence upon them. But Vernon felt that the seminary itself could do a better job of equipping students to care for the psychological, ethical, and spiritual needs of people, and in the early 1970s he was able to secure funding for the creation of a master's degree program in counseling at the seminary and established a major leading to an M.A. degree in counseling. As a consequence, in addition to his presidential duties he began to serve as Cauwels Professor of Pastoral Care and Christian Ethics and head of the Counseling Department.

In announcing the good news about the new addition to the curricula, *The Seminarian* reported that the purpose of the program was not to train "professional psychologists" but "paraprofessionals" who would engage in "pastoral counseling." Qualified individuals from the Denver area were to serve as adjunct faculty and special lecturers. When the 1974 fall term commenced, Vernon had enlisted Dr. John C. Faul, Dr. Charles Holton, and Dr. Richard Scheideman as adjunct faculty members to join him in the teaching.

One day about this time a lifelong friend of Vernon and Ann called to ask a favor of him. This woman had felt the power of Dr. Grounds's gospel-centered "theory" in her life even as a student back in New York.

"I have to appear in court, and I wonder if you would go with me," she said, a slight tremor in her voice. "It's a very serious charge." She spoke nervously, first explaining how she happened to be charged and then the importance of the court appearance. If the charge appeared on her record, she said, she could be fired from her position in professional circles.

"Of course," Vernon said without hesitation. "I'll be glad to come to court with you."

A few days later, just before the two of them walked into the court room, Vernon asked her if he could speak to the district attorney on her behalf.

"Please, do!" she said. And he did.

As a result, the district attorney not only erased the charge from the records but also assigned her to report to Dr. Grounds for several weeks.

The woman gladly agreed to that! And she walked out of the courtroom with a spotless record. Once again, Vernon's faith was active in love.[6]

Problems in Print

Despite his new responsibilities in the seminary's degree program, Vernon's hectic weekly schedule continued unchecked: flying, speaking, befriending. In 1976, the year of America's bicentennial celebration, Vernon delivered a series of lectures at several schools. These later appeared in a little book called *Emotional Problems and the Gospel*, which reveals more of his theory and practice of counseling.

"The gospel," he asserted, "is an unrivaled antidote for neurosis. Dare I say that, if mental health and healing demand self-understanding, self-identity, self-acceptance, self-release, and self-investment, if this is their demand, then the gospel of Jesus Christ seems to possess extraordinary resources for alleviating mental illness?"[7]

In these lectures he spoke specifically of anxiety, pride, guilt, and anger. Basic to the healing of all four, he said, is faith in that "aggressive Lover" of the Bible. Christianity is concerned about the individual's relationship to God. "It sees him as a creature whose overriding responsibility is to get his wrong relationship readjusted . . . it sees him as the bearer of destiny which stretches out beyond time into eternity, and this relationship is determined by his God-relationship.

"How different . . . the God of the Bible is from the God of the philosophers! They talk about a First Cause of the cosmos, the Ground of Being, the unmoved Mover of unruffled serenity and imperturbable perfection, a sort of cosmic Icicle. Their God is not the God of the Bible. The true God, the God of the Bible, is genuinely personal and measurelessly empathic, touched by the feeling of our infirmities."

Throughout the lectures Vernon underscored that the Bible and prayer are vital practices of faith that God uses to heal us.

> "The Bible agrees with the psychological consensus that these negative emotions are rooted in our very nature—only the Bible asserts that our nature is now depraved because we are members of an apostate race."

But at the same time the Bible is our window of the soul. It gives us access to the light of God Himself. "When we perceive God as He really is, there comes a release from distrustful dread. Knowledge plus practice enables us to enter more and more deeply into the significance of 1 John 4:17: 'Herein is our love made perfect, that we may have boldness in the day of judgment: because as he is, so are we in this world.' Knowledge plus practice enables us to rejoice with John Donne, 'The love of God begins in fear, and the fear of God ends in love; and that love can never end, for God is love'" (KJV).

And there is also therapy in prayer. "We must expectantly ask Him to reach down into the subterranean depths of our psyches and cut through the roots of worry and fear. . . . Usually this means prayerful verbalization because in verbalization we exteriorize our anxiety and thus by the grace of God and the power of the Holy Spirit exorcise anxiety."

Vernon then led his young audiences to Hebrews 4:16 and reminded them that "God's throne is the throne of grace. . . . Keep nothing back, verbalizing with no attempt at logic or control. It means doing exactly what a client does with a psychotherapist, letting accumulated and suppressed emotions spill out. This is the apostle's urgent invitation. Spill out all the meanness, the filth, the despair, or whatever else may have been dammed back inside. Tell it in full detail. Come *boldly* to the throne of grace.

"The King who sits upon that throne is a High Priest full of love and compassion and forgiveness. The King who sits upon that throne is a Father with a mother's heart. Before that throne we need not grovel like a captured spy begging for mercy from merciless captors. Before that throne we bow in gratitude and thanksgiving.

"In His omniscience He knows the fright and agony of a sparrow seized by a hawk. In His omniscience He knows the ache and pain of a bereaved mother's heart. Yet according to this text [Hebrews 4:16], He knows our feelings not by virtue of divine omniscience but by virtue, rather, of personal experience." The omnipotent God entered human existence at Bethlehem. He became one of us!

To help his young audiences feel the power of this cardinal Christian doctrine, Vernon often said to them, "Let me make a suggestion. Take a small piece of towel, a piece no more than an inch square. Put it in your wallet or billfold. Carry it with you everywhere. Look at it daily for the first few weeks after you voluntarily join the highest and noblest of all fraternities, the Order of the Towel. Do that, if you are able to do it sincerely. Let the towel become your insignia. Let the towel remind you of your Master. Let the towel motivate you to follow the example of our God who humbled Himself."

CHAPTER 9

Gaining New Heights

How different Jesus was! Different because he was totally God-centered and completely self-forgetting; different because of his intense and steadfast fellowship with his father; different because he came into the world not to be served but to serve. He was, as we read in Hebrews, "holy, harmless, undefiled, separate from sinners," but he loved the world, taking delight in the beauty of flowers, the gracefulness of flying birds, the joyful innocence of "Children's faces looking up—holding wonder like a cup."

— VERNON GROUNDS,
Loving the World: Rightly or Wrongly

By the third quarter of the twentieth century, Billy Graham had become "the most successful evangelist in Christian history," and in the process he had restored evangelical Christianity to a prominent place in American public life. In 1964, during a taxi ride to the airport after a visit to the White House, Billy told Carl Henry, the editor of *Christianity Today*, that he wanted to convene a global conference on evangelism. He felt, however, that the Billy Graham Association didn't have the "intellectual respectability" to gather the type of conferees he wanted—"professors and presidents of seminaries and people like that." The best solution, he thought, would be for *Christianity Today* to undertake the conference as a tenth-anniversary project, to be held in 1966. He also wanted Henry to head the conference, although Billy agreed to serve as honorary chairman.

Carl Henry asked Vernon Grounds to serve on one of the planning committees for what was being called "The World Congress on Evangelism" in West Berlin. Twelve hundred leaders from more than 100 countries were invited to attend the conference. Some American evangelicals grumbled when the congress leaders set a limit of 100 invitees from the United States and they were not included. Vernon Grounds, however, one of those "professors and presidents of seminaries" whom Billy Graham wanted to lend "respectability," was there in the Kongresshalle and on the streets with the other 1,200 delegates concerned that evangelism regain its position of priority in the life of the church. Vernon called them "never-to-be-forgotten days. . . . My soul was thrilled."[1]

In his opening address to the congress, Billy Graham announced the primary purpose of the gathering: to dispel all confusion about the meaning, motive, and message of evangelism. The confusion came, he said, from the devious strategies of "the enemy," a category that included both natural and supernatural foes. But Graham also, uncharacteristically, attacked a specific source of the confusion: the ecumenical advocates of universalism, the widespread but soft-headed belief that God would not really let people go to hell.

At one evening service, Kimo Yaeti and Komo Gikita, two of the Auca Indians who had participated in the 1956 killing of Jim Elliot, Nate Saint, and three other missionaries in the jungles of Ecuador, appeared on the platform. Their interpreter was Rachel Saint, sister of Nate Saint. Ten years after the five men were martyred on a beach along the muddy Curaray River, Rachel Saint was interpreting for two Auca converts to Christianity. Vernon could hardly believe it. "Two triumphs of divine grace," he called them.

"I rather think that many eyes were misted with tears," Vernon told his friends, "especially when we stood and sang together 'How Great Thou Art.' And certainly tears of joy flowed unchecked when, as we were still singing, an African delegate, unable to control his emotions, ran to the platform and threw his arms around those two Aucas, embracing them as his brethren. What a symbol of the Gospel's reconciling power!"[2]

Overall, the congress held few surprises, but the appearance of two particular individuals did provide what historian William Martin called "a dash of panache." Oral Roberts, the Pentecostal evangelist, was there, although mainstream evangelicals tended to avoid him until he took the platform in an unplanned address to a plenary session. Billy Graham introduced him to lead in prayer by saying, "Our prayer is going to be led by a man that I have come to love and appreciate in the ministry of evangelism. . . . I am speaking of Dr. Oral Roberts, and I am going to ask him to say a word of greeting to us before he leads the prayer."

When the applause subsided, Roberts charmed the assembly with his confession that he had been "out-preached, out-prayed, and out-organized" by the men in whose presence he stood. "I thank you, Billy, and Dr. Henry, for helping to open my eyes to the mainstream of Christianity and to bring me closer to the Lord."

The other man was uninvited but nevertheless clearly visible. Carl McIntire, the militant fundamentalist, neither received nor expected an invitation to attend. For years he had been sharply critical of Billy Graham and his "cooperative evangelism." He was there, he said, "to report." But when he was told that he had applied too late for press credentials and would not be permitted to attend press conferences or interview delegates, McIntire issued a statement and taped it to the glass partitions at the entrance to the Kongresshalle. Then, for the duration of the conference "the Fundamentalist fulminator," as William Martin called him, "stood outside the entrance, distributing mimeographed tirades against Graham and the apostate evangelism he represented."

To conclude the Congress, delegates gathered inside the great foyer of the Kongresshalle before a huge map of the world on which were faces of little children and the slogan "A soul to win every second" in four languages. Against that backdrop stood a time clock recording the number of births every second around the globe. The clock, as Vernon Grounds explained, "had been started when the Congress began; steadily it had been ticking away all those days and nights, its inexorable click ... click ... click always audible even above the hubbub of conversation. And when on that Friday morning the clock was stopped, it registered 1,774,216—not digits but souls for whom Jesus Christ died, souls who must be evangelized. Nothing further was said; nothing needed to be said."

Berlin, however, represented much more than a call to global evangelism. It represented a milestone in the history of evangelical Christianity. As one historian put it, it established evangelicalism "as an international movement capable of accomplishing more than its constituents had dreamed possible."

Signs of Fire

Vernon returned to Denver with rekindled zeal, trusting the fire to burn steadily and ever brighter. He was fully persuaded that the emphases of the World Congress were the same emphases that should mark his own ministry and the ministry of Denver Seminary.

The most obvious signs of the fire on campus were sparked by the seminary's alliance with the Conservative Baptist Home Mission Society. Vernon and the Home Society's General Director, Rufus Jones, were sometime "soul brothers," sharing a social concern and daring to venture where many Conservative Baptists feared to tread.

Under the Home Society's canopy a few young men with experience in Campus Crusade for Christ circles formed the Campus Ambassadors ministry to evangelize university students and disciple them within the life of an evangelical congregation near the campus. Bill Johnson in Flagstaff, Arizona, Bob Burger in San Jose, California, Larry Marlott in Boulder, Colorado, and Don Orvis in Denver, along with their wives, were pioneers in this venture. Don Orvis and Larry Marlott were Denver Seminary students during the "Vietnam era" and were instrumental in bringing the Campus Ambassadors Summer Institute to the seminary's campus. This meant long hair, guitars, "One Way" signs, and "Jesus the Liberator" T-shirts on campus. But it also meant a few signs of that fire that Vernon had seen and experienced in Berlin.

During these same years the Home Society sent missionary Donald Davis to work in Denver's inner city. Davis, a Fuller Seminary graduate, with the help of a few Denver students and their spouses, was able to form a congregation just south of Denver's civic center. This enabled him to teach an urban-ministry course or two at the seminary with well-deserved credibility. Another sign of the Berlin fire.

⸻

Eight years after the World Congress on Evangelism in West Berlin, the Graham team and an international sponsoring committee invited an even larger and more representative assembly of evangelical Christians to gather at the Palais Beaulieu in Lausanne, Switzerland, overlooking the lovely waters of Lake Geneva, for the Lausanne Congress on World Evangelization. The nearly 2,500 participants at the Congress were from 150 countries, and all eyes were upon the 2.7 billion of the world's people yet unreached with the gospel.

The Palais Beaulieu was just up the mountainside from Ouchy where the boats on Lake Geneve docked. Around the lake was tiny L'Abri, where Francis Schaeffer, Vernon's friend from seminary days, had established his unique ministry center and was writing a series of influential books interpreting the shifting tides of Western culture. Schaeffer crossed the lake to be one of the major speakers.

At the concluding communion service led by African bishop Festo Kivingeri, thousands of evangelical Christians signed the Lausanne Covenant, pledging to give themselves to cross-cultural missions, Christian unity, and a simple lifestyle. Lausanne stood for many of the values that Dr. Grounds and Denver Seminary had long embraced. The Congress aimed to proclaim the biblical basis for true evangelism, to relate biblical truth to contemporary issues, and to awaken Christian consciences to the implications of "expressing Christ's love in attitude and action." Vernon himself could not have stated it better.

But while Denver Seminary was well represented at Lausanne by faculty members and graduates, Vernon was not there. Scores of people asked faculty and friends at the conference, "Where is Vernon?" His birthday was at least a partial answer.

In the summer of 1974 while the great Lausanne Congress on World Evangelism was unfolding in Switzerland, Vernon Grounds turned sixty years of age. His dark-rimmed glasses highlighted the same dignity in his face and the same determination in his eyes. But his buoyant bow tie was no longer a daily feature, and his hair was now white and a bit thinner on top.

As Vernon marked his sixtieth birthday, he could also look back over a quarter of a century at Denver Seminary with a great deal of satisfaction. He had made the right choice in 1951 when he decided to stay in Denver to lead "Operation Survival."

Two months later, in September, Vernon had an unusual opportunity to "express Christ's love in attitude" when he participated in the Enabling Conference on the Evangelistic Life Style sponsored by the American Baptist Convention.[3] As a representative of Baptist evangelicalism, he shared the platform in Detroit with two prominent non-Baptists, Colin Williams, dean of the Yale Divinity School, and John Cobb, professor of theology at the Claremont School of Theology. Asked to speak autobiographically and relate some of the pivotal decisions in his own spiritual pilgrimage, Vernon recalled the hymn:

> "'Suffer a sinner whose heart overflows,
> Loving his Saviour to tell what he knows;
> Once more to tell it would I embrace,
> I'm only a sinner saved by grace.'

"Standing here today," he said, "I look back beyond my own life, through the centuries before my own time, to the Cross. And looking back I am reminded of Erik Erikson's eight stages of man, the last of which is old age. At sixty I have arrived at that stage in my life-cycle. This, as you know, is the stage of either ego-integrity or of disgust and despair.

"According to Erikson, if an individual has made the right decisions in the preceding seven stages, he now achieves a post-narcissistic love which enables him to look back and affirm the dignity, worth, and meaningfulness of his own lifestyle. He is also able to look ahead serenely because, in Erikson's words, when one has achieved ego-integrity, 'death loses its sting.' Or does it? It strikes me that Richard Rubenstein is more realistic when he laments, 'Few men of any condition can look with equanimity upon old age or death.'

"But as a Christian, committed to an evangelistic lifestyle, I look back today and with humble gratitude bear my witness. Because God in Jesus Christ has lovingly chosen me to be His own forever, my past and my future are embraced within His forgiving mercy. So despite sin and failure I can look back with joy and ahead with expectancy."

Cancer Crisis

As a psychologist Vernon knew all about life's "passages," "stages," and "turning-points." In his Christmas letter of 1970 he recalled that familiar passage in Dickens' *Tale of Two Cities*: "It was the best of times, it was the worst of times. It was the spring of hope, it was the winter of despair. . . . For our little family it has been a trying year, the most trying, I suppose since we were married."

On the hopeful side, Vernon and Ann had welcomed a son-in-law and a granddaughter into their lives. Their daughter, Barbara, had graduated from Bethel College. Then, on February 21, 1969, she had married Robert Owen in a lovely ceremony held in the Grounds's Lakewood home, with Vernon officiating. Almost a year and a half later, Emily Grace Owen was born on June 19, 1970.

But the year also brought troubled times. Vernon's mother-in-law, Sarah Barton, now in her eighties, was showing all the signs of human frailty, and Vernon and Ann had to place her in a nursing home. This brought some major changes, as Ann's mother had lived with them and been an integral part of their lives for almost twenty-five years.

At about the same time, they decided to sell their home in Lakewood and move to a new house on a hillside in southwest Denver. It was in some ways a larger place, two levels, with a large picture window overlooking the mountains and the coral sunsets to the northwest. But no sooner had they endured the throes of moving and resettling when Ann had a series of painful attacks, one requiring a trip to the emergency room and hospitalization. Eventually, the continued pain compelled her to resign as organist at Trinity Baptist Church, where she had played almost weekly for nearly twenty years. She also had to discontinue her piano teaching. For Ann, this was a terrible blow—yielding up a significant part of her life.

Then came the most shocking and disheartening news of all: "You have cancer!"

Weeks of daily cobalt therapy followed, which meant that every day, sometimes alone, Ann slipped behind the wheel of their car and drove herself to the hospital. Through these weeks of anxiety and uncertainty, Vernon did his best to maintain his normal routine.

Ann had always been the mainstay of Vernon's life. He was out in front, preaching, teaching, counseling, and traveling, but, as his daughter, Barbara, says, "without the support of my mother, Dad wouldn't have been able to accomplish so much."

Sometimes Ann was in the limelight when she served as church pianist or accompanist for the seminary's men's chorus. She was also visible in her role as hostess for all the entertaining required of a seminary president. But Ann saw other needs and endeavored to address them. She began a support group for the wives of the seminary faculty and administration. The Alethians met once a month to hear a speaker or enjoy a program or just to encourage and advise each other. Later she organized a monthly prayer meeting for faculty wives.

Now in 1970, as Christmas drew near, and with the cobalt treatments completed, Ann underwent surgery. It proved a complete success, and the doctors found no evidence of any spread of the malignancy. A few days later Vernon wrote in his Christmas letter, "While both Ann and I would have been inexpressibly grateful had God seen fit to exempt her from this dangerous illness, it has been the means of measureless blessing to us. We have been surrounded and sustained by love and concern and encouragement and intercession.

"I am sure you will understand me when I say that throughout our ministry we have, as a rule, been in a position to give rather than receive help. In recent months, however, we have been the recipients of God's overflowing help through His people. Hour by hour we have literally sensed the uplift and comfort which come from an invisible host of intercessors. And intercession has availed."

Through these few years of highs and lows—the birth of their granddaughter Emily, the frailty of Mrs. Barton, the sound of that dreadful word *cancer*, and Ann's recovery—Vernon wrote, "We have come to understand much more profoundly that there is one Constant—a Who not a What—that never changes."

Seminary Success

With the dawn of 1975, the seminary began a yearlong celebration to mark its twenty-fifth anniversary. As the months passed, Vernon recalled a visit he and Ann had made to Hawaii in 1964 to celebrate their own twenty-fifth wedding anniversary.

The highlight of the trip, he wrote, was a tour of Pearl Harbor that stirred reflections and feelings nearly impossible to express. "Whenever I recall Hawaii, I think of stepping on board the Memorial to our service personnel killed in the attack December 7, 1941. A very familiar piece of music was being played softly: 'When the Roll Is Called Up Yonder'; and only people like ourselves who knew the words of that hymn could appreciate its poignant appropriateness. Directly inside we saw inscribed on the wall the names of those who had died—name after name after name, the names of the men who laid down their lives for our country. Since that day Mrs. Grounds and I never hear 'When the Roll Is Called Up Yonder' without remembering Pearl Harbor and those names."

Then he compared that honor roll with the faithful supporters of Denver Seminary through the years and recalled a text in Hebrews 6:10 where "the apostle reassures his readers that our Lord eternally remembers everything which is done for His sake." We may forget, he wrote; "one by one we are called into eternity and eventually the memory of what has gone into Conservative Baptist Seminary will be erased. But God will never forget. God remembers, and God will reward."

It was becoming increasingly clear who some of those "faithful supporters" were as memorials began to appear on the campus. The long-awaited new library, created from the old Kent School gymnasium in 1975 by Harold Simpson and his development company, was named for Dr. Carey Thomas, who had sacrificially served as the seminary's first president. The renovated academic building was named Hannay Hall for the Clifford Hannay family in Westerlo, New York, a little village outside Albany. The Hannays owned and operated the Hannay Hose Reel Company there. George Hannay, a son, was sales manager for the company; he served on the seminary's board of trustees for many years and gave invaluable advice to Douglas Birk at significant crossroads along the way. But behind George and his family were his parents, Clifford and Hazel Hannay, who had supported the school in its early, tender years.[4]

There were, of course, many other "faithful supporters" unnamed and unknown, and there were some who appeared in the dedications of several of Dr. Grounds's books: Mr. and Mrs. Jerry Lewis, among his many Denver friends; and the Frank Cauwels family from his early days in Paterson, New Jersey. And when the faculty volume titled *A Call to Christian Character* appeared in 1970 it was dedicated to Robert and Marion Dugan.

Robert and Marion Dugan Sr. made an enormous contribution to "Operation Survival." While living in Saddle River, New Jersey, in the early 1960s, the Dugans volunteered to give their early retirement years in travel as representatives of Denver Seminary. Bob Dugan had served with Dugan Brothers, Inc., a large, well-known baking company in the East. During most of these years he was vice-president in charge of advertising and sales. But the Dugans were also ardent Christians and faithful church members who taught Sunday school and served on boards of Christian schools and missionary agencies.

As the field representative of Denver Seminary, Bob Dugan, usually with Marion at his side, began to drive hundreds of miles to out-of-the-way churches and church meetings. They often took some young pastor and his wife to lunch, listened to their stories of the burdens and blessings of ministry, and discovered their perceptions of Denver Seminary from some distant perspective, perhaps a New Hampshire village or a small town in Iowa.

Dugan always gave Douglas Birk and Vernon a full report of his travels and his conversations from his meetings. In one six-month period, he reported, he and Marion had driven 22,500 miles, made more than 250 visits, and spoken at forty-four church meetings.

Vernon maintained a steady correspondence with the Dugans, responding to Bob's requests and encouraging him in his labors.

Understanding full well the benefits and drawbacks of constant travel, Vernon wrote, "I am sure that your work in Arizona will bear an abundant harvest in due season. No doubt there have been discouragements... and in some instances I know you must have experienced rebuff and criticism. But fortunately you are a hardened veteran whom God prepared by such experiences... Thus I trust that your spirit is still high, maybe even higher than ever. We have a demanding job to do in the face of serious handicaps; nevertheless we rejoice that our Lord has promised to make us sufficient for our ministry (2 Corinthians 3:5)."[5]

A New Translation

On the campus, the twenty-fifth anniversary honor roll included some of Vernon's closest colleagues. The two nearest at hand were Douglas Birk and Earl Kalland, the other two members of the "troika." Douglas Birk's contributions to the seminary were, by 1975, clearly visible on the corner of University and Hampden: the new campus. Earl Kalland's accomplishments were in the less conspicuous life of the academy where the primary marks of success came with the accreditation of the school in the early 1970s by both the North Central Association and the American Association of Theological Schools.

Earl Kalland was a Norwegian scholar of the old school. When his colleague in the Old Testament Department, Robert Alden, spoke in memory and tribute of Kalland at the seminary's 1993 commencement, he called him "the decisive dean." Stories, he said, abounded "about how frightening he was to students summoned to his office for one shortcoming or another." Dr. Alden then told of the student who had failed Hebrew. Dr. Alden said that he explained to the dean first, and made clear his own hesitancy to break the bad news to the poor fellow. So Dean Kalland suggested the three of them meet together. When they met, the dean opened the conversation with the trembling junior. "Dr. Alden tells me that you have not done well in Hebrew."

"Yes, sir," came the reply.

"Perhaps it would be best if you took the course over again next year."

"Yes, sir."

"Well, then," said the dean. "That's that."

The meeting was over.

This "decisive dean" was also a respected scholar in academic circles, and in this role he made another outstanding and lasting contribution to Christianity.

In 1965, after several years of exploratory study by committees from the Christian Reformed Church and the National Association of Evangelicals, a group of evangelical scholars met at Palos Heights, Illinois, and agreed upon the need for a new translation of the Bible in contemporary English. A year later a large group from many denominations met in Chicago and endorsed the conclusion of the earlier gathering, and in 1967 the New York Bible Society (later renamed the International Bible Society) assumed the financial sponsorship of this major project. The responsibility for the translating, editing, and publishing of the new translation, to be called the New International Version, was delegated to the Committee on Bible Translation, a body of fifteen evangelical scholars from colleges, universities, and seminaries. The fact that participants from the United States, Great Britain, Canada, Australia, and New Zealand worked together gave the project its international scope, and the final product was the work of more than one hundred evangelical scholars from more than thirty denominations and from all the major English-speaking countries of the world. The New International Version of the Bible was a significant testimony to the strength in unity of the renewed evangelical Christianity. (Late in 1974, just after the Lausanne Congress, the New

Testament of The New International Version was released to the public. The Old Testament was published in 1978.)

Dr. Kalland served on that original Committee on Bible Translation. Naturally, he turned to several of his colleagues on the Denver faculty to join him in the task. Dr. Donald Burdick, Professor of New Testament, and Dr. Ralph Covell, Associate Professor of Missions, served as a translation team, producing the first draft of 1 and 2 Timothy, Titus, James, 1 and 2 Peter, and Jude. Dr. Kalland, along with his colleague in the Old Testament department, Dr. Robert Alden, formed another team for translating several of the longer books of the Old Testament.

Because of his involvement in the NIV translation project, Dean Kalland began to cut back on his administrative responsibilities at the seminary. He stepped down from his position as dean in 1972, and retired from the seminary in 1975, which allowed him to devote the following three years to his work on the translation and editing of the NIV Old Testament.

For Denver Seminary, Earl Kalland's departure brought to an end the original "troika" administration that made possible Vernon Grounds's itinerating presidency. It also revived old questions about the effectiveness of the administrative structure.

"Now what?" was the question on many hearts and minds, including Vernon's.

CHAPTER 10

New Perspectives

[Jesus'] heart and His arms were open wide, as they still are, to the lowest, the least, and the lost.... Concerned as He was about hunger, disease, and injustice, our Lord was concerned immeasurably more about people's relationship to God and their destiny in the world to come.... On the one hand, He would literally help restore sight, give comfort, and liberate those in bondage to destructive habits and addictive behavior. On the other hand, His ministry would be a spiritual one, enlightening the spiritually blind, liberating the spiritually shackled, comforting the spiritually guilt-ridden and distressed.... His supernatural acts of power and compassion would be dramatic vignettes of the very nature of the kingdom He had come to inaugurate.

— VERNON GROUNDS, *The Compassion of Jesus*

Denver Seminary's retirement program, like most in the country, was based on the widely held assumption that the productive years of life end at sixty-five. So, quite naturally, as Vernon approached his mid-sixties, he began thinking more and more about retirement. But retire from what? *Must I give up my classroom?* he wondered. *Or my travel? What do I retire from?*

The release of one of his responsibilities, however, caused no great concern. For years Vernon had wanted to surrender the heavy burden of administration. He had never felt comfortable making decisions that affected other people's lives. He much preferred listening to people face to face, helping them to clarify their thinking and trusting them to make their own tough decisions. Administration was too much like his father's workbench and his second-year algebra class.

At the beginning of each week, after returning from an exciting and gratifying weekend of ministry somewhere in the country, Vernon immediately had to endure a lengthy administrative meeting. Douglas Birk usually offered a somber litany of ecclesiastical and financial woes, and Dean Hayes would issue pointed appeals for new programs and faculty additions. Meanwhile, Vernon had a habit of taking with him to these meetings a stack of letters to be signed or an armful of books with little slips of paper protruding, marking the quotations he planned to use in the next-hour's class.

It was not so much that Vernon was disinterested in administration as that he never really felt that final decisions were his to make. In the accreditation self-study sent to the American Association of

Theological Schools in 1970, he had described his presidential position as a hybrid, a blend of teaching and counseling combined with some administration. But his presidency, he explained, relieved him of any direct responsibility for the academic and business interests of the school.

"My job," he said, "is not to ride herd on details or be a fund raiser, but to be a catalyst, interpreter, planner, and an agent of reconciliation." Knowing full well his lack of executive skills, he tried, he said, to think of his position as "servant leadership." He tried to lead by example and influence.[1]

Whatever its label, Vernon's leadership had served the school well through the years of struggle and sacrifice. He had nurtured a servant spirit and a deep loyalty within the small faculty and student body. In the 1960s, when several professors were receiving invitations to other schools for salaries significantly higher than Denver's, only one or two full-time professors left the school, and then not for money.

When Dr. Earl Kalland resigned from his position as dean in 1972, Dr. Edward Hayes replaced him. Hayes had served as assistant dean for several years and had led the successful efforts toward accreditation. He, too, had come to the school during the early years and had been through the thick of the battle with the militants. But he was younger than Dr. Kalland and was a more assertive administrator, eager to speak up for the faculty at administrative committee meetings.

By offering master's degrees in a dozen areas of concentration, the seminary had grown to more than three hundred students. The little community in the mansion, where everyone knew each other's names and most were ready to share lunch almost any day of the week, had been replaced by a spreading campus that drew individuals hoping to serve God in a wide variety of ministries, rather than solely the traditional missionary or rural pastor.

With the seminary growing and gaining new heights, Vernon often returned to campus to face decisions that only he could make, and the psychologist in him recognized his own weakness in this area. On the one hand, he felt compelled to cast the deciding vote; on the other hand, he felt a certain pain when the answer had to be no. Vernon found it extremely difficult to say no to anyone, and this could be frustrating both for him and for his academic colleagues. But a larger school meant more and more tough administrative decisions.

The need of the hour on campus, some said, was new leadership, and Vernon began to agree. He continued to meet three mornings a week with small, intimate groups, and he continued to make his morning stroll down the hallway and through the student center for his morning coffee, talking to students or staff members along the way. But he also began speaking to his close friends more and more often about his age.

Search for a Successor

The first public notice of Vernon's retirement plans came in the spring of 1976 when the *Seminarian* reported that he had requested the school's Board of Trustees to have his successor in place by June 1978, when he would be approaching his sixty-fourth birthday. But he also made it clear that his decision was "motivated by my own personal wishes." No one was pushing him unduly.

The board was fully aware of the strengths and weaknesses of the troika, and they knew that they could not expect the next president to serve under conditions designed specifically for Vernon Grounds. They appointed a seven-member Administrative Search Committee, with Rev. Robert Frederich of the Galilee Baptist Church in Denver serving as chairman. Several of the other committee members also lived in the greater Denver area, but three pastors flew hundreds of miles to the Colorado capital three or four times a year for the meetings at the Stapleton Airport Holiday Inn. Lesley Flynn flew in from New York City, Leith Anderson from Minneapolis, and David Falconer from Phoenix.

For over a year the committee worked through a long list of possible candidates. But when they narrowed their interest to a primary candidate, the man refused to consider the candidacy. As a result, when the full board met in February of 1978, Robert Frederich reported that the committee was unprepared to present a presidential candidate.

With this news, Vernon rather abruptly rethought his earlier decision and informed the board that he would postpone his retirement. "It now seems clear to both of us [himself and Mrs. Grounds] that I ought to postpone my retirement until commencement 1980."

He expanded on these sentiments in a memo to the faculty and staff. "During the next two years I pledge myself, as God grants enablement, to give CBTS the most vigorous, progressive leadership of which I am capable. I have no intention whatever of maintaining some kind of holding operation. While I intend to do some teaching, especially in the counseling field, I will be cutting back, regretfully, on my interpersonal involvement with students in order to make time for administration, promotion, and writing."[2]

Retirement was obviously a difficult decision. For months Vernon had been listening to persuasive arguments from those closest to him—from those who did not want him to resign and those who thought perhaps he should. All of the faculty and staff would be significantly affected by Vernon's decision, but none more than his troika colleagues, Douglas Birk and Edward Hayes. The situation tested both Vernon's traditional loyalties and his sound judgment. One day he thought, *It's time to step down.* The next day he thought, *But not now.*

The committee, meanwhile, continued its search, and in the spring of 1979, after months of discussions, travel, and interviews, they voted unanimously to invite Dr. Haddon Robinson to become the third president of Denver Seminary. Dr. Robinson was, at the time, serving as professor of preaching and head of the Pastoral Ministry Department at Dallas Theological Seminary. Dr. Robinson was known as an excellent communicator, and he also had administrative skill and experience.

A few days after this announcement, the faculty, meeting on campus in the casual comfort of the student lounge, received the committee's report and voted unanimously to accept the committee's decision. The full board also agreed, the invitation was accepted, and Dr. Robinson made plans to move to Denver.

⸻

For twenty-three event-filled years Vernon had been president of Denver Seminary, his life ordered, his calendar full. Suddenly, he faced major changes. He was now President Emeritus.

With the new title came a strange, new freedom. No more administrative meetings. No more tough decisions. There was only one word for that: relief! But somewhere deep inside Vernon's psyche he also sensed a strange, new attitude. It was hard to describe, he said.

Nostalgia?

"No, not that!"

Sadness?

"Absolutely not!"

Lowered self-esteem?

"By no means!" he wrote his friends. "It is a sense of detachment and thus a new perspective on one's life, an awareness that one's major contribution to his generation has been made. I think my new mood is a feeling of muted satisfaction mingled with a keen awareness of the failure that is the shadow side of human finitude—regret that one did not more diligently, more faithfully, more wisely, more lovingly, more bravely handle assignments and challenges."[3]

During the final year of his presidency, Vernon led the chapel services in the east wing of Hannay Hall as he had done for years. Toward the end of the year, in one of those services, he spoke with unusual transparency to the seminary family.[4]

Always intrigued by Erik Erikson's eight stages in the human life cycle, he referred to Erikson's analysis as he said, "I am now in the final period as you might guess." In this concluding stage of life, he explained, people face two possible outcomes. One can either be concerned about the coming generations or he can look back to the past in disillusionment and disgust.

"I am aware," he confessed, "of how limited time is and occasionally I am tempted to pray, 'Backward, turn backward, O time in thy flight. Make me a boy again just for tonight.' But I realize that's impossible. I know that my opportunities for service in this world are rapidly running out. [Later years would reveal how wrong he was!] I recognize that I am limited in gift. I'm limited, comparatively, in intelligence. And I know I'm limited in achievement. So I confess to you my very growing awareness of finitude."

But he also looked back upon his life and recognized the significant way his faith had changed. "I realize how far short I still fall. And I realize too how little I have accomplished ... In my earlier years I suspect that my concept of Christianity was very lopsided. It was world-denial and world-withdrawal. God has helped me to discern, I think, that there must be not only love for Himself, but there must be love for neighbor which is incarnate in some social activity."

Forty-six years had come and gone since the Rutgers freshman had prayed what his fundamentalist friends called "the sinner's prayer," and since he had climbed the mountain at Camp Kanawakee and opened his Bible to meet God. But one thing had not changed. He was a Christian, not by any good fortune of birth, but by the power of God's love. He had discovered that Calvary love is far more than an inward feeling; it is a new vitality within a believer's soul. And he was fully persuaded that true faith *works*, and it works in the world through love—visible, compassionate, acts of love.

Another Perspective

Later that year, on a quiet October Sunday morning, Vernon sat in his parked car in Chapel Hill Cemetery on metro Denver's south side waiting for Ann to finish playing for the second service at their church just across Arapahoe Road. (About two years after her bout with cancer, Ann had been able to return to her music, and her improvisations on well-known hymns often drew spontaneous applause from audiences.) Enjoying the view of the mountains in the distance, he pulled out his Dictaphone to write a letter to his friends Bob and Marion Dugan.

"Life is still hectic as ever," he said. "I seem to be even busier! I suppose that, aside from my full teaching-load and my increased hours at our Counseling Center, it is because I have been attending all of our Conservative Baptist Regionals."[5]

These three-day regional meetings held around the country always included an alumni breakfast at which he served as host and introduced Dr. Robinson, the new president, to the graduates and friends of the school. During an evening banquet on the second day of the regional events he would preside over a much larger gathering and again introduced Dr. Robinson.

"My impression," Vernon reported to the Dugans, "is that people are responding with enthusiasm to this format as well as to Dr. Robinson. One of these days I hope you can hear him and be blessed by his ministry."

Then in his report to his friends who had served so long as the seminary's field representatives, Vernon mentioned that "shadow side of his finitude" and his continuing responsibility to raise large sums of money. "Hanging over my head all the time is the burden of trying to raise that Matching Million for the Learning Center." The "Matching Million" project was one of three big events marking Vernon's first year of retirement.

The first event was a large testimonial dinner on Friday night, May 9, 1980. Charles Colson gave the address, a powerful appeal for Christian social concern and action, which pleased Vernon immensely. But the great surprise that evening was a "This Is Your Life" presentation. The planning committee had gathered snapshots of a young, round-faced Vernon Grounds and his family for display on a large screen for the more than a thousand guests, and they had invited participants from great distances to share their memories. John Van Houten, Vernon's longtime friend and first tenor in the Harmony Gospel Quartet, was there from New Jersey. Several other friends who had attended the Paterson Gospel Tabernacle long years before also traveled to Denver for the evening. And Rev. Gary Gulbranson, representing the seminary's alumni, sang one of Vernon's favorite songs, "Lord, to My Heart Bring Back the Springtime." But the greatest surprise of the evening was the appearance of his sister, Mildred, now seventy-one years of age, who had flown all the way from her home in New Jersey. Vernon was nearly overwhelmed as memories of his childhood and early years came surging back.[6]

Only a month later a second banquet was held, this one in Portland, Maine, in conjunction with the Annual Meeting of Conservative Baptists. Here, the denominational family jointly honored Vernon and Ann Grounds, and Dr. Rufus Jones and his wife. Dr. Jones had been General Director of the Conservative Baptist Home Missions Society for a quarter of a century, and during those years he and Vernon had become close friends, especially by supporting each other in their advocacy of Christian social concerns.

Finally, and in many respects the most enduring of the celebratory events of that retirement year, came the "Matching Million" project. Lew Gras, chairman of the seminary board, announced that certain longtime friends of Dr. and Mrs. Grounds—the Harold Simpson Construction Company and their associates—had given a $1,000,000 matching gift for the construction of a seminary facility to be known as the Vernon C. Grounds Learning Center. The building was to mark the fact that during Dr. Grounds's twenty-eight years at the school his personal values had come to be reflected in the seminary itself, especially "his spirit of tenacity coupled with loving moderation." His name had become synonymous with Denver Seminary.

The gift was timely, to say the least, since Vernon was donating his huge personal library to the school and the board had recognized the need for larger facilities. The "Matching Million" gift called for the building and equipping of a two-story structure that would provide additional classrooms, a chapel, and abundant space for Dr. Grounds's thousands of books. (The Vernon Grounds Learning Center was completed early in 1982, providing the seminary with needed space for the growing student body and including a spacious office for Vernon, with windows facing the mountains to the west.)

This season of celebration was primarily a way of saying, "Thank you, Dr. Grounds, for being you."

———

Through the years Vernon had spoken often of his "sanguine and phlegmatic" temperament and had confessed ignorance of his deepest motives. These, he said, were impossible to unravel, hopelessly blended in the shadows of his finitude, and he was not inclined to cover up or pretend to be something he was not. Now, however, as he looked back across the years, he saw thousands of faces, thousands of personal lives, he had met along the road of life and touched profoundly at some crossroads.

For nearly half a century Vernon Grounds had been able to meet and help so many people because he had ordered his own private world. He rose early and worked late; he controlled his calendar and his clock; and he maintained his health by strict diet and regular exercise. His life was filled with appointments but still he managed to fill his "spare" moments with reading and writing. He consumed hefty books in a relatively short time and he wrote constantly—notes, lectures, articles, and countless letters. Wherever he was, be it a hospital hallway, a distant library, or an empty parking lot, when time permitted he pulled out his yellow legal pad or handy Dictaphone. He sent hundreds of birthday cards each year, cards he signed personally. But Vernon would be the first to admit that he could not have done this alone. For most of his professional life he had a secretary and could hardly function without one. It was his secretary who sent out the stacks of birthday cards he had signed, and who typed the volumes of letters and articles he dictated or wrote longhand on his yellow legal pad. She also managed the traffic into and out of his office and tried to keep up with his often "impossible" schedule.

Vernon never pretended to be a self-made man. He never hesitated to ask friends or colleagues to help him, to pick him up at an airport, look up a quotation for him, or meet him in Colorado Springs or Fort Collins or the mountains. He freely confessed his need, and most people found this both rare and appealing in a Christian leader.

All these "habits of the heart" did not suddenly change in retirement. Vernon's friendliness, courtesy, kindness, listening, and thoughtful gifts or notes all continued. In his Christmas letter, six months after retirement, he wrote, "Change? Yes! But continuity as well. I am living with the same wife in the same home. We celebrated our 40th anniversary on June 17. Continuity! I am still a full-time faculty-member at the Seminary, teaching the same courses, following essentially the same routine, enjoying the same degree of vitality (or so it seems), blessed with the same circle of friends. I am walking with the same unchanging God who yesterday, today, and forever is the same. And in Jesus Christ I possess the same hope, the same certainty, the same peace deep below all the agitations which ruffle the surface of my psyche." He was finding that faith, hope, and love, these three, abide.

New Freedom

Although he had retired from the presidency of the seminary, Vernon still carried a full teaching load at the school and met early three mornings each week with three different small groups. He managed to squeeze in his reading, his study, and his writing, and he traveled as extensively as ever. He often spoke of being "swamped with people who have problems."

His own soul-searching was also affected by the fact that more and more of his contemporaries were suffering or sitting passively on the sidelines of life. And many were dying. Few weeks passed without news of the departure of some dear friend and another invitation for Vernon to conduct the funeral. "Teach me to number my days," he prayed, even as he was profoundly thankful for his own health and vigor and his active ministry.

"I wholeheartedly share the attitude of Oliver Wendell Holmes, the distinguished Supreme Court justice," he wrote in one of his letters to the seventeen hundred friends on his mailing list. "Visited one day by President Franklin Delano Roosevelt, Holmes closed the volume of Plato which he had been reading.

"Rather surprised, Roosevelt asked, 'Why are you doing such heavy reading during your retirement? I should think you would be on a lighter diet after your long and demanding career.'

"To which Holmes responded, 'Mr. President, I am reading Plato to improve my mind. At the age of ninety I have retired from law and writing, but I have not retired from growing.'

"That's the attitude I try to copy." Dr. Grounds added. "Why vegetate mentally? Above all, why vegetate spiritually? Whatever our age, let's keep on growing and growing."

During the summer of 1980, Denver Seminary alumni in Argentina and Brazil had invited him to speak to the Conservative Baptist field conferences in South America during late November and early December. He accepted the invitation gladly, and his first stop on the trip was Brasilia, Brazil's spectacular capital, where he spoke at the Brasilia Baptist Seminary. Then it was on to northern Brazil and the field conference there.

He spent nearly a week at Fortaleza, the booming seacoast city four degrees from the equator, but found, to his surprise, that the ocean breezes kept the temperature quite comfortable. Then he flew to Sao Paulo where he met with the missionaries and lectured to a class at the Baptist Seminary. After four days he flew to Salta, Argentina, to speak to another field conference, then made a stop in Tucuman, the university city, before flying to Buenos Aires, which he toured briefly before catching his flight to Rio de Janeiro and his Pan Am flight back to Miami.

From stop to stop on this trip Vernon had carried his heavy book bag. On the return flight to Florida he had just enough time to polish a lecture he was working on: "The Problem of Proselytism." Before he could fly home, however, he had to head for Chicago and a three-day conference addressing relations of evangelicals and Jews that was meeting at Trinity Evangelical Divinity School.

Such were Vernon Grounds's "leisurely retirement years." He had long dreamed of having time to write four or five long-neglected books, and he had even arranged with the Revell company to write a book called *The Caring Lifestyle.* He announced to his friends that it might be available in the fall of 1980. But like several others, this book never appeared.

Early in his retirement, Ann pinpointed the problem. "You don't get more writing done because of people, people, people," she told her husband, and deep down he knew she was right. He had admitted as much many times in his classroom where he emphasized to students: "In the end, nothing really matters except what goes on within human psyches and what transpires interpersonally."

This conviction helps to explain why so few of the books he had hoped to write ever got written. The one book he did publish during his retirement was developed from a series of sermons he preached in 1983 during his months as interim pastor of the Bear Creek Church. The Bear Creek Presbyterian Church in Lakewood, Colorado, had lost its pastor, Rev. John Coad, earlier in the year. Vernon and John had been good friends. They first met in a gym while lifting weights, and John had invited the weight-lifting seminary president to preach at Bear Creek a number of times over the years, and the church elders and congregation had gotten to know him rather well. It seemed only natural then, when John died after a long battle with cancer, to call on Vernon to serve as their interim pastor.

He called the series "Getting Serious about Christian Growth" and in it he developed the theme he called "the Gethsemane mind-set."[7]

"Self-love or self-hate?" he asked. "Which does God want?" He assured the congregation that God was in the business of making His children "the happiest, the most productive persons we can be. But in order to maximize our selfhood, God has to help us get rid of our sinful selfishness. God has to help us to develop the Gethsemane mind-set, that attitude demonstrated by Jesus Christ on the night of His betrayal.

"Although fully God, Jesus was a real man." He desperately yearned to escape the cross. And yet "standing on the very edge of unutterable suffering and horror, He spoke those unforgettable words of self-abandonment: 'My Father, if it is possible let this cup pass from me—yet it must not be what I want, but what you want' (Matthew 26:39 Phillips). In Gethsemane, Jesus said *no* to His own will and *yes* to His Father's will."

The Gethsemane mind-set, then, said Vernon, "is the attitude of trustful self-surrender." Jesus demonstrated this when He renounced His own very human feelings, desires, and ambitions in order that the purpose of God might be accomplished. So when we set our minds on doing the will of God and follow our Lord's example, "we are going to experience, beyond loss and loneliness and pain, the joy and blessing and glory which mean unimaginable self-fulfillment."[8]

Multnomah Press in Portland, Oregon, published this series under the title *Radical Commitment: Getting Serious About Christian Growth*. Vernon has written scores of articles during his retirement years, but *Radical Commitment* is the only book he has written during that time. (*Radical Commitment* is now published by Discovery House Publishers under the title of *YBH: Yes, But How?*)

But writing was only one of his dreams, and clearly secondary to the far more compelling passion of creating his own counseling center. Vernon had talked about this for years, and two years after retirement from the presidency, the dream became reality when some generous friends in the Denver area handed him an unsolicited but sizable gift and then proceeded to provide a suite of offices and furnishings in East Gerard Place located three miles east of the seminary. Now, at last, the Vernon C. Grounds Counseling Center could provide low-cost counseling with a distinctively Christian perspective.

The center's only affiliation with Denver Seminary was the primary counselor—Vernon, who was involved in both institutions —and the seminary students who obtained training at the center. The center gave young counselors supervised experience and an opportunity to launch their own practices. Other than this, it was an autonomous agency providing low-fee and no-fee service for those who could not afford the usual charges for counseling.

The center was also personally advantageous for Vernon because he was able to employ his daughter, Barbara, and work closely with her on a daily basis, something he had wanted for years. In making the announcement to his friends he said, "I am grateful for the privilege of having my own daughter, Barbara Owen, work with me as receptionist and secretary, a colleague in the truest sense."

Vernon now spent his mornings teaching and meeting with students at the seminary and his afternoons counseling at the center.

But the center proved to be only the first distinct advantage of his retirement. Vernon could now help more hurting people, but he also felt freer to speak out more boldly about certain social issues of the day. As president of the seminary he had always been aware that his social views were left of center, and that most of the pastors and churches supporting the school did not share these views. Now he was free to speak his mind.

CHAPTER 11

The Road's Last Turn

Poet Robert Frost caught the poignancy and yet the challenge of the constrictive process of aging. He describes an ovenbird perched on a New England stone wall with summer ended, autumn quickly passing, and winter approaching. Soon there will be no more warm sunshine; soon there will be freezing weather; soon there will be snow. Yet the ovenbird sits on that wall singing gallantly "as to make the most of a diminished thing."

That's the problem aging earthlings face. How can we make the most of a diminished thing? How can we, in the words of Psalm 92:14, still "bear fruit in old age"? How can we continue to be fresh and green like some verdant pine tree? How can we experience the constrictive process not simply with resignation but with courage, peace and hope? A vital Christian faith is the answer to such existential questions that sooner or later each of us must answer. A strong trust in God plus a meaningful relationship with him through personal trust in the gospel gives a soul-fortifying, anxiety-dispelling solution to Frost's query, "how to make the most of a diminished thing."

— Vernon Grounds, *Observations of an Octogenarian*

As Vernon Grounds "survived past the biblically allotted three score years and ten," as he once described it, he knew that his life was in God's hands. But he also knew that he had never had a life-threatening illness. No heart trouble, no diabetes, no cancer. He had always exercised and watched his diet. Why shouldn't he live another twenty years? That is what the optimist in him asked.

But there was another voice, too—the voice of the realist: "What about all those trips to churches across the country and the funeral services of your dearest friends? Remember them? What makes you think you're so special?"

Vernon seemed to treasure life even more after retirement, for he lived now with a new sense of priorities: not what is good, but what is best. The burden of the seminary presidency was gone and life went on. Now what?

In many respects he spent the 1980s and 1990s just as he had spent the previous years: traveling, teaching, speaking, and counseling. Only his title at the seminary changed. First he was President Emeritus. Then, when Haddon Robinson resigned from the presidency of the seminary in 1991, Vernon became Chancellor. Although he was never quite sure what the title meant, Vernon took it to mean welcoming guests to the campus and officiating occasionally at seminary functions.

In point of fact, his life changed very little because he had, long before, determined his priorities for life: personal counseling, theological education, and peacemaking. If anything, he seemed to be freer to travel, many times to receive some award for his leadership, and he felt freer to speak autobiographically. This cast a revealing light upon the inner life of Vernon Grounds and who he had become.

One of the first changes Haddon Robinson had made when he came to Denver Seminary was to discontinue publication of the little quarterly *The Seminarian* and publish instead a larger magazine called *Focal Point*. Alice Mathews, who with her husband, Randy, had been a part of the seminary in the early 1950s, served as editor of the magazine and in 1982 asked Vernon for a brief article telling how he touched so many people's lives so profoundly. She entitled it, "People Who Touch People Are the Loveliest People in the World."

"Only people matter," Vernon wrote. "Programs, buildings, finances serve merely as instruments to enrich human lives. How can we help people know that they count? How can we assure them that somebody, dimly reflecting God's infinite care, does indeed care for them? How can we affirm people, express our appreciation for what they do, and communicate to them that they possess value to us because God made them in His image?"

To answer his own questions Vernon turned to the treasured memories of his good friend Jacob Stam, the busy lawyer and father of seven in the Paterson Tabernacle. Though thirteen years older than his young pastor, Jacob Stam had greatly influenced Vernon Grounds. At his funeral in 1972, Vernon had called Jacob Stam "the finest Christian I have ever been privileged to know."

"Though he carried a staggering load of professional and Christian activities," Vernon explained in *Focal Point*, "Jake found time for people. . . . His loving concern never seemed to suffer fatigue."

Jacob Stam and his touch with people became young Vernon Grounds's model. And across the years Vernon, too, while shepherding a congregation and teaching in a classroom, discovered the ways and means to keep in touch with relatives, friends, seminary alumni, neighbors, and individuals who providentially crossed his path on life's journey.

"Every morning," he explained, "I do not feel fully dressed until I slip my pocket-diary into my suit coat or jacket. This notebook contains lists of names—people who are ill, who have suffered bereavement, who are struggling with problems or weighed down with burdens. In it too are blank loose-leaf pages on which I scribble *immediately* a notation of births, deaths, sicknesses, marriages, anniversaries, and needs which come to my attention. Scribbling such notations can become second nature."

"In my office I keep a supply of cards, which I constantly replenish. I'm always looking for appropriate greetings. It takes special effort to find cards for men that aren't maudlin and mawkish. On those cards I usually dash off a few words, add a meaningful text and sign my name. Often I write only Ephesians 3:20–21.

"As I scan magazines, newspapers and books, I subconsciously have in mind the special interests of my friends. Thus if I see something that applies to an old acquaintance, I clip it out or Xerox it, write a brief—very brief—greeting across it, sign my name and mail it immediately.

"I also keep on hand booklets and books, together with some plaques, for weddings, births, deaths, graduations, crises and trials, as well as for the exciting and sometimes traumatic experience of moving into a new town or a new home."

For years Vernon also kept "a burgeoning file of birthdays and wedding anniversaries." Once a month his secretary would give him a list of all the cards to be mailed the following month. He would sign them, sometimes add a remark, and arrange them chronologically. While it took effort to accumulate that file, it proved to be a worthwhile effort.

"Repeatedly," he testified, "someone has told me that I was the only person who remembered a milestone on his journey through life."

At Christmas, he said, he wrote long, reflective letters to the people on his mailing list. Since he tried to make these letters a significant communiqué, more than an update to friends about family doings, he would include a few particularly striking passages from his reading during his recent months.

"Isn't all of this expensive?" Vernon asked rhetorically. "Maybe —but as yet we aren't bankrupt! In addition, the telephone provides a quick means of contacting a hospitalized sufferer, cheering a depressed pilgrim, or saying 'hello' to a friend whom I haven't seen for months.

"Above all, by prayer I can touch a life a thousand miles away. One of my favorite quotations consists of two simple lines:
'Though sundered far; by faith we meet
Around one common Mercy Seat.'

"As for the people among whom I live, interaction is much more direct. A smile, a cheerful greeting, a fleeting conversation, a literal touch in passing—these acknowledge that the other is not merely drifting past me on the sea of time; no, I have encountered a fellow-struggler, a fellow-sufferer, a fellow-seeker whom I affirm with thanks and for whose co-existence I am glad."[1]

The Big World Outside

After his retirement from the leadership of the seminary, when he was on campus Vernon spent most of his waking hours in his study on the second floor of the Vernon Grounds Center, a room filled with memories. There, in the large room with its south and west windows that caught the sunshine and framed the mountains, he would begin the day reading the Scriptures with a few friends or praying for troubled souls somewhere in the world. With his yellow legal pad he would write sermons or lectures, and with his small Dictaphone he would compose notes and letters.

Pictures, brief messages, historic figures, works of art, and scores of walking canes in an assortment of shapes and sizes covered the wall behind the desk. A print of Claire Goldrick's painting of

Jesus and His disciples sharing the Last Supper graced the wall near the door. But the overwhelming feature of the place was books. Stacks perched on the large desk, spilled over onto the counter, and filled ceiling to floor shelves in a large adjoining room. Vernon treasured his books as old and dear friends; he mourned when he lost one and rejoiced when he found it. Over the years he managed to provide a home for at least nineteen thousand of these friends. But they never replaced his love for people. If visitors happened to comment on the thousands of books, Vernon would point out a cartoon on a wall from *Leadership Journal* showing a pastor, surrounded by books and responding to a visitor, "I can't help it if people think I've read them all."

When seminary graduates returned to their *alma mater,* they would climb the steps of the Grounds Center to this spacious office/study to visit Dr. Grounds. As soon as he looked up from his desk and saw someone standing in the doorway, Vernon came to the door, greeted the person warmly, and immediately asked about his welfare and his activities. Then he would lead his visitor to a round table surrounded by four comfortable chairs. At the center of the table was a shining lazy Susan with powdered milk, sugar, paper napkins, and coffee brewing nearby.

Comfortable and inviting, this room was Vernon Grounds throughout: his books, his round table for easy conversation, his many canes given by friends, his desk for writing personal notes, his comfortable chair for easy listening. By reading, writing, and listening here, he had made the room a memorial of his life. Here were the reminders of his greatness, the thoughts he read in his books, the times he spent with his friends, and the comfort he brought to weary pilgrims.

In his office/study Vernon's personal touch continued largely unchanged, but beyond it he was becoming something of an evangelical statesman, traveling from conference to conference in the interests of Christian counseling, church renewal, and, most significantly perhaps, world peace.

In December of 1980, at a conference held at Trinity Evangelical Divinity School, Vernon served on a panel that discussed "Evangelicals and Jews in an Age of Pluralism." In 1981 he spoke at a second conference in La Grange, Illinois, on the topic "Biblical Foundations for Peace in the Holy Land." And in 1984 he addressed a conference at Gordon College in Massachusetts on the subject of "Evangelicals and Jews: Coming of Age."

Conservative Christians at the time had become a visible presence in American society and, with their growing numbers, a political power politicians could no longer ignore. Many of them had supported Ronald Reagan for president in 1980 and rejoiced in his public approval of their efforts.

In the late 1970s, televangelist Jerry Falwell, by launching his Moral Majority, had "nudged Billy Graham out of his traditional spot as the nation's most newsworthy Christian leader." Falwell was soon joined on the political right by Pat Robertson and a "gaggle of other religious broadcasters and parachurch leaders" in forming "the new Christian Right."

Graham, himself, wanted no part of it. In *Christianity Today* he warned his newly politicized brethren to "be wary of exercising political influence" lest they lose their spiritual impact. And this was only his opening salvo. In a number of press conferences he warned against "the mingling of spiritual and political goals." In clear contrast to many of his earlier statements, he noted that "we clergy know so very little to speak out with such authority on the Panama Canal or superiority of armaments. . . . I do not intend to use what little influence I may have on [such] secular, non-moral, non-religious issues."[2]

Vernon Grounds, enjoying the freedom of his retired status, chose to join a tiny band of progressive evangelicals associated with a group called Evangelicals for Social Action (ESA), led by Professor Ronald J. Sider, a theologian at Eastern Baptist Theological Seminary. The ESA refused to endorse Falwell's Moral Majority, believing it too far right on most social issues, especially in its unquestioning support of almost every American military action in the nuclear age. Vernon found that his own views were generally applauded within the Evangelicals for Social Action, which was based on "commitments to the authority of the Scriptures, to a balance of prayer and action, and an emphasis on evangelism with a special calling in social action." These usually added up to positions on social issues somewhat left of the evangelical center.

When ESA introduced a publication called *The ESA Advocate,* Vernon became both president and primary spokesman for the movement through his articles in the *Advocate.* The monthly newsletter was devoted to public-policy analysis of key developments in Washington, and said in its first issue, "We will tell you when a letter or phone call to the president, member of Congress, or foreign leader can make the most difference."

For years, since his days as a freshman in the sound truck at Rutgers, Vernon Grounds had thought deeply about the beatitude, "Blessed are the peacemakers," but it was his retirement from the seminary that gave him a new opportunity in that regard. When he was invited to speak at a two-day conference on May 1 and 2, 1981, at the John F. Kennedy Center on Harvard University's campus, he gladly accepted. Months later he wrote in his Christmas letter that he was asked to participate "chiefly because no better known evangelical was available" to discuss the horrendous threat of a nuclear war. That, at any rate, was his humble explanation.

Representatives of all shades of religious belief were there, and with his self-confessed trepidation he spoke late Saturday afternoon to a crowded auditorium on the subject, "An Evangelical's Concern About Evangelical Unconcern." He joined many other speakers in pleading for an end to the arms race. Vernon specifically endorsed the kind of arms freeze urged by his "Conservative Baptist brother," Senator Mark Hatfield of Oregon.

Upon leaving the conference he told friends that he felt his speech was warmly received by "the heterogeneous audience" that was perhaps surprised that there actually were evangelicals who held to a pro-life morality, pleading for a search of every possible resource to fight against whatever "destroys, demeans, or diminishes human life, not only abortion, pornography, drug addiction, alcoholism, and family breakdown, but bombs as well."

In his Christmas letter to friends he wrote, "I have addressed this same subject on three other occasions, and I hope to address it as often as I can with all the persuasiveness of which I am capable. Have I, then, turned crusader? I certainly have if being a crusader means being a Christian who takes with increasing seriousness our Lord's beatitude, "Blessed are the peacemakers."

Peacemaking in Pasadena

As Ronald Reagan came to office in 1980, one of the trouble spots in the world was in a near-neighbor country, Nicaragua. Controversy of the U.S. policy there deepened after the Sandinista revolution overthrew dictator Anastasio Somoza in 1979. The new Reagan administration threw its support behind the "contras" who opposed the Sandinista regime. This decision pitted the American president against Christian groups in Nicaragua sympathetic to the Sandinistas.

Vernon Grounds was drawn to this crisis in no small measure by his long-standing friendship with Dr. John Stam, Jacob's son. John and his wife, Doris, had spent almost three decades in Central America, and their influence, as well as Vernon's extensive reading, led him to believe that the purpose of the Sandinista regime was either tragically misunderstood or misrepresented by President Reagan and his advisors.

In early December 1982, Vernon, along with several members of ESA, made a trip to Nicaragua to survey the scene firsthand. Upon his return he wrote to Colorado Senator William Armstrong and "shared his burden for Nicaragua." In his opinion, he told his senator, "governments can be Marxist without being Communist or functioning merely as tools and fronts for Moscow. Indeed, it strikes me as a realistic as well as a Christian policy to do all we can in order to cultivate amiable relationships with a country that is engaged in a socialist economic and political experiment. By so doing we can to some extent change our distorted image as ruthlessly imperialistic and capitalistic."[3]

The Nicaraguan crisis led Vernon deeper and deeper into what he considered his calling as a "peacemaker." In 1983 he also played a significant role in a four-day conference, "The Church and Peacemaking in the Nuclear Age," designed to clarify evangelicals' views of the nuclear arms race. The organizers hoped to create a public forum at which evangelical Christians could discuss their various views of the nuclear arms race. On a lovely day, May 25, 1983, over fourteen hundred participants assembled in Pasadena, California, to hear speakers representing the extremes in American evangelicals' attitudes toward war and disarmament. Vernon Grounds was at the center of the event, serving as master of ceremonies throughout the proceedings.

A few speakers reneged on their tentative commitments to participate, voicing a fear that the conference would be taken over by pacifists, but their fears proved unfounded. Only two of nearly two dozen speakers and panelists made any brief for pacifism, while four identified military strength as the guarantor of peace. A large majority embraced traditional just-war views. An outburst from an individual, haranguing conference participants from the balcony, brought one plenary session temporarily to a halt, but spontaneous singing of a stanza of "Amazing Grace" helped to ease tensions.

The most revealing session proved to be a panel discussion. First, Ron Sider, Vernon's colleague in ESA and co-author of a recent book *Nuclear Weapons and Christian Hope,* argued that faithfulness to the commands and the example of Jesus demands that Christians sacrifice for others and refuse to adopt violent means even at the cost of their own lives. Jesus' messianic mission, said Sider, replaced Jewish hopes for a political leader with a vision of God's love revealed in the suffering servant. To condone violence, therefore, is to accept a shallow view of the atonement. Christians today, Sider concluded, should work first of all for bilateral nuclear disarmament but ought ultimately to seek the elimination of all weapons in favor of a system of nonviolent national defense.

Then a second participant in the panel, Richard Mouw, then professor of Christian philosophy at Calvin College in Grand Rapids, Michigan, and another of Vernon Grounds's longtime friends, responded with a frank admission that just-war teaching has more often been used to rationalize political decisions than to sound the call for justice, and he urged that nonpacifist Christians repent of the anger and resentment they have often shown toward pacifist brothers and sisters.

Yet the just-war theory, Mouw argued, rests on a sound biblical basis, for willingness to fight a just war shows the depth of our love for neighbors. When the danger of distortion is admitted, and when specific questions of war are grounded in a broader ethical and theological framework, the just-war doctrine remains a vital element in the church's witness for justice and peace.

Finally, radio evangelist David Breeze, representing many conservative evangelicals, argued that we live in a world gravely threatened by communism, Arab nationalism, Islamic fundamentalism, and liberation theology—and in such a world we must not expect to formulate in the abstract moral rules that military leaders would be willing to follow in the heat of battle. Breeze found immediate support from another participant who argued that disarmament means "surrender of our most precious values." Peace is our objective, he urged, "but let us seek it through strength."[4]

With the conclusion of the conference, John Bernbaum of the Christian College Coalition began drawing together representative papers for a book. When *Perspectives on Peacemaking: Biblical Options in the Nuclear Age* was published in 1984, Bernbaum had secured two additional chapters. One from Senator Mark Hatfield, who had been unable to attend the conference, and one from Vernon Grounds, whose "gracious, loving spirit set the mood" for the three days.

In his chapter, "A Peace Lover's Pilgrimage," Vernon chose to write autobiographically and spoke of his earliest memories of war and his pacifist views.

He recalled the effigy of Kaiser Wilhelm hanging on a street corner in 1918 and his own crusade against war at Rutgers in 1934, but he confessed ignorance of the origin of his feelings, only that he had read scores of books and was most influenced by John Yoder, Jacques Ellul, and Gordon Zahn.

"As a Christian who takes the Bible as his all-sufficient rule of faith and practice," he wrote, "I am convinced that I must hold to a nonresistant position. In the name of Jesus my Saviour and Lord I must do more than hate and deplore war. I must stand against it absolutely and adamantly as a blatant and ghastly denial of all that the gospel proclaims and all that obedient discipleship demands. . . ."[5]

"Thus as my career and my life are in their sunset phase, I am giving myself increasingly to what I consider the top priority moral issue of our time. . . . I am doing my limited best to articulate the Christian's role of peacemaker as I have come to understand it. This is a multi-dimensional task which includes peace between God and man through faith in the reconciling Saviour. It includes, too, peace of heart and soul as a fruit of the Holy Spirit in one's own experience. It includes, as well, peace on every level of relationship

—peace in marriages, families, churches, businesses and industries. It must therefore include peace among the nations of the world. . . . If my life, my discipleship, my witness are to be shaped in keeping with the Jesus pattern, the *morphe* of Christ, I have no option but to give myself to the multidimensional task of peacemaking."

And throughout the 1980s and 1990s that is what Vernon continued to do. In a 1987 issue of the *ESA Update*, he wrote, "Interpersonally . . . peacemaking is problem number one. In marriages, malignant relationships and snarling unhappiness often erupt into physical abuse. In thousands of families, parents and children are angrily estranged. In neighborhoods, suburbs no less than inner city, nasty feuds drag on. In posh executive suites, cutthroat rivalry belies the genteel ambiance.

"Emotionally, peacemaking is also problem number one. Chronic anxiety, dark depression, gnawing guilt, bleak hopelessness —this is what therapists encounter day after day. And relief is sought from many sources—substance abuse, compulsive sex, frenetic activity. Which is why in describing self-frustrated mortals the prophet Isaiah resorts to vivid language. They are, he says, 'like the raging sea when it cannot rest, whose waters cast up mire and dirt.'

"What, then, is our primary responsibility as Christians? Peacemaking.

"The assignment is so overwhelming that we may conclude the only realistic hope for peace is eschatological. And it is if we are thinking of universal, permanent peace. But God wills that we work and pray for peace here and now. Empowered by His Spirit, we must employ every resource at our disposal to help minimize violence and maximize biblical shalom."

"Above all," he wrote, "by the proclamation of the Gospel we must augment the ranks of peacemakers. For it is the transforming experience of spiritual peace that motivates individuals to undertake the task of peacemaking—and stick to it. . . . And we who have been reconciled need constancy to have our peacemaking ministries renewed and recharged by that same Spirit."[6]

What is the secret of Vernon's peacemaking power with people? Jim Oraker, one of Vernon's former students in Young Life Institute class from the late 1960s, explains it well. Vernon's language, he says, is the language of trust, "his motions the motions of acceptance, his challenge the challenge to openness." His special type of hospitality offers the opportunity to listen, hear, reflect, dialogue... and help find God. What is it in Vernon Grounds "that fosters such ties?" It is Vernon's "gift of hospitality," which Jim sees as a synonym for making peace.

"He gives people space. When I meet him he expresses curiosity about me. I am often the first topic of conversation when we meet. I cannot remember a time when he has queried my theological allegiances, but he freely and comfortably shares his own when appropriate. Even with his busy schedule he gives one the sense that he is available—much of this has to do with his presence in the moment. I never feel pre-empted by more important things. He humors me respectfully, touches me warmly, and shares openly things of a personal nature.

"In my relationship with Vernon," Jim says, "I experience God as the great finder and the great respecter of persons, not only in the abstract sense, but of me personally. I become the sheep, lost and alone, that the shepherd carries home on his shoulder (Luke 15: 3–7)."[7]

The New Millennium

When the new millennium dawned, Vernon and Ann Grounds were comfortably situated in their apartment eight blocks west of the seminary. In his Christmas letter for the year 2000, Vernon wrote, "Ann and I have both turned 86, she on August 24, I on July 19. And on June 17 we quietly observed our 61st wedding anniversary. Life for us flows along in well-worn grooves.

"Every Sunday we hold a vespers service in the apartment complex where we live. Early in December we conducted a well-attended Christmas Sing-A-Long for our fellow-residents at the Meridian. To everyone's delight Ann played the whole program from memory; she was appropriately applauded for her talent. Almost daily from 6:30 A.M. on I host a procession of groups and individuals at the round table in my office as we enjoy bagels and coffee (of course!), talk and fellowship. Several afternoons each week and all Saturday morning I am at our Counseling Center. (Ah, what problems plague the human family!) I still teach a few Seminary courses and serve with several agencies, and I do some writing, chiefly devotional articles."[8]

The following spring, on May 18, 2001, Denver Seminary marked its fiftieth anniversary. The commencement celebration was held at the spacious Colorado Community Church just a half mile east of the seminary. Since it had also been a half century since Vernon Grounds arrived from the East Coast to assume leadership at the infant school in the old Bonfils mansion, the new president, Craig Williford, an alumnus, thought it appropriate to ask Dr. Grounds to speak on this grand occasion. Vernon happily accepted and ambled up the aisle in his academic robes as he had done so many times in the past.[9]

As he climbed the stairs to the platform, he appeared a bit stooped and certainly slower than in earlier days. But once he began to speak, his voice carried the same old resonant power and conviction.

"The past is a bucket of ashes," he began. "Do you agree with that harsh verdict pronounced by the American poet Carl Sandberg? Do you consign the past to the scrap heap of history?

"Some think that the only way to achieve success in the future is to leave the past behind. Doesn't the apostle say in his letter to the Philippians believers, 'Forgetting what is behind, I press on?'

"Is that God's message for Denver Seminary as it celebrates a half century of service for Jesus Christ? Is God charging us in this academic community to forget what has taken place since 1950, consigning it to the trash can of the past? By no means!

"That's not how I interpret God's will as expressed by Paul in his Philippian letter. Forget God's own faithfulness?" he asked. "Forget God's sustaining grace and goodness? Forget the steadfast love and sacrificial support of families and friends? Forget the lessons learned through failure and success? Not at all!

"What then is Paul's imperative? Don't let any past achievements inspire a mood of indolence, a spirit-stifling tendency to rest on yesterday's laurels and thus block future growth and progress. Keep pressing on! Into whatever future lies before us.

"What we must do," he said, "is remind ourselves of our heritage and cherish it." He then told the new generation the old story of fundamentalism and the birth of Denver Seminary. Fundamentalism, he said, was all about the defense of the gospel—in a life-and-death struggle with liberalism, which denied essential, redemptive truths of biblical Christianity. Granted some of those fundamentalists were not always gracious and scholarly. Granted some were guilty as charged: narrow, negative, and at times rather nasty. These liabilities made them easy targets for scoffers. Nevertheless, fundamentalists were on the side of the angels.

To support his appeal he introduced the audience to the latest book by his longtime friend Richard Mouw, now president of Fuller Theological Seminary. In *The Smell of Sawdust,* said Dr. Grounds, "the president of Fuller Seminary urges evangelicals not to forget their tradition in 'the sawdust trail,' because fundamentalists, in spite of their well-known liabilities, were courageously defending biblical truth and historic Christianity. That," Vernon stressed, "is our past, too. Cherish it!"[10]

During the following summer months one could usually find Vernon in his office/study in the Vernon Grounds Center, slumped in his chair at the round table listening to some graying graduate or troubled student. But September 11, 2001, the day of the terrorist attack on the World Trade Center in New York, was a memorable exception.

It was once again Convocation Day on campus, and faculty members were scheduled to robe in Vernon's spacious office before marching into the chapel across the hall. But when they made their way up the steps and into the office, the eighty-seven-year-old chancellor was nowhere to be found. He was across the campus in President Williford's office discussing what should be said at a convocation on such a day.

The faculty robed, the students assembled, and the convocation was held, but not as usual. The dean announced what had happened in New York City and Washington and Pennsylvania and prayed for friends and family members who were scheduled to fly out of Boston or New York. Later he interrupted proceedings to issue the call for all reservists to report to their duty stations. The chapel was permeated by an unusual blend of solemnity and concern.

When President Williford stood to speak, he invited Dr. Grounds to join him at the podium and announced that he had decided to discard his speech in favor of conversing with Dr. Grounds about the significance of the moment. They talked for about ten minutes, and then the president asked Vernon, "What do you think our response to this crisis should be?"

"Well," Vernon said, "we certainly must pray. And then we must be, in every way possible, agents of reconciliation."

The new students had no idea what to make of such a statement in such an hour, but a number of alumni understood completely, as did the faculty, sitting on the front row, a few with tears in their eyes. They had come to expect nothing less from the aging statesman, who for decades had lived out before them the words of the apostle: "God was in Christ reconciling the world unto himself... and hath committed unto us the word of reconciliation." All who are reconciled to God are ambassadors for Christ, and our mission is peace.

With gentleness, strength, and dignity, Vernon Grounds has, through his life and his work, been an ambassador for Christ. Traveling to and fro, year after year, he has shown, in word and deed, the transforming love of God to those along the way. And, of course, the story has not ended.

Vernon concluded one of his recent Christmas letters with his customary, and fitting, bit of verse from one of his favorites, Henry Van Dyke:

> So let the way wind up the hill or down,
> Through rough or smooth, the journey will be joy;
> Still seeking what I sought but when a boy,
> New friendship, high adventure, and a crown,
> I shall grow old, but never lose life's zest,
> Because the road's last turn will be the best.

In His Own Words

Selected Readings from
the Writings of Vernon C. Grounds

Do All Things Really Work Together for Good?

On February 15, 1947, D. Glenn Chambers of New York boarded the powerful DCA of the Avianca Airlines en route to Quito, Ecuador, in order to begin his ministry with the "Voice of the Andes." But he never arrived! Not far from Bogota, rising 14,000 feet toward the sky, is the towering peak, "El Tablazo." Glenn's plane crashed headlong into that peak and dropped, a flaming wreck, into a ravine far below.

The last letter he wrote was addressed to his mother. At a Miami airport he picked up an advertising pamphlet. On the front page was the single word, WHY? Around that word Glenn scribbled a hasty and final note. So when his mother received it, having previously learned of his death, staring up into her face was that question: WHY?

Whenever stark tragedy breaks into life, all of us instinctively wonder *why?* Why does God permit such experiences? Why does God allow us to suffer? Why does a loving and almighty God tolerate evil in His universe? Why?

When stark tragedy breaks into his life, the man without Jesus Christ may respond in one of several fashions. Cynicism may be his response; he may unwittingly follow the advice of Job's wife, "Curse God and die." Or stoicism may be his response: "Grin and bear it, and if you can't grin, then grit your teeth and bear it anyhow." Or Epicureanism may be his response: "Eat, drink, and be merry for tomorrow ..."

But when tragedy breaks into his life, the Christian, instead of responding with cynicism or stoicism or epicureanism, falls back upon Romans 8:28, attempting to make that text a soft pillow for his heart: "We know that all things work together for good to them that love God, to them who are the called according to his purpose." Yet, if we are going to be candid, the Christian does not always find that

Paul's radiant certainty proves a soft pillow for his heart. Often, on the contrary, because of two facts it turns out to be a hard problem for his head.

The text is too unqualified, too glibly inclusive. Do "all things" indeed work together for good? Who can possibly believe that? The accident which imprisons a young man in a wheelchair as an incurable cripple; the emotional breakdown which puts the mother of a large family out of her mind; the agonizing frustration which causes an idealist to degenerate into an embittered skeptic, mocking and denying God; the death which leaves an unhealed scar upon a heart —are these things good?

Some things may indeed work together for good, but how can any person of even limited discernment conclude that all events, without exception, turn out for our highest welfare? A few things, many things, even most things, yes! But *all* things? No.

The text is much too dogmatic. Paul states with unshadowed certainty:

"We *know* all things work together for good." He does not say that this is our faith; he does not say that this is our pious hope; he does not say that this is a proposition which we are unable to prove but which we embrace with a trust that appears to defy logic and reason. Paul's affirmation, we uncomfortably feel, is overly confident.

Thus, the text seems too sweeping and too dogmatic. Yet implicit in it are four truths which, when once grasped, transform Paul's assertion from a hard problem into a soft pillow.

Not a Cosmic Freak

The apostle declares: "All things *work* together for good." A better translation is given in the New American Standard Bible, "God causes all things to work together for good." So Paul does not declare that every event, every episode, and every experience of life achieves good by luck or chance or accident. He does not declare that by some cosmic freak or by the mere random whirling of senseless matter, good is eventually produced. Paul declares that God causes all things to work together for good. Thus he teaches here the same truth which he teaches in Ephesians 1:11, "[God] worketh all things after the counsel of His own will."

Why does everything, even heartbreaking tragedy, turn out for good? The answer is simple. God is at work in the whole process! By His infinite wisdom, power and love, God is causing all things to work together for good.

Visit a huge, sprawling plant where automobiles are manufactured. Watch the bewildering mass of raw material—metals, wood, fabrics, glass and what not—as it pours into the factory. Then, without entering the doors of that mammoth structure, walk around to the ramp where the finished product, a sleek and shining mechanism, rolls out, ready for shipment to every corner of the world. Can you possibly believe that by luck or chance a mass of raw material assembles itself into an automobile? But when you realize that extraordinary skills and power have been brought to bear upon that raw material, you can understand why the finished product is so beautiful and efficient.

Similarly, who can believe that all the mass of our raw experience—sickness, disappointment, broken bodies, blasted hopes, blighting sins— just by luck or chance or accident achieves good? Introduce God into the picture, however, a God of infinite wisdom, power and love, and it is possible for even the most searching mind to believe that everything will eventually work for good. God is making all things work together for good, bringing to bear upon the raw stuff of our experience all of His limitless resources.

Confessedly, there may be aspects of existence which will baffle us until we see our Lord face to face. But still, embryonically, we have a solution to this tantalizing mystery. Our cosmos, we realize, is not a self-existing chaos of atoms which swirl about senselessly. Undergirding our universe is the everlasting purpose of a Person who is perfect in wisdom, love and power, and Who uses the vast process of nature and history for the fulfillment of His gracious purpose which is supremely good.

Notice, finally, one other fact implicit in this text. Paul's confident assertion is not so unqualified and inclusive as at a first glance it may strike us. It embraces only those "who love God" and are "the called according to his purpose." Thus, before any of us attempts to appropriate this shining guarantee, he must be utterly sure that he comes within the category Paul lays down. How can we determine whether or not we are embraced within this blessed category? Very simply! Have we as yet in simplest trust accepted Jesus Christ as our Savior, responding to the invitation, "Whosoever will may come"? Have we as yet looked to Calvary and beheld there the convincing demonstration of divine grace? Have we said our "yes" to God's call of love? If we have, then the promise applies to us— but not otherwise!

Take into account these four truths and Romans 8:28 will not be any longer a tough problem for your head. It will become a soft pillow for your heart.

From *Eternity*, August 1958, 15, 17, 38.

The Price Love Paid

"But may it never be that I should boast, except in the cross of our Lord Jesus Christ" (Gal. 6:14). What a strange exclamation! Why boast about the cross?

No one writes hymns praising the hangman's noose, wears a replica of the guillotine, or decorates a church with an electric chair. Why, then, do Christians glory in the cross — that ghastly symbol of cruelty, shame, and death?

We do so for one overwhelming reason. The cross of Calvary is our time-abiding, heart-assuring, all-sufficient revelation of God's love. . . . Apart from Calvary, there is no convincing evidence to support the New Testament claim, "God is love."

In nature, for example, we find no support for the love of God. Whether we study snowflakes under a microscope or survey the heavens from an observatory, the verdict is the same. . . . Nowhere do we find convincing evidence that this Creator is a holy Father of infinite love.

Imagine a Minnesota valley in autumn, apparently tranquil and calm. But in reality the scene is a battlefield. For men are killing foxes, foxes are killing hawks, hawks are killing sparrows, sparrows are killing worms, and worms are eating men who once killed foxes. And we say that God is love. . . . The belief that God is love lies at the heart of Christianity. But nowhere in nature do we find any convincing evidence.

Nor do we find convincing evidence in history. Do we find God's love revealed in the tortures of the Spanish Inquisition, the Nazi gas chambers, or the concentration camps of Soviet Russia? . . . Then why do we Christians assert it?

We believe it because of one world-transforming fact that unbelief ignores — the fact of Calvary.

Consider what Calvary cost God the Son:

It cost Him agony of body. To appreciate that agony, watch our Lord in Gethsemane as He prays alone beneath the trees until He breaks out in a bloody sweat. See Him as He is betrayed with a treacherous kiss and is hurried about sleeplessly all through the hours of the night. Watch Him as He is brutally flogged and, weary and exhausted, is compelled to carry His cross through the streets of Jerusalem toward Golgotha.

Watch our Lord as He is dragged to the hilltop where Roman legionnaires drive spikes through His hands and feet. Men are killing their God!

Watch as our Lord hangs in naked shame and anguish and dies for us. Why is He suffering like that? Love alone is the answer. . . .

But Christ also endured indescribable agony of spirit. Paul writes: "[God] hath made him to be sin for us, who knew no sin; that we might be made the righteousness of God in him" (2 Cor 5:21).

Whenever we talk about the cross, our human language breaks down under the weight of inexpressible truth. On Calvary Jesus Christ was made sin. Who can fathom what that cost Him?

In His holiness, He abhorred evil. In His moral perfection, He could see sin in all of its hideousness, as we cannot possibly see it. In His divine sensitivity He could feel the crushing weight of sin as we cannot possibly feel it. And He could taste all of the foulness of sin as we cannot possibly taste it.

That was why He prayed, "If it be possible, let this cup pass from me" (Matt. 26:39). Yet at the cross He lifted that cup and drank it to the dregs. He became sin.

Perhaps we can understand in part our Lord's reaction to sin if we take some of our own reactions and multiply them by infinity. Years ago as a pastor, I regularly visited a hospital where two men were dying of a malignancy that had attacked their faces. Week after week I was driven to ask God for grace to camouflage my feelings.

Or think of Henry Drummond, the scientist-preacher of Scotland who came to the United States sponsored by D. L. Moody. He was a popular college lecturer, and after his meetings, students would request personal help.

One day after a long series of such counseling, Drummond was in his room with his head in his hands. A friend came in, glanced at him, and exclaimed, "Why Henry, what's the matter? Are you sick?" Drummond replied, "Yes, I'm sick. I'm sick of sin! How does God stand it?"

God's endurance of man's sin is indeed a mystery. But the far greater mystery is why Jesus Christ was willing to become sin for us. . . . The heart of God the Father must have broken when God the Son was dying on the cross. . . . But why did God the Father and God the Son undergo such agony? The New Testament gives just one reason: because of love for you and me and the whole lost world. Only through God's redemptive agony could His purposes for His creation be brought to fulfillment. And God was willing to pay the price.

That is why we glory in the cross.

That is why we are sure that behind all history and nature there is a God of infinite love.

And that is why, in our world of darkness, we seek to share the message of the cross—the message that floods the darkness with the light of redemptive love.

From *Moody Monthly*, April 1985, 42–45,
adapted from *The Splendor of Easter*
(Word Books, © 1972) and used by permission.

Liar, Lunatic or Lord of All

Judged by human standards of success, the life of Jesus Christ was a pathetic failure. Born in a manger, He was buried in a borrowed grave. His family was poor, and for thirty years He lived in an obscure village of Palestine working as a carpenter.

His own brothers thought He was mad and tried to dissuade Him when He started out to preach. His teachings were hated and scoffed at by theologians of the day. Some of His followers came from the lowest level of society. His intimate friends misunderstood Him and in the end, like cowards, let Him die alone at the hand of His enemies. He never wrote a book. He never commanded an army. He never addressed a senate, or spoke to an applauding parliament. He never occupied a throne. At the age of thirty-three He died in torture and disgrace, nailed up against the sky between two thieves.

Yet Jesus Christ spoke about Himself in a way that is astonishing. He asserted that He was a teacher whose doctrines should be accepted unquestioningly; that He was the perfect example of human character and conduct; that He was an absolutely sinless Being; that He was able to work miracles such as no other man had ever wrought; that He would rise from the dead; that He would be the final Judge of the world; that He was equal with God in power and authority.

Indeed He even asserted that He was God! Yes, He commanded His disciples to love Him, obey Him, follow Him, sacrifice for Him, believe in Him, worship Him and, if need be, die for Him exactly as they would for God.

Now in the light of these assertions, what is one to think concerning Jesus Christ? Faced as you are with these amazing claims and all their implications, what is your opinion of Him?

This strange Carpenter of Galilee, who somehow steps across 20 centuries and breaks into our lives even today, cannot be pushed to one side as a profound teacher and nothing more; or a courageous martyr and nothing more; or just a religious genius.

For if Jesus was and is really God as He claimed to be, you cannot with knowing condescension dismiss Him as a mere teacher or a mere martyr or a mere genius. To dismiss God in that way is blasphemy! If He really was and is Deity incarnate, you must fall before Him in faith and love, and surrender.

On the other hand, however, if Jesus Christ was not and is not really God as He claimed to be, how can you possibly look upon Him admiringly as the noblest example of the good life, a life of unselfish humility and lowly service? If His claim is false, you must agree that this Galilean carpenter was either a liar or a lunatic. Of necessity He must have been one or the other, if He was not Deity incarnate.

Now, which was He? A liar? Is that what He was? Not according to David Strauss, the world-renowned German scholar. Listen to the opinion of this man who made no claim to being a Christian: "He represents within the religious sphere the highest point, beyond which posterity cannot go; yea, whom it cannot even equal, inasmuch as everyone who hereafter should climb the same height could only do it with the help of Jesus, who first attained it. As little as humanity will ever be without religion, as little as will it be without Christ; for to have religion without Christ would be as absurd as to enjoy poetry without regard to Homer or Shakespeare. . . . He remains the highest model of religion within the reach of our thought; and no perfect piety is possible without His presence in the heart.". . . .

Well, then, if Jesus was not a liar, was He a lunatic? Was He a deluded fanatic? George Bernard Shaw, to whom nothing and nobody was sacred, ventured to assert that Jesus is "a man who was sane until Peter hailed Him as the Christ and who then became a monomaniac. . . . His delusion is a very common delusion among the insane and . . . . such insanity is quite consistent with the retention of the argumentative cunning and penetration which Jesus displayed in

Jerusalem after His delusion had taken complete hold of Him." But was Jesus Christ really a lunatic?. . . .

If we can trust the judgment of William Lecky, one of the most noted historians of Great Britain, Jesus Christ was not a lunatic. Lecky writes: "It was reserved for Christianity to present to the world an ideal character which through all the changes of 18 centuries has inspired the hearts of men with an impassioned love; has shown itself capable of acting on all ages, nations, temperaments and conditions; has been not only the highest pattern of virtue, but the strongest incentive to its practice. . . . The simple record of these three short years of active life has done more to regenerate and soften mankind than all the disquisitions of philosophers and all the exhortations of moralists."

Was Jesus a lunatic? Not according to William Lecky who spent his life in an attempt to destroy organized Christianity!

And if you are still in doubt as to this point, consider these words of John Stuart Mill, one of the keenest philosophers of modern times: "About the life and sayings of Jesus there is a stamp of personal originality combined with profundity of insight, which must place the prophet of Nazareth, even in the estimation of those who have no belief in His inspiration, in the very first rank of the men of sublime genius of whom our species can boast. When this preeminent genius is combined with the qualities of probably the greatest moral reformer and martyr to that mission who ever existed upon earth, religion cannot be said to have made a bad choice in picking on this man as the ideal representative and guide of humanity; nor even now would it be easy, even for an unbeliever, to find a better translation of the rule of virtue from the abstract into concrete, than to endeavor so to live that Christ would approve our life."

And John Stuart Mill, like William Lecky, had little use for Christianity.

Whenever anybody seriously argues that Jesus was an extreme pathological case, I like to point out how strange it is that the most learned, cultured, critical intellects of all ages have bowed in reverent homage at the feet of this young fanatic, addressing Him as Master. And whenever any critic insists that He was demented, I like to exclaim, "Would to God that the whole world were affected with His kind of insanity!"

Well, then, since Jesus Christ cannot be pushed aside as a liar or waved away as a lunatic, what conclusion must we draw? Jesus Christ is what He claimed to be! He is the Lord of glory, Deity incarnate, God humbling Himself to become man in order to redeem His lost creation. And since that is so, it is blasphemy for us to talk patronizingly about Him as a teacher or a martyr or a religious genius. Instead, we must bow down at His nail-pierced feet in adoration and faith exclaiming, "My Lord and my God."

From *Reason for Our Hope*
(Chicago: Moody Press, 1945), 30–35.

The Love That Keeps on Forgiving

Let me tell you a story, a story of forgiving love, a story without equal in the literature of mankind. It is a story which we can piece together only with the greatest difficulty from some fragments of biography embodied in the Old Testament. It is the story of a husband and his wife, the story of a good man who married a bad woman.

In the Book of Hosea . . . we read that God commanded a prophet of Israel to do a strange thing: "The Lord said to Hosea, Go, take unto thee a wife of whoredoms and children of whoredoms: for the land hath committed great whoredom, departing from the Lord." Now God had a good reason for this strange command, since the marriage which He thus commanded was to serve as a symbol and even become a vehicle of revelation. More than that, Hosea really loved Gomer, who may have been sold by her parents into harlotry, as happened occasionally in those days. A good man in any case married a bad woman. In love he redeemed her from slavery; in love he gave her his name and his home; in love he lavished all of his tenderness upon her, and she became the mother of his three children.

Then tragedy, stark and sudden, overwhelmed Hosea, leaving him dazed, like a man half electrocuted by a bolt of lightning. For Gomer ran away to live in adultery. Yes, after all that Hosea had done for her, after all his sacrifice, after all his compassion, after all his affection, she broke his heart. With no concern for her children and with no gratitude for her husband's redeeming love she ran away to live in brazen and terrible shame.

But before long the fires of passion were burning low, and her paramour cast Gomer aside like a squeezed-out orange rind. Down she went to the very bottom, a common street-walker, dirty, hungry, and miserable. And soon she had sold herself into vile slavery again, and there she was back in the living death from which Hosea had redeemed her. Once the prophet's beloved wife, now a slattern, unkempt, unloved, and unwanted—except for lust.

When Hosea's neighbors learned what had happened to Gomer, they no doubt exclaimed with self-righteous joy: "Good! That serves her right! She got what was coming to her! She has made her bed— let her lie in it! Poor Hosea! How he must hate her for all she had done to him and their children. Well he'll be glad to hear what's happened. It will be a sweet revenge."

So the neighbors in their self-righteousness very probably thought. But they failed to reckon with the possibilities of a God-like love, a love which forgives and forgives and keeps on forgiving. For what did Hosea do when he learned about Gomer? He did the incredible thing told us in chapter 3: Hosea redeemed Gomer from harlot slavery. In spite of all she had done to him and their children; in spite of all the heartache which she had caused him, all the shame, all the tears, all the sleepless nights; in spite of the burning pain of ingratitude and betrayal; in spite of her disgraceful adultery, he freely forgave her and once more redeemed her and made her his wife. What an incredible thing to do!

And why did he do it? His shocked friends asked that. Why? His bewildered neighbors asked that. Why? Who had ever heard of such a thing? Why did he do it?

In that prophecy which constitutes his priceless legacy to the world Hosea explains why. As he brooded over his domestic tragedy, a great light began to dawn on him, a great insight, the gift of the Holy Spirit, flashed across his mind. Israel had treated Jehovah just as Gomer had treated him. For God had redeemed that nation from Egyptian bondage. . . . So in grace and compassion and mercy God had loosed Israel from slavery. Besides that, He had made Israel His wife. . . . He had brought her into Canaan, and there He poured out his choicest blessing upon her. . . . How lavish had been Jehovah's love for Israel!

Do you see the touching picture which Hosea has drawn? As a father with patience and pride teaches his little son to walk, carefully upholding the tottering baby, so in patience and pride Jehovah had watched over Israel and guided her steps. And yet in return for all His love, she had abandoned Him; in return for all His love, she had become a spiritual harlot. She had been as thankless, as shameless, as sinful as Gomer.

That was the truth which Hosea saw as he brooded over his own domestic tragedy.

But that was not the only truth he saw. By no means! He saw a complementary truth, a truth which was breathtakingly amazing. For when His faithless wife forsook Him, flouted Him, forgot Him, what did Jehovah do? Did He wash His hands of Israel? Did He give that harlot nation up? No, no! God continued to love His faithless wife; He continued to care for her; He continued to yearn over her with all His heart. "How shall I give thee up, Ephraim? how shall I deliver thee, Israel? . . . I will not execute the fierceness of mine anger, I will not return to destroy Ephraim; for I am God, and not man; the Holy One in the midst of thee." Though Israel had turned away from Him, God was unwilling to abandon His people. . . .

Now this was the tremendous truth which Hosea glimpsed as he brooded over his domestic tragedy; this insight came to him as a gift of the Holy Spirit. He was enabled to look into the very heart of God. And he saw a Heart of infinite love, a Heart of love which in its out-flow can never be dammed back, a Heart that in love forgives and forgives and keeps on forgiving.

That was why the prophet forgave his sinful wife. If God loves like that, he reasoned with himself, I too must love like that. If God clings to harlot Israel, I must cling to harlot Gomer. If God cares for harlot Israel, I must care for harlot Gomer. If God forgives harlot Israel, forgives and forgives, and keeps on forgiving, I must forgive harlot Gomer, forgive and forgive and keep on forgiving. And thus it was that Hosea's domestic tragedy became a redemptive triumph, a human parable of God's forgiving love, even a vehicle of revelation. And what a story the forgiving prophet has written for us, a story which has no equal in the literature of mankind!

Did I say that Hosea's story has no equal? There is one Story which equals it. Indeed, there is one Story which infinitely surpasses it, rising above it as the blue sky overarches the mountains. And that story is the Story of Calvary. For listen! God created man; God blessed man; God loved man with all His infinite love. Yet man rose up against God; man disobeyed God; man turned away from God. He became a sinner, an enemy of his very Creator. He spat in God's face! In ingratitude he attempted to usurp the position of God, living in self-love, self-concern, self-worship. And as a result, cut off from the only Source of peace and joy, man entered upon an existence of misery, frustration, and suffering.

What did God do, then, this God who had created man, blessed man, and in love crowned his life with goodness and mercy? Did God rejoice over man's misery, frustration and suffering? Did God allow His love to change into hate? No! Hosea, as he brooded over his domestic tragedy, had glimpsed the great truth that God's love is inalienable. God in His love forgives and forgives and keeps on forgiving. And, therefore, just because of God's love, a bloody cross one day thrust its arms across the skyline of Jerusalem, and a dying Man in agony cried out, "Father forgive them; for they know not what they do."

And therefore today, just because of God's forgiving love, we can preach *the evangel of forgiving love.* We can declare that in Jesus Christ all of us may have redemption and forgiveness of sins. God became Man that He might shoulder the burden of our guilt and as our Substitute make forgiveness a possibility; God became Man that He might restore us to eternal fellowship with Himself.

Today, therefore, because of God's forgiving love, we can promise repentant sinners *the experience of forgiving love.* For when in faith a man opens his heart to Jesus Christ, the peace and joy of divine pardon become his abiding portion.

Today, therefore, just because of God's forgiving love, we can press upon Christian hearts and minds *the ethic of forgiving love.* We can remind pardoned transgressors of Paul's entreaty in Ephesians 4:32: "And be ye kind one to another, tenderhearted, forgiving one another, even as God for Christ's sake hath forgiven you."

But have we allowed the ethic of forgiving love, grounded in the evangel of forgiving love and springing from the experience of forgiving love, to govern our own lives? Though forgiven by God, have we been forgiving? Or have we refused to forgive someone, a wife, a father, a relative, a friend, a brother in Christ—anybody in fact? And are we refusing to forgive because in our judgment we have been too greatly sinned against? Ah, what a sham, what a pretext!

Have we been sinned against as Gomer sinned against Hosea? Have we been sinned against as Israel sinned against Jehovah? Have we been sinned against as we ourselves have sinned against our God? Then by the enablement of the Holy Spirit, in full view of Calvary, and for the sake of the world's supreme Forgiver, let us bow our souls and in His name forgive!

From *The National Voice of Conservative Baptists,*
March 1953, 4–5, 22.

Love: Poetry or Power

Many people in modern America . . . wonder whether Christianity is really all that it's claimed to be. As far as they can see, Christianity makes next to no dent on life in the twentieth century.

Christianity is good, of course, and it is certainly right, yet it seems so impractical. It has a great deal to say about love, for example; its hymnals are full of sweet sentiments regarding love for God and Jesus and the benighted multitudes dying in darkness. Love, however, seems hopelessly irrelevant in a power-conscious, power-mad world.

For what is love, anyway, this love which Christianity puts in the spot-light? Isn't it merely a sensation, an emotion, something that has to do chiefly with romantic song-hits, Mother's Day and poetry? How can it be relevant in our present world? Christianity with its pious poetry, its sweet sentimental message of love is apparently as practical as a horse-drawn buggy on a California freeway.

Our world is a world ruled by science and its favorite child, technology.

This is the age of bombs, the destructiveness of which we measure by megatons. This is the age in which bacteriological and radiological warfare will soon be perfected. In an age like this Christianity does indeed seem irrelevant. Its stress on love seems to be a pretty relic from yesterday, an interesting museum-piece which we gaze at with respect and veneration, but which we simply wouldn't dream of using — because it's useless.

So a 20th century Christian opens his Bible to a passage like I Corinthians, chapter 13. There he reads about love and reading that passage, he understands why a generation ago Henry Drummond, a famous scientist-preacher, called love the greatest thing in the world.

A 20th century Christian shuts his Bible, though, and wonders. Is love actually the greatest thing in the world? Surely a sweet sentiment doesn't count in a world of space exploration, a world where bombs and missiles make a mockery of love. What's the value of Paul's poetry in a world where power speaks the last word?

But maybe this matter of love is more complicated than it first appears. Maybe the message of Christianity—God's love for a lost world revealed in Jesus Christ and therefore our need to love people just because God in love has redeemed all of us on the Cross—isn't as irrelevant as we might think. If love is merely poetry and not a power, perhaps even the greatest power in the world, why do you suppose that so many top-flight thinkers stress it just as heavily as the Bible does?

Listen to one of our leading sociologists, Pitirim Sorokin. Caught up in the Russian Revolution of 1917, he saw with his own eyes ghastly results of cruelty, hatred, violence, and injustice. Emigrating to the United States, he was eventually appointed chairman of the department of sociology at Harvard University.

Yet Sorokin finally gave up that position because he had concluded that the world is literally dying for love. Quoting his own journal *Leaves from a Russian Diary*, he declares, "Cruelty, hatred, violence and injustice never can and never will be able to create a mental, moral or material millennium. The only way toward it is the royal road of all-giving creative love, not only preached but consistently practiced."

Today, Sorokin is devoting himself to the development of "a new applied science of amitology."

If only love can save the world, love is vastly more than a feeling. It is a force, a measureless force, a redemptive force.

In Matthew 22:36–40, our Lord Jesus Christ replies to a far-reaching question, a trick question put to Him by an expert in the Old Testament: "Master, which is the greatest commandment in the law?" How could that possibly be answered without triggering a heated argument? In the Old Testament there is a great mass of commandments which God gave to the Jews. . . . How, then, could Jesus possibly pick out one imperative and be sure that it was unquestionably the greatest?

He did just that, however, and He did it infallibly. He took Leviticus 19:18, a text from an obscure passage compounded of directives which range from the trivial to the tremendous; and He fused that text with Deuteronomy 6:4, a text which was the very heart of Israel's faith. In so doing, our Lord achieved a master-simplification. He reduced all of religion and all of ethics to a single imperative with a concave and a convex side: "Love God and love your neighbor."

The enormous complexities of theology and morality are thus summed up in love. Only this love, bear in mind, is not a little feeling or a trifling emotion. It roots back into the nature of God, expresses itself in a bloody cross, and does not operate in human experience apart from our faith and the Spirit's enablement.

What is the fulfilling of the law? What meets the entire sweep of God's demands? Love! Of course it does. When you love God, you honor His person, His name, His day, and His representatives on earth, our parents, who share in the creative process. That fulfills the first table of the Decalogue. And when you love your neighbor, you protect his life, his home, his property, his reputation, everything he has. That fulfills the second table of the Decalogue. So when you love, you keep the Ten Commandments. Love, then, is indeed the fulfilling of the law. . . .

I Corinthians, chapter 13 . . . is a piece of poetry, though we know now, that love is far more than poetry: it is a measureless force. As a matter of fact, this passage is a hymn in which Paul sings the praises of love—not ordinary love, of course, but the supernatural love which the Holy Spirit creates within us when we accept Jesus Christ as our Savior. And this hymn voices one major idea: love, God's redemptive love in Jesus Christ working out in our own lives by faith, is the greatest thing in all the world.

From *Eternity,* September 1964.

Is Love in the Fundamentalist Creed?

A fundamentalist . . . holds tenaciously to doctrines like the plenary inspiration of the Bible, the virgin birth of Jesus Christ, His substitutionary atonement, His bodily resurrection and His literal return. And, hence, of course, we are fundamentalists theologically. But very frankly some of us do not like to be tagged fundamentalists. For fundamentalism in many quarters has degenerated into a quarrelsome bickering over incidentals: indeed, it is incidentalism rather than fundamentalism. In many quarters, moreover, fundamentalism displays an unhappy ability to forget certain fundamentals which it finds troublesome.

Take, for example, the duty of neighbor-love. That it is a fundamental of Christianity cannot successfully be disputed. Our Lord seizes upon that seemingly peripheral duty mentioned in Leviticus 19:18 and in Matthew 22:37–40, He exalts it into a life-embracing, world-girdling, age-spanning principle, a supreme fundamental. In reply to the question, "Master, which is the great commandment in the law?" He says: "Thou shalt love the Lord thy God with all thy heart, and with all thy soul, and with all thy mind. This is the first and great commandment. And the second is like unto it, Thou shalt love thy neighbor at thyself."

Neighbor love is not something trivial. It is the fruit which springs from the root of unfeigned Christian faith. Yet, strangely enough, this supreme fundamental has been grossly ignored. And perhaps that neglect explains to a large degree why fundamentalism has in many quarters degenerated into a legalistic Phariseeism: hard, frigid, ineffective, unethical and loveless.

"Whom are we to love?" is simply a repetition of the question addressed to Jesus long ago by a self-justifying theologian. In the deep-cutting parable of the good Samaritan "a certain lawyer stood up, and tempted him, saying, 'Master what shall I do to inherit eternal life?' He said unto him, 'What is written in the law? how readest thou?' And he answering said, 'Thou shalt love the Lord thy God with all thy heart, and with all thy soul, and with all thy strength, and with all thy mind; and thy neighbour as thyself.' And he said unto him, 'Thou hast answered right: this do, and thou shalt live.' But he, willing to justify himself, said unto Jesus, 'And who is my neighbour?'"

Now the lawyer mentioned here is not a lawyer in our contemporary sense of the term. He is an Old Testament scholar, an interpreter of God's law, a theologian, in other words. And Luke declares that this lawyer is attempting to "justify himself." Like some of us modern fundamentalists he has apparently been forgetting that fundamental of fundamentals, the duty of neighbor-love, and to camouflage his sinful failure he is kicking up a cloud of theological dust.

Observe, however, the divine adroitness of our Saviour as in answer to this lawyer's self-justifying inquiry He tells what seems to be a simple little story. But that simple little story is actually a moral atom bomb. In this simple little story our Lord asserts that neighbor-love—the kind of mercy exhibited by the good Samaritan—"foolishly" takes in everybody. The good Samaritan was a good neighbor, Jesus tells us, because he was willing to help a stranger and a foreigner at that, a man who had no claim whatever upon his mercy; and he helped that man in spite of possible danger, in spite of difficulty and delay—yes, in spite of inconvenience and expense.

"Who is my neighbor?" that question is largely bypassed, and the issue is radically changed as the lawyer comes face to face with the probing question, "Am I truly a neighbor as God commands me to be?"

And as we ponder the story which Jesus told, we too are compelled to confront that probing question, "Am I truly a neighbor as God commands me to be?" We are compelled to inquire searchingly: "Do we love everybody? Are these hearts of ours big enough to hold a global concern?"

One word, therefore, answers the question of that self-justifying lawyer, "Who is my neighbor?" *Everybody!*

―――――――――

"Why are we to love?" Why ought we to love people everywhere? How unnatural it is to demand a love like that! Well, what good reason is there for us as sinners to love in any other way?

God loves us in precisely the way which He commands us to love our neighbors. He loves unconditionally, indiscriminately and globally. He loves us although we have no claim upon His love. So Jesus says: "Love . . . your enemies, and do good, and lend, hoping for nothing again; and your reward shall be great" (Luke 6:35).

There we have it! God even loves His enemies, expecting no gratitude and no profit from His love. And since God loves like that, we ought to love like that!

Why ought we to love everybody? "When we were yet without strength, in due time Christ died for the ungodly" (Rom. 5:5). In love God died for us when we were ungodly rebels against His holy sovereignty. Why ought we to love everybody regardless of his nationality? "God commendeth his love toward us, in that, while we were yet sinners, Christ died for us" (Rom. 5:8). In love God died for us when we were hostile rebels against His holy sovereignty. The cross is the climatic exposition of the logic underlying the law of neighbor-love.

―――――――――

"How are we to love?" Recall that overwhelming phrase in the teachings of Moses, Jesus, Paul and James: "as thyself." That indicates the mode and measure of neighbor-love: I am to love my neighbor as myself. And how do I love myself? I do not necessarily approve of everything about myself or admire everything about myself. In fact, I may criticize myself, abhor myself, and in some respects hate myself. Nevertheless, I love myself with a powerful, instinctive, over-riding emotion which springs from the passional urge of self-preservation.

And, consequently, if I love my neighbor, I will want for him everything which I want for myself; I will hope for him everything which I hope for myself. Loving him, I will long for him to get the best which life has to give and I will do everything I can to help him get it.

And what is the best which life has to give? Unquestionably it is God's salvation through faith in Jesus Christ. Not amusement, not money, not prestige, not health, not peace of mind—no! Life's best is the experience of forgiveness, the indescribable beatitude of fellowship with God the Father through Jesus Christ the Son and by the enablement of God the Holy Spirit. That is life's best.

Maybe as Christians, and especially as fundamentalists, we have been lacking in Calvary-love. Maybe we have wanted to vindicate the rightness of our position and we are persuaded, in truth, that the position we embrace is right. Maybe we have wanted to justify ourselves. Maybe we have wanted to add converts merely to strengthen our churches because they are *our* churches. What we need is to cry out for Calvary-love. If and when we do, the aftermath may prove astonishing.

From *Eternity,* June 1954, 13, 14, 41.

Check Up on Your Commitment

Once when Wendell Wilkie visited Franklin Delano Roosevelt at the White House, he asked bluntly why the President had made Harry Hopkins his confidant, that half-man as Roosevelt jokingly called him because of his extreme frailty.

"Why do you keep him so close to you?" Wilkie asked. "People distrust him and resent his influence over you."

"Some day, Wendell," President Roosevelt answered, "you may be sitting here in my place. And when you are, you will be looking at that door and knowing that practically everybody who comes through it wants something from you. You will learn what a lonely job it is, and you will discover your need for somebody like Harry Hopkins who asks for nothing except a chance to serve you."

And this is what the Lord Jesus was referring to when He gave the great commandment: "Love God with all your heart and with all your mind and with all your life" (Matt. 22:37). Love Him so completely that all you want is a chance to serve Him.

This is not an optional request; it is a totalitarian demand. It is a call for a Christian commitment which acknowledges God's sovereignty in every dimension of your experience, enthroning Him as Lord of your heart, Lord of your mind, and Lord of your life.

But how, you may ask, can I make Christ the Lord of my heart? Does it mean that I give up my friends, neighbors and family?

No, rather it means that you continue to love them. In fact, when you love Jesus Christ with all of your heart, your human loves are strengthened and purified. Yet Jesus said, "He that loveth father or mother more than me is not worthy of me: and he that loveth son or daughter more than me is not worthy of me" (Matt. 10:37).

When you make Him the Lord of your heart, your love for Him must have unconditional priority. And you do this gratefully. It is not done under pressure, nor is it motivated by a subtle fear. You do this because you love Jesus Christ supremely.

Why? Because you have been to Calvary. You have seen Him dying for your sins. You have knelt in adoration and amazement before your Creator as He agonized to become your Savior. And now your heart belongs to Jesus Christ.

Perhaps you feel that you cannot express adequately the love you have for Jesus. Perhaps you feel like William Morris, the famous artist, who was enamored of a beautiful girl, Jane Burden. He asked her to sit for a portrait, and when she did he spent a long time in silence, apparently at work on his canvas. But when he turned it around for Jane to see, it bore no picture. Instead it bore these words: "I cannot paint you, but I love you." Thus it may be with you. With Simon Peter you cry out: "Thou knowest all things; thou knowest that I love thee."

You may have made Jesus Christ the Lord of your heart, but have you made Him the Lord of your mind? Your allegiance to Christ is certainly not won by philosophy and logic, but rather by the vision of Calvary. However, you cannot stop with a merely emotional commitment.

You must make Jesus Christ the Lord of your mind for two reasons.

First, if your commitment to Jesus Christ is to be complete, it must include your head no less than your heart. It is unthinkable that the King of Truth asks you to dedicate everything to Him but your brain.

Secondly, unless your commitment to Jesus Christ includes your mind—if your faith is solely emotional—it is liable to crack up under the pressure of criticism and tragedy. A purely emotional faith is like a ship without ballast, tossed to and fro when the seas are running high. It needs the stabilizing weight of intellectual conviction.

As Plato put it, "An unexamined life is not worth living"; but neither is an unexamined faith worth having.

Since God is the source of all Truth and consequently since all Truth comes from Him and leads back to Him, to be afraid of Truth is to commit sacrilege. To adhere knowingly to error is sheer blasphemy. It is an act of idolatry, for it means that you are withholding your allegiance from the King of Truth and sinfully bowing down at an idol created by the imagination of men.

Facts, no matter how distasteful, must be faced fairly, honestly and accurately, with a sense of your own pride and prejudice, your own fear and hate and your own human fallibility.

But there is something else, too. You already possess God's Truth in the Holy Scriptures. Hence you are not pursuing Truth; you possess it. And for that reason your job is to appropriate Truth more and more fully, understanding it with increasing clarity, outgrowing whatever minor misconceptions you may once have cherished.

Your job is to study and ponder the truth you have, lost in wonder and worship, overwhelmed by the goodness of God and the glory of the Gospel, overwhelmed as Tintoretto was when he tried with all his genius to do a picture of the ocean only to throw down his brushes and cry, "It keeps growing greater. Nobody can paint it."

That is your job: to appropriate more and more fully the truth you already possess. You come to the task as a Christian committed and convinced. You do not come with complete neutrality and cool detachment analyzing Scripture with the attitude of a zoologist who indifferent dissects a worm. Not in the least. You come as one who has first been to Calvary.

Since you are persuaded that Jesus is the full and final truth, you are willing to do what Paul exhorts, "Examine all things; hold fast to that which is good" (I Thess. 5:21).

Yes, the Lordship of Christ means that you must love Him with the top of your mind as well as the bottom of your heart. It means that you must pray with Frances Ridley Havergal:

> *Take my intellect and use*
> *Every power as Thou dost choose.*

But commitment to the truth is not enough. It may become simply an academic matter, an impersonal and painless subscription to a set of dogmas. But God wants more than that from you.

Listen to Jesus: "If any man will come after me, let him deny himself, take up his cross daily and follow me."

What It Means

This is not the mere lifting of a hand at an evangelistic service, not the painless signing of an orthodox confession. This is a daily bearing of whatever cross God may appoint. This and nothing less is God's command, the commitment of all you are and all you have and all you do to Jesus Christ.

What did it mean for the Apostle Paul to make Jesus the Lord of his life? That is what it meant. See him, for example, as he lies one day outside the city of Lystra under a heap of cutting stones. He has been left there for dead, and dead he nearly is. Watch him as he twitches in anguish. Watch him as he struggles slowly to his feet. Watch him as he wipes his eyes, blinded by blood and tears. Watch him as he stumbles down the road alone like a man half-drunk. This is Saul of Tarsus, once the brilliant young star of the Sanhedrin, once the protege of Gamaliel. And what is he doing here? He is living out his commitment to Jesus Christ.

Or see Paul as he clings to a broken spar out in the Mediterranean Sea. His ship has been wrecked, and a day and a night he has been drifting in the waves. His teeth are chattering. His hands are numb and blue, scarcely able to keep their grip on the splintered wood. His body is weary beyond weariness and he is hungry beyond hunger. His lips are cracked by the salt spray and his throat is parched and burning with thirst. He stares death in the face, the strangling death of drowning. And what is he doing here? He is living out his commitment to Jesus Christ.

Or see Paul as he stands at the window of a Roman prison. He is haggard, bent, and prematurely old, worn out by journeyings, hardships and sufferings. He stares wistfully through the bars, wondering how soon Timothy will arrive, Timothy to whom he has written, "Bring my cloak. And please hurry. Come before winter if you can." Why hurry? The prison is chill and damp; the nights are long and Paul's bones are wracked with rheumatic pain. Please hurry, Timothy. He had written that because Timothy, though he does not know it, is racing against the hour when an ax will fall and Paul's head will roll between the executioner's feet.

Ah, Paul, once the shining young star of the Sanhedrin, once the protege of Gamaliel, what are you doing here in Nero's jail, marked out to die? Is this how your sun will set, Paul? Look into those steadfast eyes. He need not answer. Those steadfast eyes answer eloquently for him: "I am living out my commitment to Jesus Christ."

Living Not Dying

Probably you will not have to endure what Paul endured. Probably you will not have to die for your faith. But death is not necessarily the supreme test of a man's commitment.

Dr. William Stekel, a noted psychiatrist, said: "The mark of the immature man is that he wants to die nobly for a cause, while the mature man wants to live humbly for one."

Are you willing to live humbly for Jesus Christ? Are you prepared to say as Paul did: "I am committed. My life belongs to Jesus Christ and He may do with it precisely as He pleases. I follow after, asking nothing except a chance to serve the Savior whom I love." Are you prepared to love God with all your heart and with all your mind and with all your life?

From *Eternity*, April 1960, 22–23.

Books That Helped Shape My Life

The Christian View of God and the World, James Orr, Eerdmans

As a young student struggling to reconcile faith and reason, wondering whether evangelicalism in the full blaze of scholarship and criticism could be vindicated as a convincing interpretation of existence, I read and reread James Orr's Christocentric vision of reality. Though not designed to be devotionally edifying, it exhilarated my spirit as it stretched my mind. It freed me from the haunting suspicion that belief in the gospel must be maintained by faith alone in defiance of learning and logic. It made me realize that the Christian has no rival when it comes to seeing life steadily and seeing it whole. I still regard Orr's book as a magnificent statement to which after all these years I can return with profit.

The Magic Mountain, Thomas Mann, Knopf

I first read this literary masterwork for a course I took at Rutgers University. It fascinated me. Later I spent much of a summer's spare time working my way through this slow-paced novel which unfolds panoramically the issues and options that confronted man in the early twentieth century and which confront man perennially. It offers no solutions but reveals starkly that without the gospel all culture and philosophy and experience reaches a self-destructive impasse. *The Magic Mountain* was a powerful piece of negative apologetics in my intellectual and spiritual pilgrimage: either ironic tragedy or redemptive grace.

Works of Love, Søren Kierkegaard, Harper

Introduced to the writings of this enigmatic genius during the travail of a protracted doctoral program, I came to prize his remarkable treatment of the major New Testament passages on love. In fact, for several years I made it my habit to read a few of its thought-packed, thought-provoking pages almost every day. Old texts, rather hackneyed because of familiarity with them, took on gripping freshness. I came to realize overwhelmingly the centrality and multidimensionality of love in biblical faith. My concept of Christianity, if not my practice of it, was permanently influenced by Kierkegaard's probing discussion of *agape.*

From *Eternity,* March 1972, 72.

The New Morality?

Unlike other creatures, human beings come equipped with a sense of ought. We undergo agonies of remorse and guilt; we find ourselves perplexed repeatedly over issues of right and wrong.

Why do we rationalize, whitewash our actions and seek psychotherapeutic relief from emotional tension? The stubborn fact must be admitted: Even when we repudiate morality, we are ineradicably moral.

Christianity has traditionally given a quite simple solution to this mare's-nest of problems. It has insisted that good is any action or attitude that conforms to the will of God; evil, accordingly, is any action or attitude that contradicts His will.

The logic undergirding this position is rather simple. God by nature is good. The will of God is dictated by His nature. Therefore whatever God wills is *ipso facto* good.

Recently ethicists within the Church have vigorously advocated a different view. Popularly known as "the new morality," it criticizes and challenges the traditional position. The name itself comes from *Honest to God,* a re-examination of Christian belief which Dr. John A. T. Robinson, an Anglican bishop, published in 1963. Chapter VI of that theological bombshell, entitled "The New Morality," argues that the old morality perverts the New Testament by teaching slavish obedience to a legalistic code rather than absolute loyalty to the uncodifiable demands of Christian love.

Robinson puts it, "In Christian ethics the only pure statement is the command to love. There is not a whole list of things which are 'sins' *per se.* St. Paul makes it as clear as Jesus—the various commandments are comprehended under the one command of love and based upon it. Apart from this there are no unbreakable rules."

Notice Robinson's conclusion: When rules get in the way of love, they ought to be broken; if love so requires, it is right to do what otherwise would be wrong.

It Is Right

Scripture is our infallible rule of faith and practice, yet we ourselves are not therefore endowed with infallibility either in ascertaining God's will or in obeying it. The simplest way of showing this is to turn to the ten commandments.

"Thou shalt not steal." How unambiguous that is. What about the refugee father whose children are starving and who has no means whatsoever of saving them from lingering death except to steal? At once ambiguity rears its head and threatens our absolutism.

So the new morality offers a corrective to the lopsidedness, the exaggeration, the self-righteous pride which is much too prevalent in the camp of the old morality.

In compelling the old morality to acknowledge the situational relativity of all laws except the law of love, the new morality has been a needed corrective.

It has forced all of us Biblical absolutists to realize again that the Christian ethic is an ethic of personal responsibility. Grace-enabled and Spirit-guided, the believer must reach his own decisions before God in order to practice obedient love. By underscoring this often-obscured fact, the new morality has challenged the old morality to a more realistic confrontation of the possible ambiguity and agony of ethical experience, especially among Christians.

And It Is Wrong

"The new morality is the true Christian morality," they claim. But is it? Is an ethic "genuinely Christian" if it teaches that God gives Himself in the Holy Spirit indiscriminately and equally to everybody no matter what an individual's faith-relationship to the cross?

In his *Theological Ethics* Helmut Thielicke, the noted University of Hamburg professor, focuses attention on what he calls boundary-situations, crises in which Christians are caught between two divine demands, both of which cannot be obeyed. What we must do is act *Christianly* in the boundary situation. Like conflict-torn Abraham, when he was commanded to offer up Isaac as a sacrifice, we must exercise faith, and we must exercise faith and trust for the simple reason that through Jesus Christ we are believers in God.

The Christian is aware that, as he makes his decision in some boundary situations, he becomes guilty. Though he acts as lovingly as possible, he knows that his act is nevertheless wrong. "He is willing to take this guilt upon himself not in the name of the tragics, but in the name of forgiveness."

Guilt and grace, sin and forgiveness—these are Christian realities and essentials which Thielicke magnifies in his handling of ethical dilemmas. The dialectic of guilt and grace in the experience of a conscientious Christian who in a boundary-situation realizes that, acting as lovingly as possible, he is nevertheless doing wrong.

Finally, love is central in this new morality. Yet nowhere are we told in detail what love *is.* It is this very deep confusion about the definition of love which makes the *new* morality virtually useless as a system of ethics. By what criteria does one know that he is acting in love? We are never told. And yet all of life is to be lived under the direction of this amorphous norm, a word without specific content which benignly blankets everything from Calvary to the latest issue of *True Story* magazine. . . .

Our problem is not so much perplexity regarding right and wrong as it is impotence, the dearth of desire and dynamic to do what we know we ought to do. . . . Prolonged reflection deepens our suspicion that the new morality is dangerously inadequate as a guide for conduct, wretchedly qualified to help human beings as they struggle with the tangles and tensions of their existence. . . .

The new morality is actually not quite so new as its propagandists claim, at least in their unguarded outbursts of enthusiasm. . . . All through the centuries, from Paul on down to modern times, Christian ethicists have taught that the law of love is the central and commanding principle of morality. . . . The new morality leaves us floundering in a semantic fog. In a desert of ambiguity it bids us to plot our course by the pursuit of tantalizing mirages. . . . Fundamentally the new morality is a species of impractical idealism built upon a defective view of human nature.

> From "The New Morality: What's Wrong with the New View of Right?" *His,* October 1967, and "The New Morality: the Right and Wrong of Sex," *His,* December 1967, 14.

A Theology of Interpersonal Relations

In his early days of teaching at Denver Conservative Baptist Seminary, Dr. Grounds taught a course in which he developed "a dynamic theory of personality." In the class he defined personality *theologically, philosophically, biophysically, and, most fully, psychologically. From this definition he turned to the question of basic "human needs" or the fundamental drives, urges, and impulses that clamor for satisfaction within the human breast. From this discussion he moved on to develop the whole idea of the self-image or distinctive behavior-pattern that human beings seem to reveal through their unique lifetimes. This, then, led to the discussion of interpersonal relations in their various social contexts of family, cliques, marriage, and work. Finally, he concluded with his theology of interpersonal relationships.*

God made man to live in love with Himself and his neighbor. A fellowship of love is therefore the goal of human life, a fellowship patterned after the community of eternal love within the Godhead. And love needs no higher teleology: it does not require any other end as its justification. It is an end in itself.

Made to live in love, man experiences self-fulfillment only as he achieves human relationships which give him a secure feeling of "at-one-ment." In such relationships he is understood, accepted, and valued. Apart from such relationships he exists in loneliness, insecurity, and frustration.

Hence love is vastly more then a matter of verbalization. Indeed, love can be expressed only in relational language. It is communicated by relationship not by verbalism or the use of words, though verbalism may nevertheless be necessary in order to explicate the love-relationship. By loving a person in the whole gamut of our vital interaction, we define love for him. More than that, we elicit a love from him.

This is what a mother continually does. Instead of attempting to teach love verbally, she defines that word relationally in her whole interaction with a child. The mere word has no meaning until experience packs it with content.

Because he is a sinner, man has a tendency to love things inordinately and use persons instrumentally. In so doing he not only hurts others but he also hurts himself. Made in love, he can experience self-fulfillment only as he lives in love. This means that he must love persons supremely and use things solely in order that person-love may be enhanced and augmented. Hence when he loves things inordinately and uses persons instrumentally in order to obtain more things for himself, he lives in frustration, estranged from his neighbor. And our human tragedy lies precisely at this point: everybody is guilty of loving things inordinately and using people instrumentally, and thus the tangle of estrangement becomes more and more knotted.

And why does everybody do this? Ignoring the key-factor of an historic fall when Adam in self-love disobeyed God, we may point out that everybody does this because he has undergone person-hurt. To some degree everybody has been misunderstood, rejected, and exploited; and often person-hurt has been inflicted by the very individuals from whom he might have expected love—even including his parents.

Now person-hurt cannot be healed by a heaping up of things. Person-hurt requires person-healing, the healing of a love which accepts, understands, and forgives. But no human being is sufficient to supply adequately the love which is needed to heal person-hurt. There are several reasons for this inability.

1. All of us have a need for healing love because all of us have undergone person-hurt. And person-hurt has created within all of us a sense of insecurity and self-concern which renders it impossible for us to give love with complete freedom and unselfishness.

2. Nobody can fully understand anybody else because of the blinding factors of finitude and sin. Struggle as we may to overcome these handicaps, we always condemn and reject people, regardless of how subtly this may be done.

3. If we do succeed in giving love to a neighbor rather generously, we suffer from unloving pride, and pride reintroduces the element of estrangement.

The Gospel of Jesus Christ alone can rescue us from this predicament. For what is the Gospel? It is a message of Person-healing for person-hurt. It tells of a Person who loved and loves us unconditionally with a love which is completely unselfish and which can give everything because it needs nothing. This love gathered into itself on Calvary's cross all of our sinful hate; it triumphed over our hate in the miracle of resurrection; and now as we believe the Gospel, it produces healing love in our lives by the power of the Holy Spirit who is Himself the Giver of Love.

Loving the World: Rightly or Wrongly

You see, worldliness is not essentially a matter of externalities and negatives. It is rather essentially a matter of motives and attitudes and values. We need to examine ourselves, then, asking whether our motivation is honestly to glorify God, sharing his grace and truth with a lost world, or whether our deepest motivation is to please men as we conform to evangelical traditions that have a very debatable biblical sanction.

We need to ask ourselves whether our attitudes, our deep-down attitudes, are honestly attitudes of love for God and love for the ungodly world God loves, or whether they are attitudes of coldness towards God and harsh, judgmental, uncaring indifference toward the unreached masses of humanity. Is it possible that deep inside we are not worried about what God thinks of us as long as we can kid our fellow Christians into thinking we are spiritual? We need to ask ourselves whether our values, our deep inner values, are honestly the values of the New Testament, or whether they are the values of American society—money, cars, clothes, comfort, security, success. Or are we indifferent deep down to earthly riches and concerned about God's concerns?

We need to ask ourselves whether as Christians who preach nonconformity to the world we may be blind to our own subtle worldliness, our sensualism, materialism, and egotism. We need to ask ourselves whether our churches, despite their codes of externalities and negatives, are worldly. We need to ask ourselves whether our relationship to the world is like that of our Lord Jesus Christ. How different he was from the worldly people of first-century Palestine—and twentieth-century America! Not that he was otherworldly, detached from the world. He was in the world, immersed in it for some 30 years, yet he was not of the world, never a captive of its motives, attitudes and values.

How different Jesus was! Different because he was totally God-centered and completely self forgetting; different because of his intense and steadfast fellowship with his father; different because he came into the world not to be served but to serve. He was, as we read in Hebrews, "holy, harmless, undefiled and separate from sinners," but he loved the world, taking delight in the beauty of flowers, the gracefulness of flying birds, the joyful innocence of "Children's faces looking up — holding wonder like a cup."

He was holy, yet he loved the world. Think of his unwearying compassion expressed so concisely in Peter's words, "He went about doing good" (Acts 10:38). Jesus was holy, yet he loved the world. Think of his courage in confronting and challenging evil. He was holy, yet he loved the world. Think of his refusal to be bound by legalistic taboos about Sabbath keeping. He was holy, yet he loved the world. Think of his willingness to share in weddings and feasts and to be labeled the friend of publicans and prostitutes. Jesus was holy, yet he loved the world. Think of the humility that prompted him to wash the feet of his disciples. Jesus was holy, yet he loved the world. Think of his optimistic faith in the divine redeemability of such social scum as thieves and robbers. He was holy, yet he loved the world with a love that cost him misunderstanding, hate, loneliness, and an agonizing death on a Roman cross.

If we evangelicals in the twentieth century are to be anything like Jesus, then our otherworldliness must be just as worldly as that of Jesus, who did not love the sinful structures and self-centered values of the world-system, but who did indeed love lost mankind in all of its pain and frustration and need. If we are to be holy as Jesus was holy, our lifestyle must be that of holy worldliness and worldly holiness, the lifestyle Charles Wesley celebrates:

Not in the tombs we pine to dwell,
Not in the dark monastic cell
By vows and grates confined.

Freely to all ourselves we give,
Constrained by Jesus' love we live
The servants of mankind.

From *Christianity Today*, April 4, 1980, 22.

The Compassion of Jesus

German philosopher Fredrich Nietzsche said that pity is a slave-morality fit only for weaklings. Lenin, the founding father of communism, insisted that his disciples be steel-like and ruthless. "You can't make an omelet," he told them, "without cracking a few eggs; neither can you have a successful revolution without cracking a few skulls." . . .

Pity and *sympathy* are, of course, words that we use every day. They express how we feel when we observe another person undergoing affliction of body, mind, or heart. We recall what was taking place within ourselves as we underwent some similar experience. In our imagination we spontaneously project ourselves into that person's situation, maybe involuntarily tightening our muscles, clenching our fists, drawing in a deep breath, even getting tearful.

If the shared experience is intense enough, we call it *empathy.* It's as if we somehow crawl inside the sufferer's skin, and the two of us merge into a sort of emotional oneness. Physically, of course, we remain two separate organic entities; yet we may become psychologically unified. In some cases that sense of togetherness may be intense and prolonged as when day and night a mother in-dwells the anguish of a seriously ill child. When we empathize, we are so identified with the other person that it's as if we are hearing with her ears, seeing with her eyes, resonating with her heart, and thinking with her mind.

Aroused by an encounter with need and distress, an empathic reaction elicits a heartfelt sense of concern. It is that identifying emotion that arises from the innermost center of our being. . . . By the exercise of focused attention, we achieve an insight different from the knowledge provided by logic or science. In the biblical sense of the word *know,* we experience a profound perception. We know with a sort of deep intimacy similar to that ultimate intimacy Adam had when he knew his wife Eve and they became one flesh (Gen. 4:1).

Jehovah God

The god of the philosophers is the Unmoved Mover that imparts motion to whatever exists. Untouched by our creaturely concerns, He (really It) is the inexhaustible source of energy for the throbbing dynamo of the cosmos. The god of human speculation is a god without heart. Absolutely perfect, that god exists in unruffled sameness for all eternity. That god has no emotions, since emotion involves a change from one state of feeling to another—from calmness to an upsurge of anger, for example. By definition, though, the god of the philosophers is like an icicle that never melts.

By contrast, Jehovah, the God of the Israelites, is not just a mind. He is not just thought—eternally thinking thought. The God of the Old Testament, and the New Testament too, while unchanging in His nature and purpose, is genuinely personal. Whenever the Bible talks about the true and loving God, it uses personal pronouns.

How, then, can we grasp what God is like? We take our own personhood as a clue to divine Personhood. We eliminate anything imperfect and magnify everything about God to an infinite degree. That helps us to try to understand the reality of God as he actually is in his flawless Personhood.

The Bible discloses that the one true and living God actually feels. He experiences a whole gamut of reactions that are similar to our own. But one of the emotions repeatedly attributed to Him is compassion. Scripture tells us that He is eternal, holy, just, all good, wise, powerful, and loving. And because He is loving, He is compassionate. That adjective points to a divine attribute that is like the trait we have in mind when we characterize a human as compassionate.

Eliminate God's compassion, and God is no longer God—the personal God who interacted with Abraham, Isaac, and Jacob. Eliminate compassion, and God is no longer the God who has experiences akin to our own states of joy, regret, grief, and merciful kindness. Eliminate compassion from God's nature, and Scripture must be rewritten, our understanding of the divine nature must be radically revised, and theology must be turned inside out. But compassion can't be eliminated. It must, instead, be given a place of honor among God's attributes. He is the caring God.

Jesus' Compassion

It follows, therefore, that if Jesus is the self-revelation of the God of the Old Testament, then compassion will be embodied in Him. And it is . . . Jesus, as compassion incarnate, made caring central in His ministry. He swept aside any legalistic distortions of, and any ethnic limitations on, the all-inclusive grace of the triune God. And caring is that compassionate neighbor-love that Paul in I Corinthians 13 declared to be the greatest of all virtue—one that our Savior and Master modeled perfectly.

During His years here on earth, our Lord went about doing good (Acts 10:38). His compassion was not inactive sentimentalism which, as Samuel Taylor Coleridge bitingly wrote, "Sighs for wretchedness but shuns the wretched." Whenever Jesus encountered a need in individuals or multitudes, His emotional reaction of intense concern motivated immediate action. He fed, healed, taught, calmed turbulent seas, cast out demons, and even raised the dead. In all He did and said, He set an example for His disciples to follow through the ages (I Pet. 2:21). They, like Jesus, were to be agents of compassion communicating by word and deed the message of God's redemptive grace. . . .

When Jesus challenged the mercy-stifling behavior of the religious hierarchy of His day, He chose a Samaritan as a model of God's own compassion—a Samaritan who had compassion on a victim of theft and violence (Lk. 10). Could He have more dramatically revealed that His own heart was beating as one with the heart of His Father?

Jesus never spurned the common people who gladly listened to Him (Mk. 12:37). The Jewish hierarchy looked down on the people contemptuously because they were religiously illiterate. They said, "This mob that knows nothing of the law — there is a curse on them" (Jn. 7:49). But instead Jesus, who was moved with compassion, taught the mob. He fed its members repeatedly. He healed their sick, and He freed those who were possessed by demons (Mk. 5:1-17; 8:1-10). . . .

His heart and His arms were open wide, as they still are, to the lowest, the least, and the lost (Lk. 15). . . . Concerned as He was about hunger, disease, and injustice, our Lord was concerned immeasurably more about people's relationship to God and their destiny in the world to come. . . . On the one hand, He would literally help restore sight, give comfort, and liberate those in bondage to destructive habits and addictive behavior. On the other hand, His ministry would be a spiritual one, enlightening the spiritually blind, liberating the spiritually shackled, comforting the spiritually guilt-ridden and distressed. . . . His supernatural acts of power and compassion would be dramatic vignettes of the very nature of the kingdom He had come to inaugurate. . . .

Jesus models and motivates sacrificial compassion. How, though, can we become conduits of His compassionate kindness? Let Henri Nouwen instruct us:

"When I pray for the endless needs of the millions, my soul expands and wants to embrace them all and bring them into the presence of God. But in the midst of that experience I realize that compassion is not mine but God's gift to me. I cannot embrace the world, but God can. I cannot pray, but God can pray in me. When God became as we are . . . He allowed us to enter into the intimacy of the divine life. He made it possible for us to share in God's infinite compassion." And by grace we not only share the experience of God's compassion. By His enabling grace we can become the conduits of that compassion, following in Christ's footsteps as did a host of our spiritual forbears. But if we indeed are copying Christ, as Paul urged in I Corinthians 11:1, our compassion will not be limited to bodily needs. It will have soul needs as its supreme priority.

> From Vernon Grounds, *The Compassion of Jesus,* abridged,
> a publication of Radio Bible Class Ministries, 1999.

Aging Bodies — Time-Immune Spirits
Observations of an Octogenarian

A plaque made by a creative friend hangs on the wall of our kitchen. It depicts a white-haired husband and wife sitting contentedly side by side on a Victorian swing. Underneath them are those familiar lines by Robert Browning:

> Grow old along with me;
> The best is yet to be.

But Browning was overly optimistic. The sunset of life, sometimes long and lingering, may be a time of health and happiness. It may, however, be the opposite—a time of debility, loneliness and despondency. In either case, it is a season of inevitable diminishment, a constrictive process.

For all members of the human family, if they survive past the biblically allotted three score years and ten, life diminishes *temporally* and *physically*. For many it brings constriction *spacially*, selling a cherished home and moving into a retirement community, an apartment, or a relative's house, and finally occupying a wheelchair or bed. For many, too, it spells constriction *financially*. And, again, for all it brings diminishment *relationally* as one's family circle is narrowed when friends, colleagues and neighbors become inaccessible or make their departure from this world.

Another poet, Robert Frost, has caught the poignancy and yet the challenge of this constrictive process. An ovenbird is perched on a New England stone wall with summer ended, autumn quickly passing, and winter approaching. Soon there will be no more warm sunshine; soon there will be freezing weather;soon there will be snow. Yet the ovenbird sits on that wall singing gallantly "as to make the most of a diminished thing."

That's the problem aging earthlings face. How can we make the most of a diminished thing? How can we, in the words of Psalm 92:14, still "bear fruit in old age"? How can we continue to be fresh and green like some verdant pine tree? How can we experience the constrictive process not simply with resignation but with courage, peace and hope? A vital Christian faith is the answer to such existential questions that sooner or later each of us must answer. A strong trust in God plus a meaningful relationship with him through personal trust in the gospel gives a soul-fortifying, anxiety-dispelling solution to Frost's query, "how to make the most of a diminished thing."

To start with, a vital Christian faith provides the comfort of an abiding Presence, the Friend who will never leave or forsake us, the invisible Immanuel who, though unseen, becomes more and more of a sensed Companion in life's process of diminishment. We may and will lose family and friends. We may be confined to some impersonal facility, cared for by strangers. Yet we need not feel lonely or abandoned because our heavenly Father has made an inviolable promise, "Do not fear, for I am with you; do not be dismayed, for

I am your God. I will strengthen you and help you; I will uphold you with my righteous right hand" (Isaiah 41:10).

Secondly, as we unblinkingly confront the possibility of aloneness, we need to be grateful that a vital Christian faith can (and often does!) provide a supportive community through the concern and devotion of one's spiritual fellowship. How crucial it is, then, for our churches to develop cadres of caregivers who understand the needs of older members and give them not only concrete helpfulness but also, and even more importantly, attention, gratitude, respect and patient love. (One prays that our churches will be characterized by a genuine *koinonia* whose members see one another, especially older sisters and brothers, as unique individuals to love and cherish.)

Thirdly, a vital Christian faith provides an unchanging awareness of self-worth. No doubt from a purely secular perspective one's value as a person grows less and less with the loss of productivity. Society may view the aged as deteriorating organisms, unproductive drones and costly burdens. But from a biblical perspective, the bedfast senescent has as much value as the crowd-applauded superstar. What is it, after all, that gives incalculable worth to any human being whether young or old, robustly healthy or sick and infirm? The foundational fact of personhood gives the answer: each of us is made in God's image. More than that, every believer is God's spiritual child by virtue of a second birth, and every believer is his treasured possession as Malachi 3:17 attests. And "the gnawing tooth of time" is unable to eat away at these value-reassuring truths. Because they don't suffer diminishment, one's biblically grounded self-worth likewise doesn't diminish.

Fourth, a vital Christian faith provides opportunities for continued usefulness. Some older people can help perform tasks in church and community that are in keeping with their strength and ability. We must never belittle the ministry our Savior praised—the giving of a cup of water in his name. When participation in even such tasks is impossible, other avenues of service are still open— for example, the great ministry of prayer which enables an immobilized intercessor to reach redemptively around the globe. And what about the great ministry of witness to those within one's relational orbit—nurses, visitors, grandchildren? Undergirding these ministries is the measureless impact of a challenging example, grace under pressure, chronic (!) cheerfulness, uncomplaining patience, steadfast trust and outreaching love.

Finally, in addition to these rich spiritual resources that a vital Christian faith provides, there is the blessing of a horizon-expanding hope. Yes, an aging person may be spatially constricted, rarely traveling anywhere, perhaps no longer capable of walking outside or even indoors, maybe confined to a room or a chair or a bed. But by faith the prospect of eternal life keeps pushing horizons back and back, horizons that are as unbounded as God's heaven.

If a vital Christian faith provides resources like these for making the most of life as it moves toward its end, wisdom dictates that a vital faith ought to be cultivated long before we begin to descend the westering slope of our pilgrimage.

As an octogenarian, I once in a while recall Erik Erikson's eight stages of our pilgrimage through time. According to that very eminent Harvard psychologist, if we survive the first seven phases of life development, we reach the last level which he calls not senescence but (tactfully) mature age. If we have genuinely matured, we can look back with affirmation and gratitude. But if we have failed to do more than merely endure as organisms, and thus lack a core of integrity, we find ourselves filled with disgust and despair. No opportunity for a rerun is available (though, to be sure, until the final few seconds before our departure, there is by God's grace the opportunity for repentance and rebirth as there was for the thief who on Calvary entreated mercy).

So here I am now at stage eight able, only because of God's controlling and guiding providence, to look back with gratitude and affirmation. In spite of my failures, my stumblings, my sometimes sinful disobedience, I can testify with Shakespeare:

There's a divinity that shapes our ends
Rough-hew them as we will.

Not only that: solely because of Christ's sacrifice and the Spirit's work within my heart and witness through the inscripturated Word, solely because of my faith, I can look ahead with confidence and serenity, as well as with curiosity, applying Browning's words to my future beyond this life's eighth stage, "The best is yet to be."

From *Focal Point*, Spring 1995, 6–7.

Selected Poetry
by Vernon Grounds

Afternoon in October

For this day's glory, God above,
My heart rejoices.
My breath, enraptured, mingles with
The woodland's voices
In ecstatic prayer.

Of maple's flame and chestnut's amber
Sing I, O God.
A copse's colored aisles and nave
From Thine abode;
Thou broodest there.

For sight of mounts bedizened
Humbly I praise.
Upon their slopes, reflected now,
Thy grandeur plays.
I hush; I stare.

Today we delve into the seas;
We penetrate the stratosphere;
We uproot mountains ruthlessly;
We smash the hills and atoms here.

And notwithstanding finite bonds
And limits to our mastery,
Without conceit we claim the right
To rank ourselves, O God, with Thee.

Nocturne

I hear a thrush at eventide
Sing his ethereal vesper hymn,
Pour out his tranquil psalm at dusk
In dark woods growing still more dim.

I hear a thrush at eventide,
And beauty stabs my heart like pain.
I linger where the shadows are
To hear God speak to me again.

Rationale

This hubbub's beyond comprehending,
This protoplasmic ebb and flow,
This turbulence unending.

This flux of doing and regretting,
This cosmic scene and comic show
Of lusting and begetting.

This froth of gaiety and grieving
Becomes unbearable below
Without a blind believing.

WRITTEN AT RUTGERS UNIVERSITY, 1937

To One Who Worships at a Different Shrine

My dubious friend:
If moonlight bronze upon the beach
More forcibly than fluent speech
Convinces you that God exists
From argument my tongue desists;
And if you glimpse eternity

In stars ablaze above the sea,
In planets spinning overhead,
My words are better left unsaid;
And if you make a sacrament
Of rainbows over hilltops bent,
Of mountains pregnant with the dawn,
Of shadows misty twilights spawn,
Of stubbled cornfields rimed with frost,
Upon deaf ears my words are lost,
Wherefore I end.

RUTGERS, 1937

Autumn Matins in the Rockies

If in after years my eyes
Must blind become or dim,
Ah, may I still see sunup, Lord,
From this high canyon's rim;

And aspen making mountain slopes
A gleaming surge of gold,
A glory which the guardian pines
In changeless green enfold;

And all these sky-upbearing peaks
With day-dawn pink aglow,
Like kings who proudly wrap themselves
In robes of ermine snow;

And deep, deep down a shimmering streak,
The river's twisting track.
Ah, God, this range can lightly bear
A continent on its back!

So paint upon my mind, I pray,
This cloudless, shining morn
That old and faraway I still
Can thank Thee I was born.

Age Speaks to Youth

Say not that in my yesterdays
The better part of life is left,
Speak not the words that make me fear
And leave my heart bereft

Say not that age is judged by years,
For snow is heaped upon my brow;
Speak not of me as though near death—
I live more fully now.

At dawn I wake with heart alert
And often shake with joy to see
A line of flame upon a hill,
Or icy cobwebs on a tree.

At night I lie awake to watch
Orion sweep across the sky,
Or wait until the gold moon wanes
And softly slips away to die.

Say not that threescore years and ten
Mark me as having played my part.
Speak not of me as being old
When youth is in my heart.

Notes

Preface

1. From "My Testimony," a mimeographed copy of Dr. Grounds's remarks at his retirement from Denver Seminary, archived in the Denver Seminary Carey S. Thomas Library.

Chapter One: Finding the Way

1. "My Testimony," Carey S. Thomas Library.

2. Many of the details about Vernon Grounds's childhood and family background come from personal interviews and, most helpfully, from Vernon's daughter, Barbara Owen, who for some time has been compiling the Grounds family history. Some information about his childhood is also found in Gordon Lewis's biographical sketch, "Vernon Grounds: Gifted Man for Others," in *Christian Freedom: Essays in Honor of Vernon C. Grounds*, ed. Kenneth W. M. Wozniak and Stanley J. Grenz (Lanham, Md.: University Press of America, 1986), 15–26.

3. Vernon wrote of his pacifism at Rutgers in *Perspectives on Peacemaking: Biblical Options in the Nuclear Age* (Ventura, Calif.: Regal Books, 1984), chapter 8.

4. From two autobiographical pieces Vernon wrote at the time, recorded in the family history by Barbara Owen.

5. Vernon Grounds, "Books That Helped Shape My Life," *Eternity* (March 1972): 72.

Chapter Two: The Reason for Our Hope

1. For the interpretation of fundamentalism in this chapter I have drawn from George Marsden, *Fundamentalism and American Culture* (New York: Oxford University Press, 1980) and Joel Carpenter, *Revive Us*

Again: The Reawakening of American Fundamentalism (New York: Oxford University Press, 1997).

2. Gordon Langley Hall, *The Sawdust Trail* (Philadelphia: Macrae Smith, 1964), 143.

3. At the time of Dr. Grounds's retirement from Denver Seminary, ninety-two-year-old Matilda Saunders recalled a typical gospel service led by the young "ambassadors of Christ." The milk bottle quote is from her letter of tribute sent to Dr. Grounds upon his retirement. These hundreds of letters are bound under the title "In Tribute: Dr. Vernon C. Grounds" and are archived in the Carey S. Thomas Library at Denver Seminary.

4. The story of Vernon's first days at Faith Seminary are from his remarks as keynote speaker at the Harvey Cedars Bible Conference, Harvey Cedars, N.J., October 16–18, 2000, hosted by the Fellowship of Faith Seminary Alumni.

5. From "My Personal Journey Through Life Decisions," an address given at the ELS National Envisioning Conference, Detroit, Mich., September 1974, 14–15.

6. Vernon Grounds, *The Reason for Our Hope* (Chicago: Moody Press, 1945), 30–35.

Chapter Three: A Fork in the Road

1. Many details in this chapter come from personal interviews with Vernon Grounds and with Gordon Lewis, who grew up in Johnson City and succeeded Vernon at the Baptist Bible Seminary.

2. The story about Hank Beukema and his girlfriend Peggie, later his wife, came from a letter they sent to me while writing this book.

3. The story about John Warwick Montgomery is in his letter to Dr. Grounds at his retirement, found in "In Tribute."

4. The correspondence between Vernon Grounds and Edward John Carnell is in the Grounds correspondence in the Carey S. Thomas Library archives, as is the correspondence about the move to Denver.

5. Ernest Sartorius, *The Doctrine of Divine Love* (Edinburgh: T & T Clark, 1884), 89.

6. Søren Kierkegaard, *A Kierkegaard Anthology*, ed. Robert Bretall, (New York: Modern Library, 1946), 418–26.

7. The details about Vernon's conversation with Dr. Jackson came from an interview with Dr. Grounds in April 2001.

Chapter Four: In Search of Camelot

1. The biographical material about Frederick G. Bonfils is found in Gene Fowler, *Timberline* (New York: Ballantine Books, 1960).

2. The larger story of the "militant" and "moderate" struggle in Conservative Baptist circles can be found in Bruce Shelley, *A History of Conservative Baptists* (Wheaton, Ill.: Conservative Baptist Press, 1981). Many details about the Colorado Baptists may be found in Paul Bordon, "The Application of Burton Clark's Organizational Saga to an Analysis of Denver Seminary" (Ph.D. diss., University of Denver, 1990).

3. The story of the young seminary's internal conflicts in 1951 is based on correspondence and board minutes for 1951 (Carey S. Thomas Library archives), on personal interviews with Vernon Grounds and Douglas Birk in the early months of 2001, and upon Bordon's dissertation.

4. This letter is in Vernon Grounds's correspondence in the Carey S. Thomas Library archives.

5. The story of the drugstore conversation between Vernon Grounds and Douglas Birk is from an interview with Douglas Birk.

Chapter Five: Winds of Controversy

1. The Russell Pavy story is in his letter in "In Tribute."

2. The institutional history of Denver Seminary, including the "troika" administration, is found in Paul Bordon, "Application of Burton Clark's Organizational Saga to an Analysis of Denver Seminary."

3. Vernon Grounds, "Coincidence or Providence," *My Most Memorable Encounter with God*, ed. David Enlow (Wheaton, Ill.: Tyndale, 1977), 67–79.

4. Ray McLaughlin's quote comes from his letter in "In Tribute."

5. "Is Love in the Fundamentalist Creed?" *Eternity* (June 1954): 13–14, 41–42.

6. Vernon Grounds gave his report of the 1956 flood in his letter to friends, October 30, 1956. The *Denver Post* also reported the event in the first week of July, complete with Dr. Grounds's picture on the front page.

7. "The Nature of Fundamentalism," *Eternity* (February 1956): 12–13, 42–43.

8. Vernon Grounds, "Fellowship Is Not for Porcupines," *Eternity* (August 1959): 18–20, 46–47.

9. The actions and charges leading to the Beth Eden meeting in 1962 are reported in the May and October 1962 issues of the *Baptist Missionary-Evangelist*, the publication of the Conservative Baptist Association of Colorado at the time. These are found in the Carey S. Thomas Library archives.

The Conservative Baptist critics were following the lead of three prominent critics of Billy Graham's cooperative evangelism: Rev. Carl McIntire in New Jersey, whom Vernon had met at Faith Seminary; evangelist Bob Jones Jr., who headed Bob Jones University in South Carolina; and evangelist John R. Rice in Murfreesboro, Tennessee. All three had publications generating a steady stream of warnings against the growing apostasy of the last days.

10. The two papers Dr. Grounds wrote for the Beth Eden meeting can be found in Paul Bordon, "The Application of Burton Clark's Organizational Saga to an Analysis of Denver Seminary," Appendix D. Vernon's report to the alumni is in his 1962 Christmas letter.

11. The "loving response" quotation is from Robert Carlan's letter, "In Tribute."

Chapter Six: A Chance to Serve

1. The story about the Meltons' entertaining Dr. Grounds comes from their letter to him at his retirement, "In Tribute."

2. The account of the injuries from the car accident is from Vernon's 1963 Christmas letter.

3. Gordon Lewis, "Vernon Grounds: A Gifted Man for Others," in *Christian Freedom: Essays in Honor of Vernon C. Grounds*, ed. Kenneth W. M. Wozniak and Stanley J. Grene (Lanham, Md.: University Press of America, 1986).

4. Vernon Grounds, *Radical Commitment* (Portland, Ore: Multnomah Press, 1984), 66.

5. From Barbara Owen's speech at Downing House, July 17, 1999, at a celebration of Vernon and Ann's eighty-fifth birthdays and their sixtieth wedding anniversary.

6. The account of the Drew oral exam is in Vernon's letter to friends, June 1960, and from a personal interview.

7. After his father's death, Vernon's mother lived with his sister, Mildred Kievit, in Clifton, New Jersey, until she had to be placed in care facilities. She died June 15, 1961.

8. The account of the visit to the Goff home is from a personal interview with Nathan Goff, February 2001.

Chapter Seven: The With'ring Leaves of Time

1. The reflections from the Canadian Keswick Conference are found in Dr. Grounds's letter to the "far-flung CBTS family," August 1969.

2. The James Reston, Gunnar Myrdal, and John Gardner quotes, as well as many details of the 1960s, can be found in the *World Book Year Books* for 1967, 1968.

3. The story of the Jesus people is well-told in Ronald M. Enroth, Edward E. Ericson Jr., and C. Breckinridge Peters, *The Jesus People: Old Time Religion in the Age of Aquarius* (Grand Rapids, Mich.: William B. Eerdmans, 1972).

4. The series of lectures on the Christian's social responsibilities were published as *Evangelicalism and Social Responsibly* (Scottdale, Pa.: Herald Press, 1969).

5. The series on love and the New Morality appeared in issues of *HIS* magazine for April, May, October, November, and December 1967.

Chapter Eight: Lifting Up the Fallen

1. The story of the young couple from Wyoming is among the letters sent to Dr. Grounds at his retirement, "In Tribute," Carey S. Thomas Library archives.

2. The story about the lawyer is from a letter sent to me during the writing of this book. He asked that his name not be used.

3. The former student's comments are found in the "In Tribute" volume.

4. The series of sermons in *The National Voice*, published during 1953, can be found in the Carey S. Library.

5. The young intern story is found in "In Tribute."

6. The story about the woman's court appearance is from a letter sent to me during the writing of this book. She asked that her name not be used.

7. The quotations from *The Gospel and Emotional Problems* are from pages 46–48, 76. and 102. Vernon dedicated the book to David and Charlotte Cauwels, "whose friendship and generosity have through the years illuminated my understanding of the text, 'Faith works by love.'"

In the late 1960s Vernon had delivered another lecture, "Christian Perspectives on Mental Illness," in which he presented his Christian case for the ministry of counseling. "The Gospel," he said, "does not shrink back from any sordid tangle of psyche or soul. The Gospel, which affirms that God loves man as he is, may rightly claim to be a humanism. . . . As I see it, any rival interpretation is at best a truncated humanism; it ignores either the heights or the abysses in man's nature." And as a genuine humanism, he said, Christianity is properly humanitarian. "The Lord Jesus" he recalled, "went about doing good. He healed all who were oppressed of the devil. He commissioned His disciples to carry on a therapeutic ministry as He Himself had done."

So any Christian who takes seriously the mandate of His Master must have a concern "about everything which shrivels human existence, everything which prevents his neighbor from enjoying freedom and fulfillment by faith, everything which hinders any fellow-creature from entering into the life and likeness of God."

Mental health and healing, in particular, demand the assurance of love and the power to love. "From Freud on down through virtually every school of post-Freudian psychology the need of this twofold experience of love has been recognized either explicitly or implicitly. A human being must know that he is the object of a love which gives him both security and status; he must, in addition, function as the subject of an outgoing love. Unless this is his experience, an individual may fall victim to a self-debilitating, neighbor-destroying hate that can end in neurosis."

For any therapist, then, a major problem is "how to siphon off hate and how to substitute *agape* for that destructiveness in human nature to which a picturesque label has been attached, the *thanatos* or death drive. I fail to see any solution for this problem apart from Christianity. What is the Gospel if not the good news that man, a pinpoint of protoplasm on a pigmy planet, in a measureless universe, is nevertheless the object of a cosmic love which gives him ultimate security and eternal status?"

This lecture is among the Grounds articles filed in the Carey S. Thomas Library archives.

Chapter Nine: Gaining New Heights

1. The accounts of the Berlin and Lausanne congresses are found in William Martin, *A Prophet with Honor, The Billy Graham Story* (New York: William Morrow, 1991). Some details also appear in Carl F. H. Henry, *Confessions of a Theologian* (Waco, Tex.: Word Books, 1986).

2. The experiences of Dr. Grounds at Berlin are from his 1966 Christmas letter.

3. The report of the Enabling Conference on the Evangelistic Life Style is in Dr. Grounds's 1974 Christmas letter.

4. The reports of seminary events are drawn from 1970s issues of the *Seminarian*.

5. Dr. Grounds's correspondence with Robert Dugan is in his correspondence files, Carey S. Thomas Library archives.

Chapter Ten: New Perspectives

1. Dr. Grounds's report to the accreditation self-study report is in Paul Bordon, "Application of Burton Clark's Organizational Saga to an Analysis of Denver Seminary."

2. Memo to faculty and staff declaring Vernon's intention to stay until 1980 is in his correspondence files, Carey S. Thomas Library archives.

3. Dr. Grounds's feelings about retirement were expressed in his 1979 Christmas letter.

4. The farewell talk given at the chapel service in 1979 is with his papers in the Carey S. Thomas Library.

5. Dr. Grounds's letter to the Dugans is in his file of correspondence to them, Carey S. Thomas Library.

6. The retirement events are reported in the 1979 issues of the *Seminarian* and in Vernon's 1979 and 1980 Christmas letters.

7. The sermon preached at the Bear Creek Presbyterian Church appears in Vernon Grounds, *Radical Commitment* (Portland, Ore.: Multnomah Press, 1984), 38–46.

8. Ibid., 41–42.

Chapter Eleven: The Road's Last Turn

1. "People Who Touch People Are the Loveliest People in the World" *Focal Point*, October-December 1982.

2. William Martin, *A Prophet with Honor: The Billy Graham Story* (New York: HarperTrade, 1992), 472–73.

3. Letter to Senator Armstrong is in Vernon's correspondence, Carey S. Thomas Library archives.

4. The Pasadena Conference was reported by Kenneth A. Briggs in the *New York Times,* Sunday, May 29, 1983, and interpreted by David A. Hoekema in "Evangelicals Confront the Arms Race," *The Reformed Journal* 33, no. 8 (August 1983). I have used Hoekema's descriptions of the various positions in this chapter.

5. Vernon's quotations from "A Peace Lover's Pilgrimage" can be found in *Perspectives on Peacemaking*, ed. John A. Bernbaum, (Ventura, Calif.: Regal Books, 1984), 171, 173.

6. Vernon Grounds, "Peacemaking: Our Number One Problem," *ESA Update* (March 1987): 3–4.

7. Jim Oraker's description of Vernon Grounds is found in "Hospitality of the Spirit." *Inside the Mission* 8, no. 3 (December 1988).

8. Dr. Grounds has served on a number of boards, including ESA, Jews for Jesus, and, in recent years, RBC Ministries. The devotional writing that Dr. Grounds mentioned in his summary of activities is primarily for the *Our Daily Bread* devotional booklet published by RBC Ministries.

9. In recent years, Vernon has received many accolades from those he has influenced during his lifetime. At the Gordon College commencement in May 2002, the doctoral honoree was Dr. Armand M. Nicholi Jr., professor of psychiatry at Harvard University and author of the critically acclaimed book, *The Question of God: C. S. Lewis and Sigmund Freud Debate God, Love, Sex, and the Meaning of Life.* As a surprise to Dr. Nicholi, Vernon joined the faculty procession and was announced during the introduction of the degree recipient. "You can't be around Dr. Nicholi very long before he mentions a person who was a very significant mentor in his life, Dr. Vernon Grounds, Chancellor of Denver Seminary in Colorado. We surprised Dr. Nicholi today by flying Dr. Grounds to campus . . . to lead in a prayer of dedication."

When Dr. Nicholi offered his own remarks, following the conferral of the honorary Doctor of Humane Letters Degree, he expanded on this: "Dr. Grounds . . . influenced my whole career. As a young teenager, growing up in a very small town in upstate New York, I met Dr. Grounds in a church I began attending soon after I had come to a personal faith. . . . He took an interest in me. He suggested I go to college. Most young people went to work in the IBM and shoe factories, where their parents worked. Once I decided on college, he suggested I become a doctor. He said we needed more good doctors who were men of faith. He wrote to me often at college—and several times suggested I consider the field of psychiatry. Once I entered psychiatry, he continued to write often. . . . He sent me books and letters and quietly and patiently encouraged me—over more than thirty years. He played a role in the courses I ended up teaching—the courses led to my being invited to give the Nobel Lectures at Harvard, the lectures, in turn, finally led to this book."

(From "Honorary Degree Commencement 2002," text of introduction by Dr. Judson Carlberg, president of Gordon College, at Gordon College, South Hamilton, Massachusetts, May 2002. Dr. Carlberg is a graduate of Denver Seminary. And from "Remarks at the Gordon College Commencement, May 2002" by Dr. Armand M. Nicholi Jr.).

10. The 2001 Commencement address is on audiotape in the Carey S. Thomas Library archives.

A Select Bibliography

of the Works of Vernon C. Grounds

Books

The Reason for Our Hope. Chicago: Moody Press, 1945.

Evangelicalism and Social Responsibility. Scottdale, Pa.: Herald Press, 1969.

What a Church Owes Its Pastor; What a Pastor Owes His Church. Wheaton, Ill.: Conservative Baptist Press.

Revolution and the Christian Faith. Philadelphia: J. B. Lippincott, 1971.

Emotional Problems and the Gospel. Grand Rapids, Mich.: Zondervan Publishing House, 1976.

Radical Commitment: Getting Serious About Christian Growth. Portland, Ore.: Multnomah Press, 1984.

Articles and Contributions to Published Works

"Christian Love and Church Problems." *National Voice of Conservative Baptists* (January 1953): 4–5, 20–21.

"The Love That Never Lets Us Go." *National Voice of Conservative Baptists* (February 1953): 4–5, 24.

"The Love That Works by Faith." *National Voice of Conservative Baptists* (April 1953): 4–5, 32–34.

"The Dimensions of God's Love." *National Voice of Conservative Baptists* (May 1953): 3, 24–25.

"The Dynamics of God's Love." *National Voice of Conservative Baptists* (June 1953): 2–3, 29–30, 36.

"The Lineaments of Love." *National Voice of Conservative Baptists* (August 1953): 6–7, 14–15.

"Faith in the Father's Love." *National Voice of Conservative Baptists* (September 1953): 6–7, 27–30.

"The Demonstration of God's Love." *National Voice of Conservative Baptists* (October 1953): 9, 25–28, 30.

"The Lash of Love." *National Voice of Conservative Baptists* (November 1953): 8, 26–29.

"Is Love in the Fundamentalist Creed?" *Eternity* 5, no. 6 (June 1954): 13–14, 41.

"How Pursuit Becomes Possession." *Eternity* 6, no. 7 (July 1955): 8–9, 46–47.

"Modern Psychology and the Gospel." Part 1. *Eternity* 6, no. 4 (April 1955): 12–13, 54–56.

"Modern Psychology and the Gospel." Part 2. *Eternity* 6, no. 5 (May 1955): 18–19, 36–39.

"The Nature of Evangelicalism." *Eternity* 7, no. 2 (February 1956): 12–13, 42–43.

"Has Freud Anything for Christians?" *Eternity* 7, no. 7 (July 1956): 8–9, 46–48.

"A Revolutionary Gospel." *Eternity* 7, no. 9 (September 1956): 12–13, 40–43.

"If Man Ever Reaches Mars." *Eternity* 7, no. 11 (November 1956): 6–7, 52–56.

"Making Jesus Master." *Eternity* 7, no. 12 (December 1956): 14–15, 45–48.

"The Theologian and the Preacher." *Christianity Today* 2, no. 18 (June 9, 1958): 15–18.

"Test Your Salvation." *Eternity* 9, no. 2 (February 1958): 20–21, 46–47.

"Do All Things Really Work Together for Good?" *Eternity* 9, no. 8 (August 1958): 15–17, 38.

"The Possible You." *Eternity* 10, no. 2 (February 1959): 13–15.

"Fellowship Is Not for Porcupines." *Eternity* 10, no. 8 (August 1959): 18–20, 46–47.

"Incarnation." *Eternity* 10, no. 12 (December 1959): 9, 37.

"Atonement," "Miracle," "Suicide." In *Baker's Dictionary of Theology,* edited by Everett F. Harrison. Grand Rapids, Mich.: Baker Book House, 1960.

"Check Up on Your Commitment." *Eternity* 11, no. 3 (April 1960): 22–23.

"The Baptists and Religious Liberty." *Christian Heritage* 22, no. 6 (June 1961): 10–15, 32.

"Fundamentalism Needs a Reformation." *Eternity* 12, no. 12 (December 1961): 21–23.

"The Christian and Human Government." *Christian Heritage* 23, no. 6 (June 1962): 22–25.

"Is Christian Education Honest?" *Eternity* 13, no. 9 (September 1962): 29–31, 38.

"Commandments, Ten," "Prayer," "Resurrection of Jesus Christ," "Stoicism," "Temptation," "Virgin Birth." In *The Zondervan Pictorial Bible Dictionary,* 5 vols., edited by Merrill C. Tenney. Grand Rapids, Mich.: Zondervan Publishing House, 1963.

"We Deny the Charges!" *Christian Heritage* 24, no. 1 (January 1963): 6–9, 32.

"The Biblical Basis of Christian Unity." *United Evangelical Action* 22, no. 8 (October 1963): 20–21, 24–25.

"Building Walls Up or Breaking Walls Down." *Christian Heritage* 25, no. 3 (March 1964): 12–15, 31.

"Church and State: A Baptist Perspective." *Christian Heritage* 25, no. 4 (April 1964): 18–19, 29–31.

"Miracle or Mirage." *Christian Heritage* 25, no. 7 (September 1964): 22–24.

"Roman Catholicism in the Sixties." Part 1. *Christian Heritage* 25, no. 8 (October 1964): 8–11.

"Roman Catholicism in the Sixties." Part 2. *Christian Heritage* 25, no. 9 (November 1964): 14–18.

"The Biblical Renaissance in Roman Catholicism." *Christian Heritage* 25, no. 10 (December 1964): 10–13, 25.

"Love: Poetry or Power." *Eternity* 15, no. 9 (September 1964): 23–26.

"The Ghetto and the Trumpet Call." *United Evangelical Action* 23, no. 4 (June 1964): 8–10, 16.

"The Word of God and Protestant-Catholic Reunion." *Christian Heritage* 26, no. 1 (January 1965): 6–9, 28–29, 32.

"Perspective on the Papacy at the Midpoint of the 1960s." *Christian Heritage* 26, no. 2 (February 1965): 12–15.

"Have the Issues Really Changed?" *Christian Heritage* 26, no. 3 (March 1965): 14–15, 25, 28.

"Rome's Tempest in Theology." *Christian Heritage* 26, no. 4 (April 1965): 6–7, 13–15.

"The Ironical Paradox in Catholic Theology." *Christian Heritage* 26, no. 5 (May 1965): 6–7, 31–32.

"The Roman Catholic Church and Contraception." *Christian Heritage* 26, no. 6 (June 1965): 6–9.

"A Crisis in Authority." *Christian Heritage* 26, no. 7 (September 1965): 10–13, 31.

"A Ghost Haunts the Council." *Christian Heritage* 26, no. 8 (October 1965): 6–9, 25.

"The Conflict Within Catholicism." Part 1. *Christian Heritage* 26, no. 9 (November 1965): 12–15, 18.

"The Conflict Within Catholicism." Part 2. *Christian Heritage* 26, no. 10 (December 1965): 6–9.

"The Graveyard Theology: A Brief Introduction to Brash Infidelity." In *Is God "Dead"?* A symposium with chapters contributed by Billy Graham, Bernard Ramm, Vernon C. Grounds, David Hubbard, 9–56. Grand Rapids, Mich.: Zondervan Publishing House, 1966.

"The Essential Unity." *Christian Heritage* 27, no.1 (January 1966): 16–18.

"Is Objective Analysis Possible?" *Christian Heritage* 27, no. 2 (February 1966): 8–10.

"Post-Conciliar Protestant-Catholic Relationships." *Christian Heritage* 27, no. 3 (March 1966): 6, 8, 32.

"The Ark and the Rowboat." *Christian Heritage* 27, no. 4 (April 1966): 16–19, 32.

"The Church or the Churches?" *Christian Heritage* 27, no. 5 (May 1966): 9–11, 21.

"The Crisis in Authority." *Christian Heritage* 27, no. 6 (June 1966): 10–12, 29–30.

"The Shaky Case for Missions." *Christian Heritage* 27, no. 8 (October 1966): 26–28.

"Seven Steps to Survival." *Christian Heritage* 27, no. 9 (November 1966): 22–24.

"Building on the Bible: A Seminary President's View of God's Infallible Word." *Christianity Today* 11, no. 4 (November 25, 1966): 9–10, 12.

"The Peril of Pious Idolatry." *Eternity* 17, no. 6 (June 1966): 24–26, 34.

"Roadblocks to Ecumenicity." *Christian Heritage* 28, no. 1 (January 1967): 22–23, 26.

"The Predicament of Post-Conciliar Catholicism." *Christian Heritage* 28, no. 2 (February 1967): 22–25.

"Who Needs the Bible? A Protestant View." *Christian Heritage* 28, no. 3 (March 1967): 11–12, 23–25, 32.

"Post-Biblical Means Post-Christian." Part 1. *Christian Heritage* 28, no. 4 (April 1967): 10–12, 32.

"Post-Biblical Means Post-Christian." Part 2. *Christian Heritage* 28, no. 5 (May 1967): 24–25, 29, 32.

"Rebaptism and Protestant Converts to Catholicism." *Christian Heritage* 28, no. 8 (October 1967): 26–28, 31.

"The Virgin's Place." *Christian Heritage* 28, no. 9 (November 1967): 10–12.

"Dogmas That Divide." *Christian Heritage* 28, no.10 (December 1967): 8–12.

"The New Morality: the Problem." *HIS* 27, no. 7 (April 1967): 14–16, 21–22.

"The New Morality: What's Right with the New View of Wrong." *HIS* 27, no. 8 (May 1967): 6–10.

"The New Morality: What's Wrong with the New View of Right." Part 1. *HIS* 28, no. 1 (October 1967): 6–9.

"The New Morality: What's Wrong with the New View of Right." Part 2. *HIS* 28, no. 2 (November 1967): 15–16, 23–27.

"The New Morality: The Right and Wrong of Sex." Part 1. *HIS* 28, no. 3 (December 1967): 12–16, 28–30.

"Sacramental Absurdities." *Christian Heritage* 29, no. 1 (January 1968): 22–25, 32.

"Roadblock: Mystery of the Mass." *Christian Heritage* 29, no. 2 (February 1968): 6–9.

"Dogmas That Divide: 'Sacramental Grace.'" *Christian Heritage* 29, no. 3 (March 1968): 26–27, 30.

"Scandalized!" *Christian Heritage* 29, no. 4 (April 1968): 6–7, 22–23.

"How Deep the Chasm!" *Christian Heritage* 29, no. 5 (May 1968): 6–7, 28–29.

"We Are 'Other Christs.'" *Christian Heritage* 29, no. 6 (June 1968): 22–23, 30–31.

"Most Unusual Situation." *Christian Heritage* 29, no. 7 (September 1968): 26–28.

"A Gesture of Fellowship?" *Christian Heritage* 29, no. 8 (October 1968): 28–29, 32.

"A Case of Miscarriage." *Christian Heritage* 29, no. 9 (November 1968): 22–25.

"The Issue Is Infallibility." *Christian Heritage* 29, no. 10 (December 1968): 24–25, 31.

"How Can We Face God?" *Eternity* 18, no. 9 (August 1968): 22–23, 40.

"The New Morality: The Right and Wrong of Sex." Part 2. *HIS* 28, no. 6 (March 1968): 17–18, 23–25.

"The New Morality: The Right and Wrong of Sex." Part 3. *HIS* 28, no. 7 (April 1968): 6–9.

"The New Morality: Why Wait for Marriage?" *HIS* 28, no. 8 (May 1968): 31–35.

"The Achilles Heel." *Christian Heritage* 30, no. 1 (January 1969): 24–26.

"The Bishop's Blockbuster." *Christian Heritage* 30, no. 2 (February 1969): 30–32.

"A Papal Pandora." *Christian Heritage* 30, no. 3 (March 1969): 28–30.

"A Dishonest System?" *Christian Heritage* 30, no. 4 (April 1969): 10–12.

"The Fiction of Infallibility." *Christian Heritage* 30, no. 5 (May 1969): 8–9, 26–27.

"Infallibility: Fact or Fiction?" *Christian Heritage* 30, no. 6 (June 1969): 10–12.

"Reform or Revolt?" *Christian Heritage* 30, no. 7 (September 1969): 6–9.

"Rome's Real Revolution." *Christian Heritage* 30, no. 8 (October 1969): 22, 25–26.

"Faith and Doctrine: Contemporary or Contemptible?" *Christian Heritage* 30, no. 9 (November 1969): 30–32.

"Sophisticated Perversion." *Christian Heritage* 30, no. 10 (December 1969): 30–32.

"Evangelical Seminaries and Negro Students." *Freedom Now* 5, no. 2 (March-April 1969): 22–25.

"Christian Education 2001: Ethics and Morality." *Teach* 11, no. 1 (fall 1969): 31–32.

"Holiness and Healthymindedness: (Piety and Psychology)." In *A Call to Christian Character,* edited by Bruce L. Shelley, 123–32. Grand Rapids, Mich.: Zondervan Publishing House, 1970.

"Is the Church a Cultural Fossil?" *Christian Heritage* 31, no. 1 (January 1970): 6–7, 32.

"The First Man: Real or Religious Myth?" *Christian Heritage* 31, no. 2 (February 1970): 24–27, 32.

"Scandalous Dishonesty." *Christian Heritage* 31, no. 3 (March 1970): 24–26.

"Turning Theology Topsy Turvy." *Christian Heritage* 31, no. 5 (May 1970): 28–30.

"The Anonymous Christian." *Christian Heritage* 31, no. 6 (June 1970): 6–9.

"Every Christian's Business—Theology." *Christian Heritage* 31, no. 7 (September 1970): 26–28.

"Spiritual Discernment Versus Scholarly Denial." *Christian Heritage* 31, no. 8 (October 1970): 10–12.

"Redefining the Doctrine of God." *Christian Heritage* 31, no. 9 (November 1970): 28–31.

"The Modern Idolatry." *Christian Heritage* 31, no. 10 (December 1970): 10–12.

"What Dare We Hope For?" *Eternity* 21, no. 1 (January 1970): 14–15.

"The Future of Theology and the Theology of the Future." *Journal of the Evangelical Theological Society* 13, no. 3 (summer 1970): 147–71.

"Mountain Manifesto." *Bibliotheca Sacra* 128, no. 510 (April-June 1971): 135–41.

"Seer or Saboteur." *Christian Heritage* 32, no. 1 (January 1971): 10–12.

"A False Prophet." *Christian Heritage* 32, no. 3 (March 1971): 24–26.

"Revision or Perversion?" *Christian Heritage* 32, no. 4 (April 1971): 30–32.

"Mythomaniacs." *Christian Heritage* 32, no. 5 (May 1971): 22–25.

"The Gospel of Hope." *Christian Heritage* 32, no. 6 (June 1971): 6–9.

"Infallibility: An Insider's Inquiry." *Christian Heritage* 32, no. 7 (September 1971): 30–32.

"The Challenge Rome Faces Today!" *Christian Heritage* 32, no. 8 (October 1971): 30–32.

"Religious Toleration." *Christian Heritage* 32, no. 9 (November 1971): 8–11.

"Radically Protestantized?" *Christian Heritage* 32, no. 10 (December 1971): 24–27.

"Bombs or Bibles? Get Ready for Revolution!" *Christianity Today* 15, no. 8 (January 15, 1971): 4–6.

"Therapist and Theologian Look at Love." *Christianity Today* 15, no. 22 (August 6, 1971): 14–16.

"Revolution Is Brewing." *Eternity* 22, no. 3 (March 1971): 12–13, 44–45.

"Existentialism: A Net to Catch a Fog." *Eternity* 22, no. 8 (August 1971): 16–17, 36.

"Authority: Neither Authentic Nor Mature." *Christian Heritage* 33, no. 2 (February 1972): 22–25.

"The Continental Divide." *Christian Heritage* 33, no. 4 (April 1972): 26–29.

"The Not-So-Great Infallibility Machine." *Christian Heritage* 33, no. 5 (May 1972): 30–32.

"Infallibility — A Dead Duck." *Christian Heritage* 33, no. 6 (June 1972): 30–32.

"Is There Any Immunity Against Apostasy?" *Christian Heritage* 33, no. 7 (September 1972): 22–24.

"Books That Helped Shape My Life." *Eternity* 23, no. 3 (March 1972): 45.

"Genocide," "Murder," "Naturalistic Ethics," "Probabilism," "Satan," "Suicide." In *Baker's Dictionary of Christian Ethics*, edited by Carl F. H. Henry. Grand Rapids, Mich.: Baker Book House, 1973.

"Understanding the Neo-Mystical Movement." *Christian Heritage* 34, no. 1 (January 1973): 4–7.

"The Revolt Against Rationalism." *Christian Heritage* 34, no. 2 (February 1973): 26–28, 32.

"Neo-Mysticism Versus Supernaturalism." *Christian Heritage* 34, no. 3 (March 1973): 26–28.

"The Sad Story of Western Culture." *Christian Heritage* 34, no. 4 (April 1973): 26–29.

"Neo-Sacralism Versus Supernaturalism." *Christian Heritage* 34, no. 5 (May 1973): 4–7.

"Neo-Mysticism Versus True Supernaturalism." *Christian Heritage* 34, no. 6 (June 1973): 8–11.

"Neo-Mysticism Versus True Supernaturalism." Part 7. *Christian Heritage* 34, no. 7 (September 1973): 26–28.

"Neo-Mysticism Versus True Supernaturalism." Part 8. *Christian Heritage* 34, no. 8 (October 1973): 26–29.

"Neo-Mysticism Versus True Supernaturalism: Poor Humpty-Dumpty or Blowing the Mind." Part 10. *Christian Heritage* 34, no. 10 (December 1973): 22–25, 32.

"How to Keep the Peace." *Eternity* 24, no. 4 (April 1973): 33–34, 38.

"Hope Beyond Hopelessness." *The Other Side* 9, no. 5 (September-October 1973): 12–15.

"Neo-Mysticism and the Nature of Man." *Christian Heritage* 35, no. 1 (January 1974): 30–32.

"Neo-Mysticism and the True Supernaturalism: Where Will It All End?" Part 12. *Christian Heritage* 35, no. 2 (February 1974): 26–28, 32.

"Neo-Mysticism Versus True Supernaturalism: Are Mysticism and Christianity Enemies?" Part 13. *Christian Heritage* 35, no. 3 (March 1974): 10–12, 32.

"Neo-Mysticism and the True Supernaturalism: Evangelicalism Versus Neo-Mysticism." Part 14. *Christian Heritage* 35, no. 5 (May 1974): 4–7.

"Neo-Mysticism Versus True Supernaturalism: New Testament Mysticism." Part 15. *Christian Heritage* 35, no. 6 (June 1974): 24–27.

"Premillennialism and Social Pessimism." Part 1. *Christian Heritage* 35, no. 7 (September 1974): 24–27.

"Premillennialism and Social Pessimism." Part 2. *Christian Heritage* 35, no. 8 (October 1974): 22–25, 28–29.

"The Bible and Emotional Problems: The Bible and Anxiety." Part 1. *Christian Heritage* 35, no. 10 (December 1974): 24–27.

"Why We Should Say 'Yes.'" *Eternity* 25, no. 8 (August 1974): 17, 44.

"The Beatitudes," "Confession," "Humility." In *The Zondervan Pictorial Encyclopedia of the Bible,* 5 vols., edited by Merrill C. Tenney. Grand Rapids, Mich.: Zondervan Publishing House, 1975.

"Childbearing," "Children," "The Christian Faith," "Rule of Faith," "Faithfulness." In *Wycliffe Bible Encyclopedia,* vol.1, edited by Charles F. Pfeiffer, Howard F. Vos, and John Rea. Chicago: Moody Press, 1975.

"The Bible and Emotional Problems: The Bible and Anxiety." Part 2. *Christian Heritage* 36, no. 1 (January 1975): 10–12, 21.

"The Bible and Emotional Problems: The Bible and Anxiety." Part 3. *Christian Heritage* 36, no. 2 (February 1975): 24–27.

"The Bible and Emotional Problems: The Bible and Anxiety." Part 4. *Christian Heritage* 36, no. 3 (March 1975): 20–23.

"The Bible and Your Emotions: The Bible and Pride." Parts 4 and 5. *Christian Heritage* 36, no. 4 (April 1975): 22–24.

"The Bible and Your Emotions: The Bible and Pride." Part 6. *Christian Heritage* 36, no. 5 (May 1975): 26–29.

"The Bible and Your Emotions: The Bible and Anger." Part 7. *Christian Heritage* 36, no. 6 (June 1975): 24–27.

"The Bible and Your Emotions: The Bible and Guilt." Part 8. *Christian Heritage* 36, no. 7 (September 1975): 28–31.

"The Bible and Your Emotions: The Bible and Guilt." Part 9. *Christian Heritage* 36, no. 8 (October 1975): 22–25.

"The Bible and Your Emotions: The Bible and Guilt." Part 10. *Christian Heritage* 36, no. 9 (November 1975): 22–25.

"Christian Counseling: Who Has the Answer to Eternity?" *Eternity* 26, no. 1 (January 1975): 16–19.

"Just Polishing Coffin Handles?" *Eternity* 26, no. 12 (December 1975): 74.

"Pacesetters for the Radical Theologians of the Sixties and Seventies." In *Tensions in Contemporary Theology,* edited by Stanley N. Gundry and Alan F. Johnson, 45–101. Chicago: Moody Press, 1976.

"The Hope of the Gospel/The Gospel of Hope." Part 1. *Christian Heritage* 37, no. 2 (February 1976): 22–25.

"The Hope of the Gospel/The Gospel of Hope." Part 2. *Christian Heritage* 37, no. 3 (March 1976): 30–32.

"The Hope of the Gospel/The Gospel of Hope." Part 3. *Christian Heritage* 37, no. 4 (April 1976): 26–29.

"The Buck Stops Here." *Christian Heritage* 37, no. 5 (May 1976): 26–29.

"Let Freedom Ring!" *Christian Heritage* 37, no. 7 (September 1976): 4–7.

"The Bible and the Modern Mind." Part 1. *Christian Heritage* 37, no. 10 (December 1976): 22–25.

"Soar with the Eagles, Sing with the Angels." *Christianity Today* 20, no. 23 (August 27, 1976): 9–10.

"God's Perspective on Man." *Journal of the American Scientific Affiliation* 28, no. 4 (December 1976): 145–51.

"Coincidence or Providence?" In *My Most Memorable Encounter with God,* edited by David Enlow, 67–78. Wheaton, Ill.: Tyndale House Publishers, 1977.

"The Bible and the Modern Mind." Part 2. *Christian Heritage* 38, no. 2 (February 1977): 10–12, 21.

"The Bible and the Modern Mind." Part 3. *Christian Heritage* 38, no. 3 (March 1977): 8–9, 27.

"The Bible and the Modern Mind." Part 4. *Christian Heritage* 38, no. 5 (May 1977): 10–12.

"The Bible and the Modern Mind." Part 5. *Christian Heritage* 38, no. 6 (June 1977): 10–12, 27.

"The Bible and the Modern Mind." Part 6. *Christian Heritage* 38, no. 7 (September 1977): 10–12.

"The Bible and the Modern Mind." Part 7. *Christian Heritage* 38, no. 8 (October 1977): 12–14.

"The Dismal Consequences of Unbelief." *Christian Heritage* 38, no. 9 (November 1977): 22–24.

"The Intellect's Terminal Cancer." *Christian Heritage* 38, no. 10 (December 1977): 30–32.

"Faith to Face Failure, or What's So Great About Success?" *Christianity Today* 22, no. 5 (December 9, 1977): 12–13.

"Hunger: Are Christians Hypocrites Concerning World Hunger?" *United Evangelical Action* 36, no. 2 (spring 1977): 13–14.

"Evangelical Views of Today's Moral Crisis." In *Evangelicals and Jews in Conversation on Scripture, Theology, and History,* edited by Marc H. Tanenbaum, Marvin R. Wilson, and A. James Rudin, 248–265. Grand Rapids, Mich.: Baker Book House, 1978.

"Lifeboat Banquet: Why Are Only a Select Few Invited?" *Eternity* 28, no. 1 (January 1978): 21, 23, 28, 30.

"Getting into Shape Spiritually." *Christianity Today* 23, no. 9 (February 2, 1979): 24–27.

"Loving the World: Rightly or Wrongly." *Christianity Today* 24, no. 7 (April 4, 1980): 20–22.

"Church: An Indispensable Institution." *Decision* 21, no. 11 (November 1980): 7.

"The Delicate Diplomacy of Jewish-Christian Dialogue." *Christianity Today* 25, no. 8 (April 24, 1981): 26–29.

"Goodness: Reflections of the Incarnation." *Christianity Today* 25, no. 12 (June 26, 1981): 28–29.

"Prevent the Postholiday Blues: How to Stay in the Saddle from Thanksgiving Through the New Year." *Christianity Today* 25, no. 19 (November 6, 1981): 48.

"The Final State of the Wicked." *Journal of the Evangelical Theological Society* 24, no. 3 (September 1981): 211–20.

"What's So Great About Success?" *Leadership* 2, no. 1 (winter 1981): 54–56.

"Physician, Heal Thyself." *Journal of Psychology and Christianity* 1, no. 2 (July 1982): 2–8.

"Caring for Teenagers: 8 Verbs That Speak Their Language." *Command* 32, no. 3 (fall 1983): 26–27.

"Challenge of Christlikeness." *Decision* 24, no. 2 (February 1983): 10–11.

"Spiritual Weapons for Waging Peace: How Can We Denounce War Enough?" *The Other Side* 19, no. 4 (April 1983): 40–41.

"The Problem of Proselytization: An Evangelical Perspective." In *Evangelicals and Jews in an Age of Pluralism,* edited by Marc H. Tanenbaum, Marvin R. Wilson, and A. James Rudin, 199–225. Grand Rapids, Mich.: Baker Book House, 1984.

"A Friend of Many Years Remembers Francis Schaeffer." *Christianity Today* 28, no. 9 (June 15, 1984): 61–63.

"A Call to Respect God's Image." *Christianity Today* 29, no. 6 (April 5, 1985): 14–16.

"Have We Learned Our Lesson? Three Books Talk About American Apathy in the Face of the Holocaust." *Christianity Today* 29, no. 12 (September 6, 1985): 40–43.

"The Price Love Paid." *Moody Monthly* 85, no. 8 (April 1985): 42–43, 45.

"Truth and Tolerance." *Moody Monthly* 85, no. 11 (July/August 1985): 99–102.

"Pondering Our Christian Responsibility for the Poor." *Urban Advocate* 1, no. 4 (summer 1985): 1, 6–7.

"The Bible and the Modern Mind." In *Interpretation and History,* edited by R. Laird Harris, Swee-Hwa Quek, and Robert Vannoy, 169–83. Singapore: Christian Life Publishers, 1986.

"The Battle for Shalom." *Christianity Today* 30, no. 1 (January 17, 1986): 18, 20.

"Called to Be Saints—Not Well-Adjusted Sinners." *Christianity Today* 30, no. 1 (January 17, 1986): 28.

"Evangelism: Techniques and Technologies." *Christianity Today* 30, no. 15 (October 17, 1986): 28.

"My Desideratum for Denver: Knowledge, Insight and Discernment." *Focal Point* 15, no. 1 (winter 1995): 8–9.

"Aging Bodies—Time-Immune Spirits: Observations of an Octogenarian." *Focal Point* 15, no. 2 (spring 1995): 6–7.

"Truth-telling vs. Truth-twisting." *Focal Point* 15, no. 3 (summer 1995): 7–8.

"Why Should We Help the Poor?" *Moody* 98, no. 2 (November/December 1997): 12–16.

"Still the World's Greatest Job." *Ministry* 72, no. 9 (September 1999): 10–13.

Sermons, Lectures, Addresses, and Letters

The Carey S. Thomas Library archives also hold many mimeographed articles, lectures, and sermons distributed in the 1950s and 1960s as "The Seminary Study Series" and "Conservative Baptist Today." In addition, the scholar interested in the study of Vernon Grounds and his thought can find many recorded messages and addresses given by Dr. Grounds over the course of his career. His correspondence, presidential and personal, is also preserved in the archives, and his doctoral dissertation, "The Concept of Love in the Psychology of Sigmund Freud," can be found in the Denver Seminary library.

Note to the Reader

The publisher invites you to share your response to the message of this book by writing Discovery House Publishers, Box 3566, Grand Rapids, MI 49501, USA. For information about other Discovery House books, music, or videos, contact us at the same address or call 1-800-653-8333. Find us on the Internet at http://www.dhp.org/ or send e-mail to books@dhp.org.